Vote Your Conscience

The Last Campaign
of George McGovern

RICHARD MICHAEL MARANO

Westport, Connecticut
London

Library of Congress Cataloging-in-Publication Data

Marano, Richard Michael, 1960–
    Vote your conscience : the last compaign of George McGovern / by Richard Michael Marano.
        p. cm.
    Includes bibliographical references (p.) and index.
    ISBN 0–275–97189–9 (alk. paper)
        1. McGovern, George S. (George Stanley), 1922–   2. Legislators—United States—
Biography.   3. Presidential candidates—United States—Biography.   4. Presidents—
United States—Election—1984.   5. United States. Congress. Senate—Biography.
6. Political campaigns—United States—History—20th century.   7. United States—Politics
and government—1981–1989.   I. Title.
E840.8.M34 M37   2003
328.73′092—dc21   2003008554

British Library Cataloguing in Publication Data is available.

Library of Congress Catalog Card Number: 2003008554
ISBN: 0–275–97189–9

First published in 2003

Praeger Publishers, 88 Post Road West, Westport, CT 06881
An imprint of Greenwood Publishing Group, Inc.
www.praeger.com

Printed in the United States of America

The paper used in this book complies with the
Permanent Paper Standard issued by the National
Information Standards Organization (Z39.48–1984).

10 9 8 7 6 5 4 3 2 1

Copyright Acknowledgment

Material from interviews and/or correspondence with the following used by permission:
George McGovern, Patricia J. Donovan, George V. Cunningham, and Paul Sullivan.

To Eileen, Michelle, Richie, and Christine
For fulfilling all of my dreams

If we really believe that we are "one nation under God," let us move forward in the quest for a peaceful world—not as Republicans or Democrats, but as citizens of a great democracy. Adlai Stevenson has said that "peace is the most important unfinished task of our generation." It is to that unfinished task that I pledge my time, my talents and my prayers.

—George McGovern, 1956

Contents

Photo Essay follows page 106

Preface

When I was growing up in my hometown of Waterbury, Connecticut, there was a fierce loyalty to the Democratic Party that rose to an almost religious fervor. The blue-collar workers, whose unions had supported Democratic candidates since the era of the New Deal, left no stone unturned in their search for votes for those whom they saw as supportive of fair wages and decent working conditions. My baptism into the Democratic Party took place at a very early age. One day in October 1962, our neighbor next door, Blanche Rinaldi, shouted over the hedges to my mother that President Kennedy was about to come through town and his motorcade was going to pass near our house. My mother put me, her two-year-old, into a stroller and quickly ran down the street. We arrived just in time to see President John F. Kennedy! An American flag was held in my young hand, and my mother watched with jubilation as the charismatic president waved to us from his automobile.

I confirmed my support for the Democrats in 1968 when my third-grade teacher, Miss Balfe, urged her students to go down to the Waterbury Green to attend a rally for Vice President Hubert H. Humphrey. The Green was packed, and to my astonishment, a few of the reserved and dignified teachers from my elementary school were standing on benches, screaming their support for Humphrey. One could have mistaken these usually conservative and proper educators for schoolgirls screaming at The Beatles on *The Ed Sullivan Show*.

Waterbury was the city made famous in Democratic Party circles by Theodore H. White in his book, *The Making of the President 1960*. We in Waterbury, as well as John F. Kennedy himself, believed that the momentum that began at the Waterbury rally in the last days of the 1960 campaign projected him into the forefront of that year's presidential election. It was on Sunday, November 6, 1960, that Senator Kennedy returned home to New England for the final stretch of his campaign. When he arrived in Waterbury at 3:00 A.M., there were 30,000 people waiting for him on the Green. As he spoke to his supporters from the balcony of the Roger Smith Hotel, he was greeted as a conquering hero, as if the ballots had already been counted and he had emerged the victor.[1]

In 1972, when Senator George McGovern came to town to speak at a rally on the Green, he too appeared to us to be another great Democrat in the Kennedy tradition. There would be no slim defeat as there had been in 1968, we thought, but an upset victory over Nixon reminiscent of Kennedy's in 1960.

The crowd that awaited McGovern on the Waterbury Green was loud and enthusiastic. It was a Thursday evening, very early into the campaign, and McGovern was almost crushed arriving and departing the rally. The crowd easily drowned out the thunderings of the Mattatuck Drum Band. McGovern was accompanied by Senator Ted Kennedy, the youngest brother of the late beloved president. McGovern and Kennedy, who had flown into Oxford Airport from New York City, arrived in Waterbury about 9:50 P.M. Despite many pleas from Democratic Town Chairman Frank Santaguida to clear West Main Street for the arriving motorcade, the crowd was far too wild with enthusiasm, and, eventually, he gave up trying. A few minutes later, McGovern and Kennedy were forced to get out of their cars and walk to the grandstand.[2]

In his introductory remarks, Congressman John S. Monagan, a former Waterbury mayor, alluded to the previous Kennedy visits and the "love affair" between the people of Waterbury and President Kennedy; Senator Abe Ribicoff also spoke of the historic 1960 Kennedy visit and said the late president told him afterward, "I am no longer the underdog; I am going to win Tuesday."[3] Ribicoff turned to McGovern on that September evening and said that, after thirty years of campaigning in Connecticut, he felt that there had never been crowd enthusiasm equal to this, at such an early stage in a campaign. He told McGovern that his "heart should swell with pride when you leave this great city . . . you are on the up-grade."[4]

"We want George" was the chant heard over and over, interrupting all of the introductory speakers. An estimated crowd of 12,000–15,000 people applauded for McGovern for more than a minute before he could gain their attention. McGovern attacked Nixon for high unemployment, but by far the most applause came when he challenged the war in Vietnam. The crowd screamed, shouted, and stomped their feet, and McGovern was obviously elated at his reception.[5]

The next day, the local newspaper, well known for its conservative slant, published a photograph of McGovern and Kennedy coming through the crowd with someone near them carrying a "legalize pot" placard.[6] I was too young at the time to understand the subliminal message: George

McGovern was no ordinary Democrat, and this was not a typical election. At stake was the real possibility of a change in direction for our country. This was my introduction to George McGovern.

Throughout his entire political career, McGovern remained true to his deep moral beliefs and possessed the courage of his convictions, regardless of the political consequences. He believes in the people's right to know the hard truth, even when mistakes have been made. "I've never tried to deceive anyone where I've stood. And I've always been willing to defend in public those convictions which I hold in private," he has said.[7]

McGovern also remained an unrepentant New Dealer who believed that the solutions once applied by Franklin D. Roosevelt remained the right solutions. He was an uncommonly courageous politician who spoke directly, while knowing full well that his candid words would be used quite effectively by his political opponents to smear him. In a speech delivered in 1967, in Aberdeen, South Dakota, McGovern described his unusual candor this way:

> To remain silent in the face of policies we believe to be wrong is not patriotism; it is moral cowardice—a form of treason to one's conscience and to the nation. It is not easy to dissent in time of war. . . . I do know how all this will come out. I do know that the people of a state can easily secure a new Senator, but a Senator cannot easily secure a new conscience. . . . I want to be reelected . . . but I do not want reelection so badly that I will ever sacrifice my convictions to achieve it.[8]

I first met McGovern and learned of his interest in seeking the 1984 Democratic nomination in March 1982. During a speaking visit at Fairfield University, McGovern, almost in jest, told a group of nearly 600 listeners that they might well be hearing from him again very soon. Later he told me privately that if the frontrunners were unable to excite the Democratic Party and failed to address those issues that he deemed critical to the debate, he might wage "a special kind of a campaign," one that would remain true to his values, never compromising them for political expediency.

During the next twenty years after meeting McGovern at Fairfield University, I visited him at his Washington, D.C., office, corresponded with him on numerous occasions, attended several events at his Stratford (Connecticut) Inn, and interviewed him about his 1984 campaign. He is a man that I came to admire and respect more and more, and for whom, ultimately, I have great affection.

This is the story of that 1984 effort. I am proud to have played a small part in it as McGovern's Connecticut coordinator, for I could not stand on the sidelines and watch as others participated in the political debate of 1984.

Acknowledgments

The idea of writing this book came to me within moments of George McGovern's departure from the 1984 presidential race. I actually began writing it back then, but was soon "distracted" by my law studies and preparaton for the bar exam.

In 1999, I again took up this project, and, thankfully, there was no turning back. I am indebted to my former law clerk, Myklyn Mahoney, for helping me organize boxes of research, which greatly assisted me in moving forward.

I am grateful to my dear wife, Eileen, and our children, Michelle, Richie, and Christine, for allowing me to spend the time to complete this project, which was a true labor of love.

My good friend, Jim Ball, gave me constant encouragement and made countless suggestions on style as well as substance. He shares my long-held admiration for the "man of conscience."

This book would not have been possible without the assistance of Neal Alpert, a promising young writer with a plethora of talent. Lisa Cerverizzo typed and retyped the manuscript with her usual good cheer. Jason Musante was of invaluable assistance in proofreading, editing, and providing encouragement, especially in moments of frustration.

I am especially grateful to Laurie Langland, archivist of the Senator George McGovern Collection at Layne Library, Dakota Wesleyan University, for her many hours of assistance with research, as well as for providing numerous helpful suggestions on style and editorial content.

Nick and Nicky Bollella provided assistance with photographic design and Ed Hahnenberg and Paul Bialobrzeski with research. I am thankful to Laurie Lidz and Betty Perugini for their help with the manuscript. I am indebted to Stanley K. Sheinbaum for use of his photographs, to the editorial cartoonists for permission to use their work, to Marc Schloss and

Melody Miller of Senator Edward M. Kennedy's Senate Office, and to the reference archivists at the John Fitzgerald Kennedy Library for their assistance.

Lastly, I am truly grateful to Ambassador George McGovern, George V. Cunningham, Patricia J. Donovan, Congressman James P. McGovern, Paul Sullivan, and Ken Swope for their generous assistance with interviews, recollections, and encouragement.

I only hope that this book does justice to a truly remarkable and much underappreciated national hero, George McGovern.

A Visit with the Ghost of Elections Past

Of all my colleagues in the United States Senate, the person who has the most feeling and does things in the most genuine way . . . is George McGovern. He is so highly admired by all his colleagues, not just for his ability, but because of the kind of man he is. That is truer of him than anyone else in the United States Senate.
—U.S. Senator Robert F. Kennedy

One of the great ironies of American politics is that George McGovern, one of the most misinterpreted and misunderstood men ever to seek the presidency, was also perhaps one of the most intelligent and farsighted. In 1971, Senator George McGovern predicted that by 1972 he would be "recognized as the most broadly based candidate and the one who has the best chance of winning."[1] In 1972, he was rejected by 47 million voters, due in large part to a complete distortion of his capabilities and convictions. He was branded an isolationist, although his Vietnam predictions later became reality; an extremist dove, although his own military record was one that merited great distinction; and unelectable, although he consistently won elections in Republican South Dakota and won a nearly impossible nomination in 1972. On his way to that nomination, McGovern won victories in almost a dozen state primaries, including New York and California. McGovern's courage to take on a popular president was refreshing and something seldom seen in modern American politics: He chose to run a campaign based on issues rather than on superficial rhetoric. Ultimately, perhaps he was guilty of choosing conviction over victory. Nevertheless, history has already shown that his 1972 campaign was one that articulated commonsense ideas—not extremist nonsense. Even after losing his own Senate seat in 1980, George McGovern remained true to his convictions and continued his fight for peace and social justice.

Senator McGovern is "an intelligent, hard-working, caring, sensitive man . . . a kind and decent man who genuinely cares deep in his heart about human beings not just in this country, but around the world."[2] Indeed, McGovern once described himself as a man of "experience" who has a "steady, dependable temperament, as well as a sense of history and some degree of imagination."[3]

It may be said that to understand George McGovern, one must understand his personality. Pulitzer Prize–winning author Theodore H. White described McGovern as "one of the great listeners of all time."[4] Yet, White also found McGovern "baffling" and observed that what he said in public was much more important than what he said or committed to in private. The mind of McGovern "was absorptive, not provocative," according to White. By this, he was referring to the fact that most people who spoke with McGovern one-on-one left with the feeling of having "swayed him deeply," when, in reality, McGovern was merely absorbing everything they had to say. He did not give the impression of disagreeing, even if that was the case. Due to the confusion that McGovern could unintentionally create in these situations, White hypothesized that McGovern's psyche "would make a fine subject of investigation" for historians someday.[5]

Although many journalists and historians see George McGovern as a paradox who was an interchangeable reflection of his ill-fated 1972 campaign, many others view him as a man whose personality was quite atypical of most candidates who seek the presidency. Indeed, this view is more of a negative reflection upon the way we Americans practice electoral politics, rather than on McGovern's appeal within this complex process.[6]

Political columnist Jack W. Germond has written that "George McGovern became a political laughingstock in a way that was all out of proportion to his qualities as a public official and political leader."[7] This is true enough, for some of the qualities that McGovern holds—old-fashioned values, integrity, candor—are necessary to effectively hold public office.[8] However, others have accused McGovern of being wishy-washy.[9] Some have observed that McGovern found it hard to sharply disagree with the people around him whom he personally liked.[10] Indeed, to some, his need for personal harmony may have been one of his weaknesses. White has written that McGovern's personality was, in fact, a key factor with some of the problems in his campaign against Nixon in 1972.[11]

Those closest to him professionally, however, disagree with such negative assessments. Patricia Donovan, who began working for Congressman McGovern in January of 1957 and was his secretary for twenty-five years, believes that the harsh criticism is completely unfounded. The Senator, she recalled quite fondly, maintained "an even disposition both publicly and privately." He was "more relaxed in private and his sense of humor was more to the fore in private." McGovern, she said, enjoyed a good joke "and especially enjoyed the banter and repartee with his colleagues, in particular Senator Mondale. The men in the Democratic cloakroom used to enjoy listening to Senator Mondale and Senator McGovern exchange barbs, and insults."[12]

George Cunningham, a long-time administrative aide, agreed with Donovan's assessment. Cunningham recalled that McGovern was "a realist" and "politics was one way to advance his views." He too found McGovern to have a good sense of humor and a personality that was very much the same in private as in public. Although he "had a certain degree of toughness which enabled him to win the kinds of tough races he did," and "could be tough especially when he wanted something done," McGovern was more of a gentle man, "both very kind and generous." There was a lot of Methodist minister in him, according to Cunningham.[13] Pat Donovan agreed and further described McGovern this way:

> His fundamental thorough knowledge of the Bible and the Judeo-Christian ethic undergirded his thinking and his statements. His compassion and concern for the less fortunate in our society and his acceptance of every person as they were stemmed from his Christian beliefs. He genuinely gives a damn about every individual and the impact of public policy on them.[14]

It is unfortunate that the American electorate never really got to know the real George McGovern. Arthur Schlesinger Jr. described McGovern as a much underappreciated man.[15] George McGovern has also been described as a "decent man, politically liberal, unwilling to use military force to achieve foreign policy objectives, quick to delegate authority, easily bored by nitty-gritty economic matters, eager to slash defense spending, and a bit fuzzy on many other issues on which his judgment may be colored by wishful thinking."[16] According to one former aide, McGovern is "extraordinarily intelligent, but he operates more on a basis of hope and optimism rather than realism. . . . That was very true of his efforts to reduce military spending and end the war. That's the premise of an educator or crusader, rather than a daily doer of things."[17]

McGovern has often been criticized on his style of public speaking.[18] Certainly, he lacked the public charisma of a Robert Kennedy, a Ronald Reagan, or a Bill Clinton. McGovern, who has been described by political columnist Jules Whitcover, as well as others, as an introspective man, was not as dynamic a speaker as some others.[19] In his autobiography, *GRASSROOTS*, McGovern wrote that his boyhood was marked by a "painful bashfulness." He credits the school debate team with having pulled him out of his shell and giving him the confidence to pursue public service.[20]

Perhaps McGovern could best be summed up by saying that he is an eternal "optimist and a dreamer, and his dreams have been as broad and

unbounded as the Dakota prairie."[21] Like most politicians, he was a product of his home state. Had he not been from a small state like South
Dakota, it is unlikely that he would have been elected to the U.S. Senate.
And had it not been for the war in Vietnam, as well as the untimely death
of Robert Kennedy, it is unlikely that he would have ever sought the presidency.[22] McGovern's educational background also defined his political
perspective and separated him from other politicians. He holds a Ph.D.
in American history from Northwestern University and had a perspective
as a historian that set him apart. He was able to step back from current
events and ask deeper questions about where we were heading as a nation. He appeared inherently able to challenge the status quo both with
Democrats and Republicans alike and pointed out that their generally
accepted assumptions were wrong.[23] McGovern possessed old-fashioned
values: candor, integrity, and hard work. His political methods were traditional: grassroots organizing, tireless canvassing, and intimate knowledge of the party rules (which he helped draft).[24] He tended over the years
"to speak with considerable candor." He did not "back away from any of
the tough issues, even though they required paying a penalty."[25]

Of course, it is apparent that how one views George McGovern depends, in large measure, upon one's political perspective. He has, of
course, been vilified by a great many Republicans and right-wing extremists. He also stands out of the crowd of politicians because he was a risk
taker and an idealist. He did not fear political defeat as most politicians
ordinarily do. For him, the exchange of ideas and the battle to direct national policy was the goal. The outcome of the election, he believed, was
pretty much out of his hands.[26] In 1971, McGovern described himself this
way:

> My greatest single asset is truthtelling. I don't duck the issues, and I'm not
> capable of deception. I'm open, honest, Midwestern and rural in back-
> ground. People think I come across like a Sunday school teacher, that I'm
> not an effective communicator. I think a lot of the American people are tired
> of flash and charisma and show business spectacles or candidates getting
> special instruction in television techniques and image-changing. I think
> truthfulness and trustworthiness are more important than flash, appeal and
> charisma.[27]

In politics, first impressions are like a piece of clay; if allowed to harden,
they are very difficult to change. And in 1972, George McGovern was not
yet a well-known national figure. He was still relatively unknown by the
American electorate at the time of the Democratic National Convention
in Miami. The electorate's first impressions of McGovern had been distorted by Hubert Humphrey in California's primary and debates, by Senator Hugh Scott's comments, and, at that time, he was still to face the

Eagleton fiasco and the radical charges levied by the Nixon campaign. During the California debates and primary campaign, Hubert Humphrey spoke of McGovern in half-truths and distorted his record.[28] *Newsweek's* June 19, 1972, story was a foretelling of McGovern's future perception with the electorate. The article was entitled, "How Radical Is McGovern?"[29] Charges of radicalism, like the clay, quickly hardened and were to remain with McGovern for the remainder of his career. However, he regarded himself not as a radical, but as an "unabashed New Deal Democrat."[30] He described his 1972 defeat as a "campaign of candor, compassion and common sense. It is history's verdict that our opponents waged perhaps the most shameful campaign in American history."[31]

The left wing of the Democratic Party may have appeared, to the electorate, to be led by McGovern. But he had attempted to use the constituency of the left to achieve the nomination, not to lead it.[32] McGovern had to remain true to his convictions.

> I never said anything I didn't believe and if people saw that as coming from the left, why, they have to make that judgment. I never thought it was leftist. I thought it was just common sense . . . but I'm sure that my political opponents did everything they could to paint me as a left-winger. That's standard in American politics.[33]

The inaccurate and false impressions were nurtured and cultivated by each of his opponents—both Democrat and Republican. When Senate Minority Leader Hugh Scott charged that McGovern favored the three As—abortion, amnesty, and acid—his radical perception cemented.[34] In the fall, the Republicans continuously alleged that the three As were the key issues for McGovern and his candidacy, and it became relatively easy to argue that he was out of step with the vast majority of Americans. McGovern's theme of shifting resources and attention from works of war to building a better America was more often perceived as a part of a radical left agenda than as a return to America's historic roots.[35] With the nomination finally won, McGovern needed to persuade the American voter that he was a responsible alternative to Richard Nixon. However, after the Eagleton fiasco, McGovern was not only perceived as too liberal, but also as incompetent—or certainly at least less competent than Richard Nixon.[36]

> I don't think I was too far to the left and I think that the factors that defeated me were not ideological factors. I think that the Wallace shooting was number one and a close second, if not equal to it, was the Eagleton matter. Neither of those things were ideological factors. But I am, you know I've won big primary elections, eleven of them and including some of the bigger states. So, I don't think that I was too far to the left.[37]

For McGovern personally, the greatest single factor contributing to the 1972 landslide was the shooting of George Wallace, not the liberal label. McGovern believed that there were two factors that turned the 1972 election into a landslide; first and foremost was "the inability of George Wallace to run as an independent after he was shot, and secondly the Eagleton affair." Looking back, McGovern believed that it would have been a Nixon victory against any Democrat running in 1972, no matter what he had done, because Nixon was riding high, having just come off a trip to China, détente with the Soviet Union, the signing of the SALT I Treaty, and the establishment of wage and price controls. Beyond all of this, the administration was pumping money into the national economy at a very fast rate and announced a week before the election that peace was at hand at long last in Vietnam.[38]

According to McGovern, Nixon's southern strategy "came into play in a diabolically clever way, in that he had been orchestrating the Wallace vote for four years with bad Supreme Court appointments, openly defying the courts on the busing decision, the tough hard line against young people, the antiwar stance, Agnew's forays into the South and orchestrating prejudices of the so-called 'silent majority.'"[39] This was calculated to appeal to the Wallace vote. Once it became clear that Wallace was not an alternative after being shot, the former Wallace supporters migrated to the Nixon camp. So, the formula for the election was the Nixon vote plus the Wallace vote combined behind Nixon. That is the statistical difference primarily between 1972 and 1968. McGovern received approximately the same vote that Hubert Humphrey did. The difference is that Nixon added the Wallace vote on top of what he had in 1968. McGovern's chances were without question dealt another severe blow by the Eagleton affair.[40]

Pat Donovan believes that the electorate's greatest misconception about George McGovern is that he was "some kind of shoot-from-the hip wild-eyed radical, when in fact he is a thoughtful, moderate, sensitive man who carefully weighed his positions and statements before speaking out." McGovern, she said, "often said that he is a true conservative in his judgments, while not disclaiming his liberalism on social issues."[41]

George Cunningham recalled that "McGovern did not object to the 'liberal label' or those it attracted, because it brought in needed troops" for the campaigns which used Vietnam as a "major battle cry in '68 and especially in '72." Although McGovern "got his early organization from the left wing of the party," which helped him build a national base, "Vietnam was not enough of an issue to allow McGovern to capture the heart of the party in '72. The Party remained too fractured and could not pull itself together behind a candidate."[42] Cunningham described it this way:

> In my view, McGovern never was a "left wing radical". . . he was a liberal
> in the sense that many political leaders from the northern great plains were

prairie populists in the long standing tradition of that area of the country. The populists mainly became liberals, but their politics remained basically unchanged.

Those who called McGovern a "left wing radical" were usually his opposition within the Democratic party . . . or others in the press and elsewhere who simply wanted McGovern to be defeated. To the best of my knowledge, McGovern never ran as a "left wing radical" in South Dakota or anywhere else.

Like anyone else running for public office . . . McGovern talked about the issues of principal interest to those whose votes he was seeking. Obviously . . . he talked South Dakota issues when he was in the state . . . as did most candidates when they were in their home states.[43]

Richard Wade, a former McGovern adviser and professor of urban history at City University of New York, believes that the "big welfare grant" was the only "radical" idea McGovern ever proposed.[44] "I don't know where people got the idea he is a radical; no man is more reserved, cautious or careful when it comes to big issues than McGovern," Wade said.[45]

Some did not know just what to make of McGovern. First came the notion that he was "too nice" to be president, then the complaint that he was a "one-issue" candidate.[46] After McGovern issued numerous specific policy proposals, he was seen by some as "fuzzy" or "overly vague" and by others as a "radical."[47]

As if there were not enough obstacles to overcome, McGovern picked Missouri Senator Thomas Eagleton for vice president, only to discover later that Eagleton had suffered from emotional depression and was treated with electric shock therapy. When Senator Thomas Eagleton's history of mental health problems came to light, McGovern's chance at being elected appeared to be completely doomed.[48] In the week that McGovern agonized over the decision and stated his 1,000 percent support of Eagleton, the story remained front-page news. Recalling in 1984 the Eagleton situation, McGovern said:

> I think that "fuzzy" label, by the way, goes back to the Nixon television commercials in '72. They just saturated (television with) a picture of my head spinning. And why? Well, for one thing, because I said I was for Senator Eagleton as my running mate 1,000 percent, and then a week later changed my mind. I'll never understand what was wrong with changing my mind on a complicated issue. Hell, I didn't know anything about mental illness. I didn't know he had a history of that.
>
> The more I talked to psychiatrists, the more I thought he should step down.[49]

Political Columnist Jack Germond has described Eagleton's failure to inform McGovern of his mental history as "the single most flagrant betrayal" in modern American politics.[50] Nevertheless, this first public test of McGovern as a decision maker raised serious doubts in the minds of the electorate as to his competence to lead the country. McGovern never understood what was wrong with changing his mind on such a complicated issue.[51]

Nixon, for his part, had visited Peking and Moscow, and remained inaccessible in the White House away from the press. His last-minute "peace is at hand" promise neutralized the war issue for the general electorate.[52] Although everything McGovern said about Watergate during the campaign proved to be true, Watergate was not a campaign issue in 1972 and had little or no impact on the result.[53] Much of Nixon's campaign literature contained attacks on McGovern's personal integrity. One brochure, entitled "The Clearest Choice of the Century," read in part as follows:

> Is Senator McGovern believable? This summer he went through six or seven men before finally finding someone who could run on his ticket with him. Then he sent a public relations man to deal secretly with the North Vietnamese in Paris while our government's negotiations were still going on. He first denied it, later he confirmed it.
>
> Such McGovern inconsistencies are not new:
>
> In 1967, Senator George McGovern said he was not an advocate of unilateral withdrawal of our troops from Vietnam. Now, of course, he says he is.
>
> Last year, Senator McGovern said he would remove all American forces from Southeast Asia. Now he wants to leave troops in Thailand and on ships in the area.
>
> In Florida, Senator McGovern said he was pro-busing. In Oregon, he said he would support the anti-busing bill now in Congress.
>
> In 1971, Senator McGovern said Jerusalem should be an international city. This year he wants to recognize Jerusalem as the Israeli capital and move the United States embassy there from Tel Aviv.[54]

As for the nominee, there was constant criticism of McGovern's understanding of his organizational needs and the lack of direction and control the candidate had over his own staff.[55] It was alleged that the three top advisers—Gary Hart, Frank Mankiewicz, and Lawrence O'Brien—lacked coordination and communication, and the McGovern campaign never changed its tactics from winning a primary to winning a general election.[56] All of the problems that were plaguing the campaign stuck to the nominee and, in the minds of many voters, were as indistinguishable from the campaign as to the man himself.[57]

The final perception in the mind of the electorate was that McGovern remained a narrow liberal, antiwar candidate. He was generally perceived neither as mainstream, nor as the candidate of the mainstream within the Democratic Party.[58] The George McGovern perception was synonymous to the divisions within the party, the radical label, and the ineffectiveness of the campaign he waged.[59]

The national press in 1972 viewed McGovern's poorly run campaign with frustration. Because they saw his campaign as unprofessionally run and with little hope of success, they gave little respect to the candidate himself. The 1972 Democratic nominee was the recipient of less than objective reporting. The press had rarely seen a candidate who appeared less carefully choreographed. Most political observers will concede that there is a degree of disdain among the party faithful for long-shot nominees. What is readily forgotten by journalists and historians is that McGovern waged a brilliant primary, the likes of which may rarely be seen again. Few outsiders in either party have come from so far behind to defeat the party establishment.[60] Perhaps the carnage necessary to win the nomination necessarily prevented a November victory.[61] That, however, is a question for another day.

The savage nature of the partisan infighting that went on right up until the time of his narrow first-ballot nomination was seen by McGovern as the third major blow to his campaign. He had agreed to three televised debates with Senator Humphrey after having virtually won the nomination. And in hindsight he viewed that decision as a very serious mistake. He had been trying to get Humphrey to debate for a year, but Humphrey had refused until he was almost out of the race and desperate. After Humphrey's money was gone, he couldn't get on television any other way so he agreed to debate McGovern in California. McGovern admitted going into those debates with the frame of mind of trying not to alienate Humphrey, whom he thought he would need in the fall. Humphrey was his old friend but went into "a kind of desperation mode"; he was looking for a knockout punch, and the attacks made in those three debates hurt McGovern very seriously.[62]

Those Humphrey supporters joined in an anybody-but-McGovern last-minute move to deprive him of the California delegation at the national convention. Instead of preparing for that convention, working on an acceptance address, picking a running mate and working on the platform, that time was spent saving a nomination that had already been won.[63]

In order to understand why McGovern came to run for the White House in 1984, it is important to first trace the events that led him to seek the presidency in 1972, as well as to speak a little about how his career and his reputation evolved. Before delving into that matter, however, it may be helpful to take a brief glimpse of what led McGovern to 1972— how the man emerged from political obscurity to become the Democratic Party nominee.

After World War II, McGovern, the son of a Methodist minister, came back from war as a bomber pilot with an idealistic sense of social justice and a belief in the need for international reconciliation. He earned his

Ph.D. in American history at Northwestern University and took a teaching position at Dakota Wesleyan University.[64] In 1952 the Dakota Wesleyan University yearbook, *The Tumbleweed*, was dedicated to George McGovern. "Often in annual dedications it is felt that the selection must be confined only to those with the longest periods of service." This principle was changed in 1952 because the students felt his excellence of service made George McGovern well qualified despite the fact that he had been on the teaching staff for two years. In that short time, he "found his place in the hearts of students both in and out of the classroom. He is one of those capable few who can associate intimately with the students and share their problems, yet command their respect in the deepest sense of the word." *The Tumbleweed* was dedicated to him; they wrote, "not only because of his excellence as a teacher, but more so because of his warm personal qualities and understanding of all sides of student life."[65]

In 1952 the South Dakota Democratic chairman offered him the job of building a statewide party and the following year McGovern resigned his full-time faculty position against the advice of all his friends, and accepted the job. To put it mildly, South Dakota was Republican territory. In the legislature, Republicans outnumbered Democrats 108 to 2, and there had not been a Democrat in the state's congressional delegation for twenty years. In his autobiography, McGovern recalled that his three years of building the party were the liveliest, happiest time of his life. He not only rebuilt the party but also created enough contacts and name recognition to win a seat in Congress in 1956.[66] McGovern believed that the most far-fetched political dream could come true if he worked hard enough. He learned "the enormous value, not only in politics, but in diplomacy, in anything, of personal contact. By getting out and meeting people face-to-face, just by working hard at it, you could overcome a lot of disadvantages." McGovern was also convinced that Franklin D. Roosevelt was right, that government programs could provide far more effective solutions to public problems than the private sector. Government should guarantee civil rights, return the unemployed to work, feed the hungry, and ensure world peace.[67]

Against the conventional wisdom of the day, McGovern succeeded in being reelected to Congress in 1958. In 1960, when he lost a Senate race to Karl Mundt, President John F. Kennedy appointed him director of the Food for Peace Program and special assistant to the president. In 1962, he narrowly won a Senate seat and began to emerge as a proponent of the liberal, activist government that he learned from Roosevelt's New Deal. Barely nine months into his Senate term, he began speaking out against increased U.S. involvement in Vietnam. Although his manner had been described as quiet and soft spoken, he gave speeches in which he passionately and relentlessly criticized the war. And although it was unpopular in South Dakota to oppose the war, McGovern could not be silent.[68]

There was no more pressing or divisive issue facing the country from 1965 until the 1972 election than the Vietnam War. Although McGovern endorsed the Tonkin Gulf Resolution in 1965, he gradually broke with the Johnson administration over Vietnam, and in 1968 he supported the presidential bid of Robert F. Kennedy, but only after Lyndon B. Johnson announced he wouldn't run.[69] "He (LBJ) was angry at his critics. . . . I never blamed Johnson for the Vietnam War but for continuing the war that he inherited," McGovern later explained.[70] At that time, McGovern, and a handful of other Democratic senators—Wayne Morse, Frank Church, and Ernest Gruening—were a thorn in the side of the Senate and House Democratic leadership with whom President Lyndon B. Johnson met regularly.[71] Democratic Party regulars, for the most part, all supported the Johnson administration's policy on the war, as did most Southerners and labor leaders. They also supported Hubert Humphrey for the Democratic Party nomination in 1968.[72]

In 1968, the two antiwar candidates, Eugene McCarthy and Robert Kennedy, competed in the primaries, but it was the party leaders who nominated Humphrey. The party, deeply divided over the war, also fostered hostility and division at the manner in which its candidates were nominated. In a large number of states, party leaders had appointed the delegates. Therefore, in 1968, a candidate such as Humphrey could be nominated by the party-appointed delegates without the need of winning a single delegate primary. The reaction of the liberal antiwar faction of the party was to force the creation of two commissions on party reform.[73]

In 1968, the year he was to seek his first reelection to the Senate, McGovern first seriously considered the idea of running for president. Only two weeks prior to the nomination, on August 10, 1968, McGovern announced his candidacy and became the leader of the 300 or so leaderless delegates of the late Robert F. Kennedy and received 146½ delegate votes at the convention. His belief that he, not Hubert Humphrey or Eugene McCarthy, was most able to withdraw from Vietnam, and that he could best lead America, convinced him that he should make a serious run for the presidency.[74] "I was so mad about the war that there was nothing that could have kept me out of that race," he later said of his decision to run in 1972.[75] For McGovern, the Vietnam intervention by the United States was a "criminal, immoral, senseless, undeclared, unconstitutional, catastrophe."[76]

After the Democratic convention in 1968, there were massive defections by antiwar activists who saw little or no difference between Humphrey and Nixon. Many did not work or even vote in the general election. Despite McGovern's significant differences with Humphrey over the war, he nonetheless pledged his full support for his old friend and campaigned hard for him. The divisions among Democrats were so deep in 1968 that Humphrey was able to garner just under 43 percent of the vote.[77]

The Commission on Party Structure and Delegate Selection caused a great division within the ranks of the Democratic Party, as well as its relationship with organized labor. And its first chairman was South Dakota Senator George McGovern. The Commission endorsed reforms requiring that all delegates to the National Convention be elected. At that time, only twenty-two states scheduled primaries for 1972.[78] The goal behind the McGovern Commission, as McGovern saw it in 1970, was to unite the Democratic Party—to pull it together—not to tear it apart. The reforms were to draw back into the party the young, women, farmers, and Wall Street.[79] Until that time, nonprimary states appointed delegates at the pleasure of the party leadership. The McGovern Commission guidelines required that party caucuses, which at that time were a mere formality and held without much notice or publicity, be held in the year of the election, open to all Democrats, and well publicized. State parties would now be required to encourage minorities, young people, and women to participate as national convention delegates. Although these reforms were meant to lead to party unity, the result was further division within the party. Party and labor leaders were less than enthusiastic, and resentment toward Commission Chairman McGovern was beginning to fester.[80]

Even though the reforms succeeded in bringing countless newcomers into the Democratic Party nominating process, many party leaders grew disenchanted with the process of running for election and dropped out of the process. Most party leaders who did run for delegate were pledged to Maine Senator Edmund Muskie. Organized labor saw the new rules as an attack by liberals upon labor's influence in the Democratic Party. The purpose of the reform, to open the process, backfired. Although McGovern balanced his delegate slate in 1972 with grassroots activists, Muskie relied heavily upon the party leadership for delegate slates.[81]

The divisions within the party from 1968 only deepened in 1972. Although the party leadership nominated its man in 1968, the antiwar supporters succeeded, in large measure due to the reforms of the McGovern Commission, to nominate George McGovern in 1972. However, neither faction could win without the support of the other.[82]

As early as October 1971, labor organizations worked to block Senator Harold Hughes from the chairmanship of the Credentials Committee, which would interpret the new rules. Hughes was regarded as a "far out" left-wing reformer by George Meany, president of the AFL-CIO.[83] Labor organizations' disdain for the eventual nominee, George McGovern, was simmering, and it viewed the reforms with indignation. For labor organizations, the new rules were seen as an attempt to take over the party and limit labor's influence. George Meany vowed early on to stop the reforms and, later on, to stop McGovern at all costs. This included labor's abandonment of the Democratic nominee and support for Richard Nixon.[84] In the delegate selection process, labor at first ignored the new rules, but later on ran slates of uncommitted delegates. Their effectiveness was minimal. McGovern's primary campaign, on the other hand, was well organized, built a machine out of antiwar protestors, and made full use of the new rules. Passionate antiwar opponents defeated party leaders pledged to Muskie in party caucuses in state after state. Muskie and labor were playing the game but using outmoded rules.[85]

Despite a twenty-year record in Congress of supporting organized labor on practically everything they tried to accomplish, organized labor opposed McGovern's candidacy primarily because of the war in Vietnam. George Meany was an ardent supporter of the American war in Vietnam and believed there was something unpatriotic about criticizing American involvement in any country.[86] The divisions were so deep that no amount of goodwill could bring labor into the McGovern camp prior to the convention. George Meany told DNC (Democratic National Committee) Chairman Lawrence O'Brien that he was "opposed to George McGovern yesterday . . . is opposed to George McGovern today, and . . . will be opposed to George McGovern tomorrow and forever."[87]

Labor wasn't McGovern's only problem at the convention. The party leadership still hoped to prevent McGovern's nomination by contesting the California delegates. Even though McGovern had won 151 delegates in California's winner-take-all primary, Humphrey's forces, who controlled the Credentials Committee, argued that they should be given votes in proportion to the popular vote. If Humphrey had prevailed, McGovern would have been denied a first-ballot nomination.[88] Despite the ruling eventually going in McGovern's favor, the party leadership and organized labor were already planning McGovern's demise and their subsequent takeover for control of the party.[89] A second and even more damaging problem for McGovern occurred with the ouster of Mayor Richard Daley's Illinois delegation.[90] At the time, Frank Mankiewicz, McGovern's campaign director, observed that "we may have lost Illinois tonight."[91]

Lawrence F. O'Brien, the outgoing Democratic Party chairman whom McGovern eventually convinced to serve as campaign chairman, later spoke of his incredulity over McGovern's indecisiveness and lack of attention to important details as the nominee of the party. He criticized McGovern's handling of the selection of the new Democratic Party chairman, the seating of the Illinois delegation, and the overall disorganization of the general campaign. O'Brien wrote a highly critical account of George McGovern as a presidential nominee and as a national political figure in his autobiography, *No Final Victories*.[92] O'Brien was frustrated by McGovern's less than decisive nature and inability to deal harshly when necessary with his inner circle. Although O'Brien found the 1972 primary effort smartly run and well organized, he found the general campaign effort inept at virtually every level. McGovern, O'Brien frustratingly observed, could not determine his own role in the campaign and would become concerned with details that should have been handled by staffers.[93] Unable or unwilling to focus on the individual feelings of those around him, he attempted instead to pursue those national policies upon which he did remain focused. The net result was a campaign organization that was poorly organized. There was no chief of staff upon whom McGovern could completely rely. The functions of the leadership of the campaign were skewed, and McGovern had (or it at least appeared to O'Brien), on occasion, the tendency to become naturally immersed in the minutia of minor issues.[94]

Much of such criticism of the disorganization within the campaign against Nixon, however, grossly overstates its effect upon the November election results. Whether many of the observations were accurate, they simply pale in comparison to the deep divisions within the party that existed at the late hour in which McGovern finally secured the Democratic nomination, Nixon's "southern strategy," the Eagleton situation, and the "radical" label.[95] For O'Brien, McGovern was judged by those he attracted, many of whom shared his policy on the war in Vietnam but who shared little else. Opposition from party regulars and organized labor, coupled with the Eagleton nomination, left McGovern, already a weakened candidate, with little possibility of a November victory. The party regulars who, by and large, were not fans of George McGovern had been convinced early on that McGovern could not win, so they did not waste the time, money, or prestige on his candidacy.[96] Although he was respected by his colleagues for doing his homework and paying attention to details, McGovern was not considered to be a major force with Senate Democrats. Even after winning major primaries in New York and California, McGovern was seen by many within the party as an upstart and an outsider. He lacked connections not only with labor, but also with mayors and black leaders.[97] McGovern, however, clearly viewed himself as a "party man."[98] His views may have been somewhat to the left of his party, but he was more than willing to accommodate them to political imperatives.[99] The party regulars complained that his positions were extreme to some and badly defined to others.[100]

Boston Congressman Tip O'Neill, the future Speaker of the House, came away from the 1972 Democratic National Convention greatly disappointed in McGovern's nomination and was contemptuous of his followers. An ardent Muskie supporter, O'Neill described McGovern's nomination as a "disaster." O'Neill told the press, "we got beat by the cast of *Hair*." He was later critical of McGovern for possessing neither the polish nor the charisma required of a national figure who sought election to the highest office in the land. As for being a legislator, O'Neill did not think McGovern had much of a record to run on.[101]

Harsh criticism of McGovern by many party regulars grew partly out of their belief that in 1968 McGovern helped cost Lyndon B. Johnson another term as president because of McGovern's alleged opposition to Johnson.[102] In truth, McGovern never did join the battle cry to dump Johnson.[103] Party regulars also objected to McGovern's candidacy because they perceived that he was going further to the left than they believed was necessary and should have taken more moderate positions.[104]

The irony is that, as *Newsweek* correctly reported in 1972, McGovern's so-called "radicalism" was the stuff of the 1930s and 1940s, not the hysterical 1960s and early 1970s.[105] In 1972 McGovern advocated reducing the defense budget by $32.5 billion within three years, and his defense advisers at the time, who included former Pentagon hand Herbert York and Herbert Scoville, a one-time disarmament official, firmly believed in the need for a credible deterrent. The McGovern plan called for building the budget from the bottom up instead of just trimming items off the current inventory. McGovern believed that adequate strength could be achieved with vastly reduced hardware.[106] His plan was not only politically inexpedient, but also challenged regulars within his own party who viewed his positions as unacceptable and extreme.[107] Perhaps they were too risky to chance with the electorate. For the average voter, McGovern's positions were difficult to comprehend, if they reached the electorate at all.

Former Senator Gary Hart, McGovern's 1972 campaign manager, has argued that, out of the field of candidates, only George McGovern could have defeated Richard Nixon. McGovern had a message of hope and change from the status quo. The acknowledged Democratic frontrunner, Senator Edmund Muskie, offered nothing new in terms of ideas. McGovern was no radical, Hart has written. His staff and advisers were all members of the Democratic Party mainstream. Yet his candidacy created a phenomenon by offering hope to millions who were disillusioned by the events of the 1960s. However, Hart concedes that the Eagleton situation shattered any chance McGovern had to emerge as a competent leader, and his campaign was thereafter doomed.[108]

In hindsight one could well argue that, in all probability, no Democrat could have won in 1972.[109] A June 1972 Gallup poll showed Nixon increasing his lead over McGovern by 43 to 30 and Humphrey by 43 to 26. The conventional wisdom of the day was that no candidate could beat Nixon.[110] With all of McGovern's campaign problems, he ran only about 4 percent behind what Humphrey had done against Nixon four years earlier. Nixon was too formidable an opponent for McGovern, the nominee of a deeply divided Democratic Party.[111] In hindsight we also know that the Democrats, from their presidential candidate on down, were hurt by dirty political money and the most money ever spent up to that time in a presidential campaign.[112] Because the extent of the Nixon campaign's dirty tricks and the Watergate scandal came to light only after the election, those issues could not be translated into votes at the time by the McGovern campaign.[113] But despite all of the campaign shortcomings, there was, as Hart has written, a "McGovern phenomenon."[114] The same cannot be said of Walter Mondale or Michael Dukakis. In the years to follow, young people, who had been brought into politics for the first time by McGovern's campaign, became state legislators, congressmen, senators, governors, and even a president.

In the course of his long and largely successful political career, George McGovern had lost tough elections and had accepted defeat. The year 1972 is the lone exception. "Nineteen seventy-two, against Nixon, that's the one. That's the one that's always been, well, been frustrating for me, been hurtful. I have never been able to get myself to accept that was a fair one. . . . If I felt that people really had a chance to hear what I was saying, that would be acceptable. . . . But I don't think that happened," McGovern explained.[115] The 1972 election is the nightmare that would not go away because it not only branded him a loser, but also the biggest loser in modern presidential politics. Eagleton's disclosure of mental illness gave McGovern a nagging sense of unfairness. "I've thought and thought about it. Was it a result of the Eagleton thing, or all the intensive negative advertising or, I don't know, but I just don't feel I had a fair shot." McGovern clearly believed that his real message did not get out.[116] It was buried, he believed, in a blizzard of negative advertising and bad press.[117] But for McGovern, the 1972 election results were not a humiliating rejection. "It doesn't seem so humiliating," he said, "when you remember that the Nixon crowd was sentenced to a total of 180 years in the penitentiary."[118]

In 1983 McGovern wrote, in defending himself from the conventional wisdom of being "too far out" in 1972, that his defeat was largely attributable to Nixon's "southern strategy" and his problem with Eagleton. He rejected the theory that a Democratic nominee must "stand in the center of the road" in order to win.[119] He believed that one of the reasons for the timidity of the 1984 Democratic contenders—especially Hart, and to a lesser degree Mondale—was their fear of falling victim to the kind of defeat he suffered in 1972. McGovern clearly believed that intellectual honesty on the issues was far more important than election results. McGovern also faulted his 1972 defeat on the inability of George Wallace, after his shooting, to mount an independent campaign as he had done in 1968. McGovern believed that the combination of the Wallace vote with the Republican vote permitted Nixon's "southern strategy" to create the formula for the Nixon landslide of 1972.[120]

McGovern wanted to be remembered "as the man who led the '72 effort that . . . put the domestic political pressure on the administration to end the [Vietnam] war. Second, he "opened up the political process and . . . brought in the women, the young people, the minorities, the poor, and people who had never been involved in a presidential selection process."[121]

The Nixon campaign did make a heavy investment in distortion and deception, and McGovern was troubled at the outset with the Eagleton problem, which received more press during the campaign than the Watergate cover-up. The conventional wisdom among many Democrats that McGovern lost in 1972 by being "too far out" is simply historically inaccurate.[122]

McGovern faced a difficult reelection campaign to the Senate in 1974. In that campaign he pledged that he would not seek the presidency again.[123] Nevertheless, the drive for the Democratic nomination was still burning. He believed that seeking the nomination was the best way to remain a force within the party. He hoped that his liberal message of 1972 would be carried into the 1976 race. By 1975 and into early 1976, many of McGovern's inner core had become involved with other candidates vying for the Democratic nomination.[124] Although he had used the Vietnam issue as well as the newcomers to the party in the delegate selection process to capture the 1972 nomination, he remained politically dead. He was treated by the Democratic establishment as some sort of leper. Not only were his positions ridiculed, but so was the man himself. It was as if the Democratic leadership had unwittingly adopted the mud-slung rhetoric on him espoused by Richard Nixon.[125]

McGovern believed that he could still put his 1972 coalition together even without the issue of the Vietnam War. If the party were to turn to him again in 1976, his plan was not to attempt to broaden his base within the party while alienating his core supporters. He believed that he should remain ideologically pure to his base and reach out to the Republicans and Independents. McGovern believed that unity of the Democratic Party was neither possible nor desirable because the result was such a fractured party, one that prohibited a November victory. Instead, McGovern believed his own base within the Democratic Party with a coalition of Independents and Republicans would succeed. By the summer of 1975, McGovern had held several meetings with his 1972 aides. Each time they tried to discourage a run for the nomination.[126]

By October, several candidates were already actively vying for the nomination. He felt (as he would feel again in 1983) that the candidates were not enunciating liberal objectives. He also felt that he was the best qualified to bring that agenda to the American people.[127] With no clear liberal candidate emerging from the pack, two draft Humphrey campaigns were organized. It was difficult for McGovern to stomach Humphrey as the beneficiary of a convention stalemate. McGovern had been right on the war, on the corrupted administration of Richard Nixon, and yet his supporters were out there supporting many of the other candidates. At one point, McGovern even suggested to Hubert Humphrey that they run as a team in 1976—Humphrey for president, McGovern for vice president.

Humphrey, for his part, quoted McGovern as encouraging him to run for president but neglected to mention the suggestion was that they run as a team.[128]

At the Louisville issue convention in November, where there was a local demonstration protesting school busing, McGovern challenged all the candidates to support court-ordered school desegregation by busing "openly and plainly." Any candidate who opposed busing would be actively opposed by him, McGovern said. Jackson and Carter, who were critical of busing, were outraged at his attack. None of the candidates, in fact, wanted busing to be a central issue in the campaign. McGovern succeeded only in being perceived as being out there further on his own.[129] For the remainder of his political career, McGovern continued to be plagued by this misperception.

Going into the 1984 race, McGovern, as expected initially, received scorn and ridicule from the press and others who were incapable of accepting anything less than the possibility of ultimate victory. This would have prevented virtually every politician from entering the race—every politician except George McGovern. McGovern took great risk in running for president again in 1984. He knew he would face ridicule from the media and from many of his former colleagues, but what troubled him most was the criticism heaped upon him by his friends and past supporters. Few stood with the former South Dakota senator in his final quest for his party's presidential nomination; it was all too clear that the man who won an impossible nomination twelve years earlier did not stand a chance of winning again. So, as in many of his political races, McGovern stood virtually alone. Armed with only a few dollars in his hand, George McGovern waited in line to make 250 copies of his announcement speech to become the Democratic Party's seventh candidate for the presidency in 1984 on September 13, 1983.[130]

This book, then, examines the issues McGovern raised, the campaign he waged, his treatment by the press, and, of course, the reception of his message by the American people. It will explore how he challenged each voter to look beyond all the glitter and hype and to simply "vote your conscience."

It will give an account of a defeated U.S. senator, the 1972 loser to Richard Nixon who jumped back into the political arena one final time in order to have an impact on the political debate. What were the issues that were so important for McGovern that he would risk ridicule, scorn, and humiliation? In just six months of campaigning, McGovern, who had been defeated in his bid for a fourth term in the U.S. Senate only three years earlier, managed to alter the course of the debate throughout the remaining months of the presidential campaign. He boldly advocated a reduction in defense spending and introduced a ten-point platform in stark contrast to the issues being espoused by the eventual Republican nominee, President Ronald Reagan.

McGovern's campaign platform, the ten-point program, was a logical extension of the New Deal liberalism once advocated by FDR, Adlai Stevenson, Robert F. Kennedy, and McGovern himself. Many members of the press believed that McGovern sought to change America's perception of him as a radical. But McGovern sought merely to articulate those policies that were not forcefully being addressed by the six announced candidates. McGovern, never the spectator, could no longer stand idly by knowing that important issues were being ignored. And by and large, he was successful. He showed liberals just how far off course liberalism had strayed. But more than that, he brought a sense of unity to the party badly torn by the resounding defeat of President Jimmy Carter in the 1980 election.

Throughout his thirty-year political career, George McGovern boldly and consistently advocated far-reaching solutions to the difficult problems of our day. He believed with all his heart that "it is possible for mankind to lay the conditions for a peaceful world," but also recognized that it is necessary to devote a considerable amount of time and energy in studying the forces at work in today's world. McGovern regarded the constant single threat to peace coming from "impatient and over-emotional individuals who see every issue in either black or white, and who expect solutions to every problem overnight." It was clear to McGovern that "building for peace is the most painstaking and perhaps the most frustrating effort in which a human being can become involved." Throughout his political career, he sought to influence public support for peace-building organizations and to promote a worldview other than one that centered our interests and our efforts on purely local considerations. "Every citizen," he said, "no matter how young or old needs to understand that it is no longer possible to draw an identifying line between domestic and international affairs."[131] His entry into the 1984 race further demonstrated his vision and determination in leading America toward the path of common sense.

George McGovern's last political campaign, like the man himself, was significant for its simple honesty and conviction. There remained a lot of the teacher in him on the campaign trail. Indeed, he spoke more like a teacher than a political orator. And, in many respects, he thought of himself "as trying to mold public opinion, educate, inform the public and . . . [be] inspiring."[132]

Like the lone voice in a crowd, George McGovern has never hesitated to espouse the values upon which this nation was founded, and for which it still strives. Unlike many post–World War II politicians, McGovern was a man with a vision; throughout his career, he had been determined to keep America on a straight course, remaining true to her ideals. He considered himself a compassionate man who knew war firsthand. That is why he detested it and sought peaceful solutions to the world's problems. "The personal trait I value very highly is my sense of history," he explained. "By that I mean the capacity to understand what forces have brought this country to a position of greatness in the world and, beyond that, a capacity to know what is important in our own day, the causes we ought to be identified with and those we ought to oppose."[133]

Pat Donovan observed that McGovern's greatest political motivation was described best in a *New York Times* profile, which began: "Food, farmers and his fellow men are the three foundation stones upon which George Stanley McGovern has built his philosophy of life."[134] That is so true.

CHAPTER ONE

The New Right and the Old Paranoia: Senate Defeat

If they [the Radical Right] disagree with you one bit, you're a no good s.o.b.

—U.S. Senator Barry Goldwater

On August 16, 1979, conservative political activists announced that they were "targeting" for defeat five liberal Democratic U.S. senators seeking reelection, using a relatively untested campaign weapon. The Democratic Senators included Birch Bayh of Indiana, Frank Church of Idaho, Alan Cranston of California, John Culver of Iowa, and George McGovern of South Dakota. The National Conservative Political Action Committee (NCPAC) announced that it would use "negative" campaign tactics to unseat liberal legislators. The committee announced at the onset of their effort to unseat the liberals that they were prepared to spend about $700,000 on the brief, intensive effort to increase the senators' negative poll ratings.[1] To achieve this in South Dakota, the New Right groups planned to attack Senator McGovern on his liberal voting record, specifically with regard to his record on abortion, in an attempt to soften him up for his conservative Republican opponent.[2]

There were several factors that the NCPAC planned to take advantage of. One such factor was the campaign spending law, which limited group contributions to $5,000 in support of a candidate, but which put no limitation on how much one could spend against a candidate. Unlimited "independent" spending was only permitted when there was coordination of any kind between the individual that was doing the spending and the candidate's organization.[3]

According to figures compiled by the Federal Election Commission, NCPAC's budget for the five-state effort, money that it raised through direct-mail campaigns, was nearly triple the amount of all independent spending for or against Senate candidates in 1978.[4]

John Dolan, chairman of NCPAC, stated at a news conference that he could turn between 10 and 20 percent of the people in South Dakota against McGovern simply by convincing them that McGovern is doing a "rotten job." Dolan believed that Senator McGovern was "basically disloyal" to his constituents by voting contrary to the philosophy of South Dakota. Dolan freely admitted that the advertising was "totally and unabashedly negative." Referring to the voters, Dolan said that he hoped they would be influenced by the negatives, although they may not remember why.[5]

One week before McGovern's announcement rally at the Mitchell Corn Palace, newspaper ads appeared in daily newspapers around the state questioning the records of McGovern and his upcoming guest, Senator Robert Byrd.[6]

The ads, which posed six questions, were taken to task by McGovern, who explained that he and Byrd had cast over 10,000 roll call votes. "If the best the opposition can do is ask six questions, I think they are in sad shape," he said. "If the campaign tricksters in the East Coast ad room who are spending all this money in South Dakota had talked to me, I could tell them a lot more than six mistakes I've made the last 17 years," McGovern added.[7]

McGovern was infuriated that his opposition chose to attack his friend, Senator Robert Byrd. "I do resent it when a guest is here from another state, and is not running for anything here to be subjected to that kind of treatment."[8]

The ad was paid for by a group that called itself "People for an Alternative to McGovern," an arm of the National Conservative Political Action Committee. "These people do not represent, in my judgment, the interests of the people of South Dakota," McGovern said.[9]

The ad also charged that McGovern voted against farmers on thirteen of fourteen critical issues, according to the American Farm Bureau Federation.[10] McGovern responded:

> That is a plain unadulterated piece of poppycock. I have never once in 17 years cast a vote against the farmers of South Dakota and the nation. I may well have voted against the Farm Bureau 13 of 14 times, but that does not mean that I voted against the farmers.[11]

McGovern described the American Farm Bureau Federation as a "big business front" that is "only right about once in 14 times. I'm surprised that I voted with them even once in 14 times."[12]

McGovern took the offensive against the "Target McGovern attacks" and suggested some questions that truly needed to be answered. "Who are you? Where are you getting your money? Why are you so interested in defeating a South Dakota senator that you have been flooding our state with right-wing money from all over the nation for the last two years?" Regarding those hiding behind his primary opponent, McGovern asked, "Who is your candidate? Are you bankrolling the visitor from Texas? How much Texas oil money is being used to pay for these ads? Do you even have a candidate, or are you just a negative bunch out to get McGovern at any cost?"[13]

On February 13, 1980, the majority leader of the U.S. Senate made a 3,000-mile round trip from Washington to South Dakota to participate in the kickoff rally for Senator George McGovern's reelection bid. Senator Robert Byrd, the keynote speaker at the Corn Palace event in Mitchell, said that he would make the trip "two or three more times if I have to." Calling McGovern a "man of integrity," Byrd said he learned of McGovern's integrity when he asked for the senator's vote in his quest for the majority leader's position. "Some people said yes, they'd support me, and then didn't. George McGovern said 'I can't do it; I've known Hubert Humphrey too long. He's been my friend. I can't vote for you; I'm going to vote for Hubert,'" McGovern told him. "There is nothing that a man can be more proud of than integrity," Byrd said to the 1,800 supporters who interrupted him numerous times with loud applause and cheering.[14]

Byrd pointed out that McGovern's seniority and strong support for farmers were great assets to South Dakota. "Don't make a mistake. It's your investment . . . and as long as you have George McGovern, you can rest assured that he will not vote against the American farmer," guaranteed Byrd. "The day he votes against the American farmer is the day I vote against West Virginia coal," Byrd said to thunderous applause.[15]

Byrd praised McGovern as an eloquent spokesman for numerous national issues touting him as a senator with "brains, common sense, and guts." The majority leader heaped praise on McGovern for his early opposition to the war in Vietnam. "It took courage for him to oppose the war . . . he was part of a small and maligned minority, but he had courage, and he was right!" Byrd described McGovern as a cooperative senator who "retains independence of thought and action." Byrd observed that, if defeated, and as next in line to chair the Senate Agriculture Committee, he would be forced to appoint a Democrat from another state who wouldn't share South Dakota's interest in agriculture. "Don't put me on that hot seat. Give me back George McGovern!"[16]

"If I think enough of him to travel 1500 miles . . . a man who said, 'I can't vote for you' . . . the people of South Dakota should think enough of him to go to the polls. . . . It's too late when the polls are closed to say, 'I wish I had.' The people who grouse around the most are the ones who won't go to the polls," Byrd said.[17]

McGovern also drew praise from former Governor Harvey Wollman, who emceed the rally and characterized his position as campaign chairman as "probably the most important job I'll ever have."[18]

Congressman Tom Daschle called McGovern a man of vision who "has guts." Daschle characterized McGovern as a senator South Dakota shares with the nation because of the great respect he generates. This admiration has benefited South Dakota "tenfold in the things he's brought back."[19]

McGovern was obviously elated at the turnout and buoyed by the excitement of the night. He advanced several reasons for deserving reelection and took aim at the antiabortion groups who targeted him for defeat.[20]

"I am the strongest pro-life candidate in 1980. This nation began with an assertion of the right to life, liberty, and the pursuit of happiness. Those have been the guiding principles of my public career during every day I have served the people of my state," he said. Explaining that he did not personally favor abortion except in the most extreme circumstances, McGovern called it "the most personal and sacred decision a woman will ever make, and she must make it by consulting her conscience and her doctor, not by waiting for the politicians in Washington to decide it for her." He criticized prolife groups for failing to recognize the complexities of the abortion issue. "To make abortion illegal under all circumstances is to drive desperate women . . . into the back alleys and unsanitary rooms of butchers . . . coat hangers . . . then we will lose not only the fetuses, but the young mothers, and that is not respect for the right to life."[21] Citing his "prolife" stand in the Senate, McGovern explained that he worked "to fight those things that degrade or weaken or exploit human life." Prolife should also include the fight against arms buildup around the world, and actions feeding underdeveloped nations, he declared.[22]

Noting that he was first in line to chair the Senate Agriculture Committee and second in line for chair of the Foreign Relations Committee, McGovern gave his seniority as another reason for deserving reelection. "Seniority in the senate doesn't mean much unless it's used in the public interest. My seniority in the senate has enabled me to prevent the weakening of our farm price support and farm credit programs. My seniority has enabled me to take the lead in utilizing billions of dollars in farm produce in Food for Peace and the nation's domestic food assistance and school lunch programs," McGovern boasted. Referring to himself as "a dove," he said he would use his seniority to oppose the reinstitution of mandatory draft registration unless the country is faced with imminent war.[23]

McGovern explained that a "dove" is a "cool headed bird who doesn't believe in taking the young men of this nation into a war unless the national interest is involved. If any aggressor attacks this nation or our historic allies, I will be a hawk ready for battle."[24]

Referring directly to Larry Schumaker, his first ever primary opponent, McGovern said:

Let me say to him and to anyone else who takes me on . . . you better know where you stand on the concerns of women because women are no longer going to be satisfied with a political run-around or second class citizenship.[25]

Both George and Eleanor McGovern had been in the forefront of the fight for equal rights for women. "It is the most rational thing in the world for me to be a strong advocate of equal rights for women because I have lived with a woman for thirty-six years who not only insists on equal rights, but who has always carried equal responsibilities," he said.[26]

In March, an ad appeared on television in South Dakota with a basketball player dribbling a ball down the court. The announcer said that globetrotter is a great name for a basketball team, but it's a terrible name for a senator. The announcer added, "While the energy crisis was brewing, George McGovern was touring Cuba with Fidel Castro. He also took a one-month junket to Africa. All at the taxpayer's expense." He then concluded, "No wonder he lost touch with South Dakota. With so many problems at home, we need a Senator, and not a globetrotter." This commercial, and others similar to it, also depicted McGovern as a radical for his stands on abortion, gun control, the equal rights amendment, and the economy.[27]

"There's no question about it, we are a negative organization that wants to get rid of . . . bad votes in the Senate," boasted Dolan. "We're interested in ideology. We're not interested in respectability." What made the negative campaign so unusual was that it sought to defeat Senator McGovern without openly promoting any challengers.[28]

Past efforts of conservatives were aimed at seeking control over the Republican Party, but the new method appeared to be aimed at creating coalitions among special interest groups, such as the gun lobby, antiabortionists, and those opposed to SALT II.[29]

According to the McGovern campaign, close to $400,000 had been budgeted against them. Dolan, however, claimed that the figure was closer to $100,000. McGovern was depicted in fund-raising leaflets as a "radical left extremist" who voted for handgun control, spoke on behalf of homosexuals, praised Cuba, and had "been an enemy of the F.B.I. and C.I.A. since he came to the Senate in 1962."[30] One newspaper advertisement stated, "George McGovern voted against you when he voted to bail out New York City and its labor unions, bureaucrats and crooked politicians and cost South Dakota more inflation."[31]

Even greater controversy was stirred by an antiabortion group, Stop the Baby Killers, which sent out letters to South Dakota and other states that stated that McGovern and his liberal colleagues were "political baby killers" who "apparently think it's perfectly O.K. to slaughter unborn infants by abortion."[32]

George Cunningham, McGovern's administrative assistant, believed that groups such as these were very dangerous to the political system because they use issues, such as abortion, as a facade to try to defeat liberals and moderates.[33]

Dolan admitted that his effort to unseat McGovern was rooted in a loophole created by the U.S. Supreme Court when it ruled in 1976 that independent groups could spend unlimited amounts on political causes, as long as they did not coordinate their efforts with any candidate.[34]

According to Dolan, images are important, not issues. He stated, "We start early and use repetition and it's bound to have an impact. Start with an image like George McGovern doesn't represent South Dakota. Keep hitting away. That's more effective than George McGovern did or didn't do X, Y, or Z for South Dakota."[35]

On June 1, 1980, churchgoers across South Dakota returned to their cars to find brochures featuring pictures of a dead fetus and of Senator George McGovern's face slashed with a large X, along with the assertion that he had "continuously voted tax dollars to kill preborn children." All that week, the week of McGovern's first Democratic primary challenge in his eighteen years in the Senate, South Dakotans heard radio commercials denouncing the senator as a big-spending liberal who was weak on national defense. These types of advertisements were pumped into South Dakota by national antiabortion and conservative political action groups that joined forces to defeat him.[36]

When asked to respond to charges against NCPAC's unfair treatment of McGovern, Dolan replied, "McGovern is a liberal Senator from a conservative state, and his record really is outrageous. Not every member of the Senate pals around with Castro. We felt that we could make McGovern vulnerable."[37] According to McGovern, the assault was effective in defeating him. "It's hurt," he remarked. "I'm always answering negative questions: 'Is it true you're a pal of Fidel Castro's, that you sold the Panama Canal to the Communists, that you want to kill the unborn?' It's all these off-the-wall right-wing ideas. They've been running this stuff for two years, and there's no question that it creates a negative mood."[38]

Among other national organizations opposed to McGovern were the National Right to Life Committee, Life Amendment Political Action Committee, Committee for the Survival of a Free Congress, National Conservative Caucus, American Conservative Union, Fund for a Conservative Majority, Young Americans for Freedom, the John Birch Society, Citizens for the Republic, National Right to Work, Eagle Forum, Citizen's Committee for the Right to Keep and Bear Arms, Gun Owners of America, Tax Limitation Committee, Committee to Defeat the Union Bosses, and Committee to Save the Panama Canal. Groups in South Dakota included People for an Alternative to McGovern, the Senatorial Research Committee, People Who Want a New Senator, and Target McGovern, an organization started by Dale Bell, a campaign aide to Ronald Reagan in 1976.

Target McGovern sent out more than 200,000 pieces of literature, enough to reach a third of the state's population.[39]

Senator McGovern, who already spent over $750,000 on his reelection effort by June 1980, said that he was troubled by the emerging alliance between antiabortion and conservative political interests. "I worry about the right-to-lifers getting into bed with these extremist right-wing groups," he said. "A lot of right-to-lifers are being used by the right-wing without realizing they're sort of political dupes."[40]

For the first and only time in his South Dakota political career, McGovern had primary opposition. In his view, the antiabortion groups were responsible for the right-to-life candidacy of his primary opponent, Larry Schumaker, a mathematics teacher from Texas, who supported a constitutional amendment outlawing abortion. Schumaker, a political novice, was born in South Dakota but left in 1961 and did not return until he announced his candidacy in the winter of 1979.[41] "The battle against McGovern on abortion was unrelenting and very vicious in the extreme," recalled George Cunningham.[42] According to McGovern, the right-to-lifers "brought Larry Schumaker up here from Texas and are providing the organizational strength, the bodies, everything."[43]

Schumaker was endorsed by the South Dakota Life Amendment Committee and his campaign was promoted by national antiabortion groups such as the Virginia-based Life Amendment Political Action Committee. The National Abortion Rights Action League contributed thousands of dollars to Schumaker's campaign. The antiabortion drive against Senator McGovern also received the active support of many religious leaders, such as the Rev. Thomas Burns, who wrote fellow Roman Catholic priests and urged them to oppose McGovern and to support Schumaker.[44]

On August 4, 1980, the week that marked the thirty-fifth anniversary of the birth of the nuclear age when the city of Hiroshima disappeared in a searing explosion resulting from a single nuclear device, McGovern came to the floor of the U.S. Senate acknowledging that most pollsters and pundits were telling America that the economy was the number one issue. But he believed that the central concern of our time was the survival of humanity in the nuclear age. He recognized that either the Soviet Union or the United States could launch a nuclear war that would not only end life in those two countries but also would end most forms of life on planet Earth. If that happened, of course, McGovern said, there would be "no worries over inflation, or taxes, or energy or government efficiency. There will be only the horrible remains of a dead or dying civilization choking in radioactive dust."[45]

McGovern called on the Senate to act on the SALT II treaty by March of 1981 at the latest, or it would be too late for the Soviets to further comply with "that particular formula," which, he believed, was clearly in the interest of the United States. Failure to do this, he cautioned, would send us back to the drawing boards and unknown years of additional negotiations before another treaty could be devised.[46]

SALT II, he said, would not diminish the importance of a firm Western response to Soviet intervention in Afghanistan. The result of U.S.-Soviet cooperation to reduce the threat of nuclear war would not diminish the competitive aspects of Soviet-American relations in other areas. "SALT is not a favor we give to the Soviets and it is not a reward for good behavior."[47]

He called upon the U.S. Senate to return SALT II to the agenda. McGovern further argued for calling the role before adjournment in the fall to test the current support for SALT II, and if the Senate could not ratify the treaty before the November 4 elections, he called for returning to a postelection special session devoted solely to the nuclear treaty. And if the nuclear treaty had not been ratified by the end of the year, McGovern called for making the ratification of SALT II the first order of business in the new administration and the new Congress in January 1981.[48]

In order to focus the attention of the Senate and the nation on this "most crucial imperative," McGovern submitted a resolution setting forth the urgency of Senate ratification of SALT II and invited his Senate colleagues on both sides of the aisle to cosponsor "that resolution of hope and common sense."[49]

Some political strategists believed that McGovern would lose his reelection fight unless Senate Agriculture Chairman Herman Talmadge was beaten in his runoff election in Georgia on August 26. The reasoning behind this theory was that McGovern was in line to succeed Talmadge and that South Dakota farmers would love to see their senator in the chairman's seat. Since Talmadge won, one can only speculate on its validity.[50]

By September, Senator McGovern was fiercely fighting an uphill battle for reelection. By his own description, he was the "juiciest target" of the well-financed and well-organized attacks aimed at liberal legislators around the country. National Democratic Party officials also believed that he was the most vulnerable Democrat up for reelection in 1980, "an unrepentant liberal in a relentlessly conservative state, a man who had never had an easy election in 24 years of public service."[51]

In the primary, where he was opposed by a political unknown, voters were inundated with flyers depicting dead fetuses and asserting that the senator regularly voted to "kill preborn children," that he was friends with Fidel Castro, that he was somehow responsible for the Panama Canal treaties, that he favored a weak military posture, and that he advocated a 50 cent a gallon tax on gasoline, which he did not.[52]

Although McGovern won the primary, with his little-known opponent receiving 38 percent of the vote, his general election campaign was badly damaged.[53]

McGovern's Republican opponent, U.S. Representative James Abdnor, was a four-term congressman with a solidly conservative voting record and virtually no enemies. According to Roger Kasa, managing editor of *The Huron Daily Plainsman*, Abdnor was seen by many as one of the few "nice guys" left in politics. If McGovern was to be beaten, Abdnor was the right man to do the job.[54]

By the end of September, things were looking slightly better for McGovern's chances. The conservative assaults, including the charges that he was antifamily, began to backfire. And McGovern campaigned steadily, pounding home his message that his small, rural home state needed a man with his influence to protect their agricultural interests in Washington. The people recognized that McGovern had been a very effective senator. "He may be liberal, but he's a South Dakotan," said Kasa.[55]

The Republican Senatorial Campaign Committee placed the senator at the top of its list of candidates whose defeat it sought. Meanwhile, NCPAC continuously flooded the state with anti-McGovern propaganda. The charges varied, ranging from accusations that the senator was prowelfare and proabortion to allegations that he was against a strong military, but the message never changed: "George McGovern is out of step with his people." Lt. Governor Lowell Hansen, a Republican, observed, "McGovern is a great Senator, but he represents the people of Massachusetts, not South Dakota."[56]

"I think it was really effective," conceded McGovern. "They created so much suspicion and resentment that I was constantly thrown on the defensive. They come in with such self-righteous arrogance," he said. "These people who are putting out the right-to-life issue: they act like God has revealed himself to them and them alone." For McGovern, it was as if the right wing had declared war against the Judeo-Christian ethic and was using the political process for waging battle.[57] Senator McGovern had never mentioned the abortion issue in the U.S. Senate. He believed he was sent to Washington to use his judgment, and if he had always listened to his constituents, he would never have led the opposition to the Vietnam War. Yet, his opposition made abortion the major issue of his 1980 campaign, costing him, for the first time in his career, much of the Democratic vote.[58]

McGovern became indignant over what was happening to him. "I resent it . . . when I come out of God's house on Sunday morning and find that some misguided political agent has put a leaflet on my car accusing me of being anti-family and a killer of babies. Who appointed these single-issue advocates to play the role of God in judging the rest of us by their standards?"

There is no question that the single most important issue of his reelection campaign was abortion. McGovern personally opposed abortion. He explained that he and Eleanor would never have even considered

abortion for any of their five children, even if her life had been endangered. But the key issue is that he didn't support a constitutional
amendment to make abortion illegal. Abdnor did.[59]

Abdnor, a fifty-seven-year-old bachelor, avoided running a highly vis-
ible campaign and refused to debate the senator.[60] Except for the debate
question, Senator McGovern was pretty much kept on the defensive. He
kept trying to explain his position on abortion, especially to the Catho-
lics who made up 20 percent of the voters. Some experts surmise that issue alone may have cost him the election. But for McGovern, the real issue
was which candidate could be the best spokesman for South Dakota.[61]

McGovern also articulated his strong support for agriculture. "If I'm
there," he said, "I'll be the dominant voice for Northern farmers. Senator
Talmadge is only interested in cotton, tobacco, peanuts and rice. I'll be able
to speak for wheat, soybeans and feed grains. I want to be there to save
our farmers." McGovern was interested in the details of agricultural policy
partly because of his longtime interest in nutrition. "That," he asserted,
"is the real way to save human lives, and nobody in the Senate has fought
harder to feed the hungry."[62] McGovern tried, but he could not make his
agricultural policy the dominant theme of his campaign. Abdnor took a
more conservative line on almost every issue discussed in the campaign:
abortion, federal spending, regulation of small businesses, and defense.
No one blamed Abdnor for the ferocious anti-McGovern campaign
mounted by those "out-of-state groups."[63]

Farmers, who accounted for about 30 percent of the state's total vote,
had historically been part of the Democratic coalition. Political observers
are divided on how much support McGovern lost from farmers on conservative issues.[64] According to most experts, however, the most emotional
issue remained McGovern's opposition to a constitutional amendment
outlawing abortion.[65]

McGovern countered antiabortion attacks by insisting that single issues
should never be allowed to decide elections and by stressing his own
personal opposition to abortion. He also expressed outrage that he, with
five children and four grandchildren, could be called "antifamily."[66]

McGovern's campaign, widely recognized as more professional and
better organized than Abdnor's, stressed service to his constituents in
response to the charge of having lost touch with the people of South Dakota. According to Loren Carlson, professor of political science at the
University of South Dakota, McGovern's most important asset was that
he was accessible and that his staff provided prompt, effective service.
Carlson added, "That may not matter in some places, but it's very important in a state like South Dakota where everybody knows everybody."
McGovern not only stressed his commitment to his constituents, but he
also began to take the offensive against Abdnor.[67] He challenged him to

a debate, and when Abdnor refused, McGovern took out full-page newspaper ads touting that "only two politicians have ever refused to debate
George McGovern—Richard Nixon and Jim Abdnor."[68]

McGovern's campaign charged that Abdnor drew much of his campaign money from oil and business donors. One of the liveliest campaign
issues centered on campaign finances. Abdnor's staff charged that
McGovern's successful direct-mail fund-raising efforts gave him an unfair edge. The McGovern forces, however, said that they already spent half
of the $1.2 million raised to counter the negative tactics of NCPAC and
other conservative groups. According to McGovern press spokesman Jeff
Brockelsby, "if you add up all the independent committees that have been
spending money . . . there's a very good chance we'll be outspent by them
all."[69]

McGovern made no apologies for being a liberal, which he defined as
"one who believes the power of the U.S. government ought to be thrown
on the side of the ordinary people."[70] He also proved to be a shrewd campaign tactician. When a national conservative group passed out handbills
that called McGovern, the father of five, a "baby killer" because he
believed women should have a right to abortions, he made an issue of
being smeared by out-of-staters. So many South Dakotans sided with
Senator McGovern in public opinion polls that Abdnor had to disavow
the group's support.[71]

Then, when former President Gerald Ford spent a day campaigning for
Abdnor, McGovern ran a full-page newspaper ad noting that he and Ford
both supported the Panama Canal Treaties, SALT II, and the Equal Rights
Amendment, all of which Abdnor opposed. As a result, Ford spent much
of his time answering hostile questions. Ford also urged that the candidates debate—apparently no one told him that Abdnor refused to debate
Senator McGovern.[72]

By mid-October, McGovern confronted the right-wing attackers head
on. He charged outsiders with bringing distortion and hate into South Dakota, and he attempted to shift public attention from himself to his opponent. He also charged that Abdnor had given up his House seat to run
for the Senate only at the urging of NCPAC and on its promise of money
and tactical support.[73]

It was estimated that by October, the anti-McGovern propaganda ran
from $200,000 to $300,000, which was a great deal of money for a South
Dakota campaign in 1980. The money was spent on television, radio, and
newspaper advertising and for hundreds of thousands of leaflets.[74]

By the time the campaign was winding down, many political observers believed that McGovern would somehow defeat Abdnor despite poll
statistics.[75] However, McGovern could sense that the campaign was in
trouble. Even some traditional Democratic voters who had previously

supported him were cold toward his candidacy, and a few even objected to putting a sign on their lawn.[76] For nearly two years, McGovern had been the target of a coalition of political conservatives and antiabortion groups seeking to oust liberal legislators. Most of the heat, however, was turned on Senator McGovern, both because of his prominence as a liberal who once ran for the presidency and because his state was regarded as fundamentally conservative.

McGovern credited the closing of the wide gap with Abdnor to a tactic of confronting both the issues and his opponent. "We took everything they had," he said. "Nobody was hit harder. We decided to take the issues head on and try to fight it out on substantive grounds."[77]

In the end, McGovern was unable to win reelection in his conservative home state due to the negative campaign tactics of NCPAC and the other right-wing groups, as well as Reagan's landslide victory over Carter in South Dakota, 61 percent to 32 percent. Although McGovern outspent Abdnor $3,237,669 to $1,675,430, he received 39 percent of the vote to Abdnor's 58 percent.[78]

His defeat was seen by many as a litmus test of the strength of these right-wing groups. Although nationally Senator McGovern achieved prominence as a liberal, he was never elected in South Dakota because of his liberal views. He won in his home state because he "shook more hands, walked more main streets, and drove down more dirt roads than his opponents," rather than by demonstrating an ability to speak out in Washington.[79] But morality and politics went hand in hand in rural America, and the ideals of the New Right have always been a basic part of rural South Dakota. In Senator McGovern's 1980 bid for reelection, the conservative political action committees tapped the morality and conservatism of South Dakota and, through "negative campaign practices," used these strong feelings to defeat South Dakota's senior senator.[80]

However, as a result of the counterattack by the McGovern campaign, there were signs of a backlash in South Dakota against the national right-wing groups. Not even the local conservatives were happy about the tactics of NCPAC or the Life Amendment Political Action Committee. By the end of October 1980, NCPAC pulled out of the race in South Dakota. By then, however, far too much damage had been done.[81]

Using the relatively untested campaign weapon of "targeting," the National Conservative Political Action Committee was successful in substantially increasing Senator McGovern's negative poll rating, and thereby softened him up for his conservative Republican opponent. McGovern was often limited to defending against charges of being a "baby killer" and a "radical leftist," rather than being allowed to clearly articulate his actual stands on the issues.

For McGovern intellectually, the 1980 race was a defeat he could accept. He believed that South Dakota wanted somebody more conservative. In a 1984 interview McGovern said, "I wasn't about to change, so they got rid of me. Okay, that's the system."[82]

What happened, you see, was that after I was defeated in the Senate race, we felt a kind of emancipation. Neither of us shed many tears over that one. Oh, sure I wanted to win, and there was the fact of a rejection by your home state and all. But in another way, I was greatly relieved to be out of the Senate. Eleanor and I felt we had lost touch with our country.[83]

Eleanor McGovern was not as understanding. According to her husband, she had been hurt the most in the family.[84] McGovern understood that the criticism was part of the price you paid for playing in the big leagues.[85] Not that he didn't get outraged at times, especially when his ideas were twisted. Of course he would get mad for a short time but then he would forget it. Eleanor, on the other hand, could not adjust to it. She reacted very sensitively to any criticism of her husband because she saw it as kind of a public stripping away of her husband's life and soul.[86]

However, personally McGovern felt like a wounded deer. According to his longtime secretary, Pat Donovan, "he was saddened and offended that the people of South Dakota, for whom he had worked so hard and sacrificed so much, rejected him. He was not so much angry as hurt and determined to go after the right wing groups that had brought him down, so he started the organization Americans for Common Sense."[87] George Cunningham concurred: "McGovern was disappointed with his defeat, but not angry." Seeing the writing on the wall, McGovern worked on his concession speech several weeks in advance.[88]

On December 4, 1980, Senator Edward M. Kennedy spoke on the Senate floor of the common sense of George McGovern. Kennedy lashed out at the New Right that helped defeat McGovern in his courageous bid for reelection. He complimented McGovern on identifying "the New Right groups as the real 'radicals' trading in emotional single issues that inflame, rather than educate or inform, American voters." According to Senator Kennedy, McGovern "based his public life on the politics of hope and the challenge of doing better." Kennedy called McGovern's new coalition, "Americans for Common Sense," another forum to continue his great service to the country and wished his friend and colleague well.[89]

McGovern's loss of his Senate seat gave him a chance to get back in touch with his country. On a Sunday in the spring of 1982, Eleanor and George McGovern got into a car and headed out of Washington, D.C. They drove south on a monthlong tour of America, with a special emphasis on national parks. Eleanor was happier than she had been in years, according to her husband. They began in the Shenandoahs, drove down into the

Smoky Mountains, and drove west across Tennessee. They also saw the Tetons and the Sangre de Cristo, but their best memory was the Great Smokies. They went back again in the spring of 1983 and bought a little cabin near Shagbark, Tennessee. "The Smokies were my compromise to Eleanor," he said. "I am not ruling out New Mexico, [but] it's just so damn far." For the moment, McGovern had a chance to step away from the political arena, but he showed no signs of staying away on a permanent basis.[90]

By the beginning of 1981, McGovern had signed on as a Washington consultant, decided to give speeches all over the country, and agreed to teach a course at Northwestern University. He had a plan to host a syndicated television show, one that would be a liberal version of conservative William F. Buckley's *Firing Line*, and he also planned to write a newspaper column. He remained focused on what he considered the nation's preoccupation with emotional right-wing political issues, and he believed that the political discussion had shifted to these issues.[91]

McGovern was outraged at the way in which the radical New Right had successfully targeted him for defeat. It had been building steam since 1976, and indeed, had even once focused its attention on Arizona Senator Barry Goldwater. It was critical of Goldwater because he backed Ford in 1976 against Ronald Reagan, due to the fact that he considered some of Reagan's positions extreme, particularly with reference to the Panama Canal. Goldwater weathered their criticism, and managed to make some interesting observations. He acknowledged what he judged to be their good qualities—conviction, hard work, and determination—but observed, "[I]f they disagree with you one bit, you're a no good s.o.b."[92] McGovern believed that the radical New Right was not a normal political group that was "able and willing to press its views in our democratic political arena and then accept the outcome, favorable or unfavorable, with a measure of good cheer." For the first time in our nation's history, we were dealing with political evangelists who were angry and intolerant, incapable of believing that they could be mistaken or that those with whom they disagreed might have honorable intentions. Although they called themselves conservative, their zealousness, self-righteousness, and vindictiveness toward those with whom they disagreed connoted something radically different from the conservatism of Robert Taft, Barry Goldwater, or Robert Dole.[93]

McGovern believed the term "conservative" to connote "care and restraint in the initiation of change; not fear for change itself, but fear of its possibly harmful, unintended consequences." He also associated the term with a connotation of careful thinking in the "marshaling of facts and restraint in the drawing of conclusions." McGovern saw true conservatism at fundamental odds with the thinking of the New Right, which proffered "its beliefs as revealed truths to which it brooked no opposition."[94] The tradition from which the New Right sprang was not in the Taft, Goldwater, or Dole tradition, nor was it in the tradition of our nation's founders. Instead, it flowed from what historian Richard Hofstadter has described as the "paranoid style" in American politics—not a mainstream, but characterized by "heated exaggeration, conspicuousness, and conspiratorial fantasy." The paranoiac in politics "tends to regard himself as a righteous innocent set upon by powerful, wicked, and unscrupulous conspirators."[95]

The New Right that emerged as a force in 1980 inherited its tradition from Senator Joe McCarthy and saw "American society as rotten with decay, disintegrating in weakness, unaccountably sold out by office holders who willfully sought to betray their public trust."[96] In 1980, two-thirds of all senators supported the Panama Canal treaties, yet they were perceived to have done so not because they considered it to be in the national interest but because "they actually wished to weaken and betray America." They were seen not merely as political opponents to be opposed and outvoted, but enemies to be eliminated—"targeted." To this radical group, political differences were not questions of judgment, to be negotiated and compromised, but were "conflicts between absolute good and absolute evil to be fought out to a finish." Their activists, according to McGovern, were best understood not as political operators, but as "political theologians, priestly exorcists, in the service of a cause without content." McGovern saw as their driving force not just fear, but paranoid fear, rooted partly in reality but extending beyond the bounds of reality into a fantasy world of "nightmare and menace."[97] When the New Right activists' pervading sense of helplessness takes hold, foreign adversaries are seen as "growing more powerful and threatening while America is seen as growing steadily weaker and more helpless." Their fears are not so much false as they are distorted and exaggerated. They feed on helplessness and do not see the rivalry with the Soviet Union as a circumstance of modern history but instead as the result of the willful stripping away of our nation's strength by the treasonist liberals. Their historical perspective has been traded in for conspiracies and scapegoats, and they direct their attacks against "liberals" such as George McGovern.[98]

McGovern was not affronted so much from the suspicion, malice, and ill will generated by the paranoid politics of the New Right, but from the degradation of political dialogue in America that is its result. The New Right distracts from serious, pressing issues that government can and should act upon and diverts political dialogue into irrelevancies such as one's private morality and personal lifestyle, which are only marginally, if at all, government's business.[99]

Personally, McGovern had no particular reluctance to discuss personal matters but preferred to do so as an individual rather than as a public official. He believed that private matters are not the business of government:

> I personally feel no need of the preachments of the radical right for guidance in the love of God and family, and I doubt that the citizens of South Dakota need or want such guidance from me or any other public servant, because that is not what they hired us for.[100]

McGovern saw a difference between "moralizing" and "morality" in politics. Prior to the 1980 election, McGovern believed that the radical right would "burn out, becoming a victim of their own narrowness, their obsession with ideological purity and their basic poverty of ideas." After his defeat, however, he took a far different posture.[101]

As soon as the elections were over, McGovern turned his attention to building a citizen counterforce to this zealous, dangerous, radical-right movement.[102] McGovern believed that our entire political process was under attack by a well-organized, well-financed, cleverly orchestrated coalition of reactionaries and extremists, many of them single-issue zealots. They had combined a new technique of direct mail, computers, public opinion polling, and radio and television advertising to disseminate the gospels of extremism, distortion, defamation, fear, and paranoia, he said.[103] To combat these zealots, McGovern formed "Americans for Common Sense," which was made up of people who refused to stand by silently while the radical right corrupted and destroyed our democratic process. As a first step, he sought to expose the Moral Majority and the radical right for what they really were. He envisioned a process involving the holding of real issue town meetings, television programs, creating a resource library on the activities of the radical right, and publishing periodic reports on their activities, and he estimated that it would require an annual budget of $147,000 just to publish the intelligence report.[104]

Richard A. Viguerie, a right-wing, direct-mail specialist who once served as executive director of the Young Americans for Freedom, boasted that they already took control of the conservative movement and that conservatives had taken control of the Republican Party. "The remaining thing is to see if we can take control of the country," Viguerie said.[105] McGovern's Americans for Common Sense sought to meet head-on the dangerous marriage of political zealots and religious extremists who used television and direct mail to impose their beliefs on America.[106] The initial fund-raising letter for Americans for Common Sense was sent to 100,000 people whose names were taken from liberal mailing lists; it raised an almost immediate $75,000.[107]

By the spring of 1981, Americans for Common Sense (A.C.S.) hoped to name a coordinator in every state, locate full-time organizers in half a dozen cities, and mail over half a million letters to potential members and contributors. George Cunningham, the group's executive director, realized that A.C.S. was probably ten to twelve years behind where the conservatives were. "We have a long way to go to catch up to them in tactics, fundraising abilities, and the techniques of organization. We hope to make a dent in the lead they have within a year to eighteen months," he said. According to Cunningham, A.C.S. would attempt to frame from consultation with grassroots members which political questions should be under national discussion.[108] By 1982, McGovern hoped to be ready to operate a political action committee to aid liberal candidates. "I don't think it's worthwhile going into that if we don't have a couple of million dollars to dispense to candidates," he said. "I don't want a PAC just to have a PAC." McGovern insisted that his group would not duplicate the efforts of the Democratic Party or other liberal groups. "I don't see any of them operating at the grassroots level across the country like the right-wing groups do," he said of liberal organizations, adding, "I want our impact to be on the neighborhoods." As for the Democratic Party, "I would love to see it do the research and grassroots organizing," he said. "I don't see that happening."[109]

A.C.S. had a twofold mission: to develop a practical agenda for the country as an issue-oriented counterforce to the negativism of the New Right and to stimulate citizens through a number of chapters around the country to be active participants in the public decisions that were being made.[110] McGovern saw Americans for Commons Sense as a bipartisan organization designed to support a progressive public agenda beneficial to the community and country at large. It was not just for Democrats who were outraged and felt the wrath of the New Right tactics and its network during the 1980 campaign, according to A.C.S. literature.[111] Between formally beginning on January 5, 1981, and May 1, 1981, over 20,000 Americans joined Americans for Common Sense, and 200 chapters were in the basic organizational stage. A.C.S. had sent over 500,000 pieces of informational membership solicitation and was working on issue sheets, data, and statistical development, as well as other projects.[112]

In the first half of 1981, McGovern had delivered more than sixty-five speeches in thirty states warning against the radical right.[113] McGovern gave a lecture at the Dr. Karl Renner Institut, Vienna, Austria, on June 29, 1981, in which he analyzed the 1980 U.S. election and the future of Soviet-American relations. He charged that both the United States and USSR possessed a shared ignorance of what was crucial in the modern world, "a common blindness both to the futility of ideological conflict and to the awful risk their rivalry incurs for themselves and all others." They shared, he said, a "willful ignorance of the extraordinary benefit that would accrue from their cooperation for world peace and order."[114]

Reagan, he said, seldom let pass an opportunity to accuse the Russians of lying and cheating to achieve their presumed goal of world domination.

In his view, the American electorate gave Reagan no such mandate in 1980. Although they felt angry, their vote registered "a protest against domestic inflation, high government spending, excessive regulation, and the perception that their country was being 'pushed around' in the world." They lost confidence in Jimmy Carter; they did not give a mandate to embark on a renewed, intensified Cold War.[115]

McGovern observed that distinguished historian Arthur Schlesinger Sr. wrote of the predictable cycle of American politics, with eras of reform and conservatism alternating at roughly fifteen- to twenty-year intervals. "When the shifts take place, they are much more commonly the result of failure and fatigue on the part of those in office than the creative visions of the party out of power," McGovern explained. Therefore, the evidence demonstrated that the American electorate did not mandate a sharp and fundamental turn to the right in 1980.[116]

Unlike the other Republican administrations of the post–World War II era, the Reagan administration came to office committed to a clear philosophy: anti-Sovietism, reliance on heavy weapons spending, mistrust of arms control, and disdain for East-West détente. He credited the Soviet Union with responding with "reasonable restraint to the verbal assaults" of the Reagan administration. McGovern warned that the clear and present danger of the time was that hard-liners on both sides might stumble into a dangerous confrontation from which neither side could extricate itself.[117]

McGovern sought to influence those events to ensure that calmer counsels would prevail, that the Soviets would not abandon détente and that the Reagan administration would moderate its philosophy as it gained experience. This could be accomplished by him and others through the media, the press, the lecture forum, and the classroom.[118]

The message for the Russians was neither "nuclear machismo" nor "better red than dead," McGovern said. Our message should be this:

> We will fight you if we must, if our values and way of life are threatened and you leave us no choice but to defend them or surrender. But that is not what we want, nor do we think it is what you want. What we want is to survive in freedom, and we want you to survive too. We do not like your system and we would not be willing to live under it ourselves. But neither do we propose, now or in the future, to challenge you or your system. We want to co-exist and we want to cooperate in areas of common interest, of which we believe there are some. Foremost among these is our common interest in survival itself. As nuclear superpowers we Americans and you Russians are both the most threatening nations in the world and also the most threatened. We are, together, both the most powerful nations in the world and also the least secure. Others may get in the way if we have a nuclear exchange, but we are each other's prime targets. If anyone comes out on top in a nuclear war, it is not likely to be either of us. All this gives

us a shared, vital interest in preventing nuclear war, in working together to bring the arms race under control and to build, step by step, a world order in which we no longer threaten each other, and all other nations, as we do now.[119]

In response to the estimated 80 million Americans who regularly tuned into sermons by fundamentalist ministers who were becoming increasingly involved in right-wing politics, A.C.S. created a series of radio spots to awaken America to the need for reason and common sense in the political arena. It was titled the "Common Sense Radio Project."[120] Americans for Common Sense also joined with the National Organization for Women on several issues to counter the effects of the Reagan economic program on the status of women. McGovern spoke out on the unequal economic hardship in the lives of so many millions of women. He estimated that between 1969 and 1978, the number of poor families headed by women increased by one-third, while the families headed by men decreased from 3.2 to 2.6 million. McGovern reasoned that this impoverishment of women was the result of both cultural and historical forces—child-rearing responsibilities, low economic expectations and realizations, societal ambivalence toward women's economic independence, and bad policies at every level of government.[121] In August 1981, Americans for Common Sense published a newsletter entitled *RightWatch* which exposed an alignment called the "Coalition for National Policy," made up not only of the most active groups in the New Right, but also of financial backers such as brewer Joseph Coors, and Nelson Bunker Hunt, the Texas billionaire who long supported the John Birch Society. This movement boasted key members from the Reagan administration, and A.C.S. exposed their influence in opposing Supreme Court appointments and legislation to reverse numerous laws and programs aimed at helping individuals and families. *RightWatch* also sought to expose Reagan's alliance with right-wing activists and their attack on the legal service program, as well as the financial growth of right-wing political action committees.[122]

In 1981, A.C.S. began appointing a board of advisers, planning film presentations, organizing regional seminars, and distributing a biweekly newspaper column.[123] McGovern and his staff met quietly with the candidates who were being targeted in 1982 and were very helpful in urging them to be prepared for the onslaught that would come again, and to have a counterattack ready to go.[124] And they did. Encouraged by the growth of his organization, which by the fall numbered over 70,000, McGovern launched "The National Campaign on Defense Policy" to speak out on and reverse the nuclear arms race.[125] He firmly believed that the road to military destruction was paved with excessive military spending. He spoke out against the Reagan administration's commitment to spending $1.5 trillion in the largest arms buildup in U.S. history. In 1981 alone, the

United States spent over $3.7 billion on the production of nuclear warheads. McGovern called the arms race one of the leading causes of inflation, which drained technological skills from the civilian economy and made domestic production inefficient. And he took his ideas on foreign policy on the road.[126]

Back on March 30, 1981, in a lecture given by Senator McGovern at Northwestern University, he argued that a sound national security policy would require us to disenthrall ourselves from the ideological obsession with communism as a centrally directed world conspiratorial force. McGovern recognized that there was indeed a global rivalry between ourselves and other superpowers, a rivalry that reflected the different ideologies. But he saw this rivalry also resembling "the traditional, age-old behavior of powerful nations." He believed that for our own security, and that of our allies, the United States "must maintain powerful, modern armed forces, both nuclear and conventional" but also press opportunities to curb the arms race.[127] In order to do that, McGovern believed that the United States must find opportunities to detach marxist states from dependence on and domination by the Soviet Union. Countries such as Angola and even Cuba should be pursued "through arms control, trade and cultural relations, and other forms of cooperation." McGovern was concerned that America was distancing itself from its traditional values in international affairs. For example, he advocated that the United States must "stop drawing intellectually ridiculous" and "politically lethal distinctions between the terrorism of left and right." "To abandon human rights in favor of combating terrorism is an operational impossibility because the suppression of human rights is itself an act of terrorism, sometimes of an exceedingly brutal nature," McGovern said.[128] He advocated that both in principal and in practice the United States should stand as the enemy of all terrorism, regardless of ideological sponsorship, and as the supporter of human rights wherever there was the opportunity to support them. As he was often prone to do, McGovern quoted Franklin D. Roosevelt as saying, "More than an end to war, we want an end to the beginnings of all wars."[129]

Also in March 1981, McGovern received an enthusiastic response at George Mason University. He warned against the "emergence of irrational forces that are a threat to both liberals and conservatives." In a pointed reference to Jerry Falwell's Moral Majority, McGovern said, "[S]ome are now using their considerable influence over millions of Americans to advance a narrow, if not extremist, doctrine that I think has no biblical foundation at all." There is no foundation in the arguments against the Panama Canal Treaty or the Arms Limitation Treaty, he said. "Don't confuse the New Right with the New Testament," he cautioned.[130]

During a lecture at Fairfield University on March 2, 1982, the former senator urged Democrats to work for education, mass transportation, alternative energy sources, and public assistance for the poor and elderly. "We should not be supporting such non-essential programs as tax relief for the wealthy," warned McGovern.[131] He chastised the New Right as a contingent of "single-issue zealots." "The New Right, unlike the old-line conservatives, tends to focus on only one, two, three or four issues such as abortion, gun control, school prayer . . . any of those emotional social issues."[132]

McGovern lashed out at Reagan's policies, outlining four specific paradoxes.[133] "We have an allegedly conservative Republican administration deliberately programming federal deficits so enormous that, if offered by a liberal Democrat, they would confirm conservative suspicions that liberals have no respect for the dollar. I am supposed to be a liberal, but I find the Reagan deficit astounding and irresponsible," McGovern said. "If I, as the Democratic presidential nominee in 1972, had even hinted at the acceptability of a 100 billion dollar deficit, I would not even have carried Massachusetts," he said. McGovern argued that he could find almost nothing to support in the Reagan economic, military, foreign, or budget policies. He said that he disagreed with virtually every action of the Reagan administration, and he believed that Ronald Reagan did not appear to understand the simplest economic truths.[134]

Second, McGovern was critical of Reagan's foreign policy of splitting the North Atlantic Treaty Organization Alliance while reuniting the Sino-Soviet block and repeating, in Central America, the mistakes of Vietnam. He believed that the Reagan administration had misread totally the military and geopolitical power struggle between the United States and the Soviet Union, and its military budget was so wasteful and poorly conceived that it was a threat to the national security of the nation. He believed that Reagan was blind to the greatest danger of our age: the mounting threat of extinction posed by an uncontrolled nuclear arms race. In that speech, McGovern urged the Democrats to stop drifting along with Reagan's policies, which were weakening the nation and threatening world peace.[135]

The Democrats, he said, should stop endorsing sweeping tax cuts that feed inflation and unbalance the budget, and they should stop endorsing ill-planned weapons while neglecting our real defense needs. "They can stop supporting budget policies that weaken such productive investments as education, transportation, energy, agriculture, job training, nutrition, drug rehabilitation, public assistance, and the dignity of our older citizens." In short, McGovern advocated that the proper Democratic agenda was to oppose Reagan at every turn and to offer an alternative of tax justice and a balanced budget, pressing for the ratification of a verifiable nuclear arms agreement with the Soviet Union, and to take steps to buttress small business and family farms. The Democrats should do this, he said, by investing more in such human capitals as education, training, and whatever is necessary to provide work for everyone willing and able. For McGovern, nothing could be more wasteful than idleness when there was topsoil to be preserved, houses to be built, railways to be modernized, and young people to be redeemed from ignorance, drugs, and crime.[136] "There is no excuse for a great country not to be able to provide jobs for every able body willing to work," he said.[137]

The third paradox was that we had an administration that "touts free enterprise, yet American capitalism cannot flourish with eighteen percent interest rates," he said. "Neither can we withstand the budget-destroying military expenses, high interest rates and major tax cuts. It is fiscal and monetary madness that cannot work."[138]

The fourth paradox was that this administration won in 1980 mainly because of Carter's inconsistent and uncertain foreign policy but now acts inconsistently and uncertainly. "Our relations with our European allies are at an all-time low," he said.[139]

As for El Salvador, McGovern warned that the United States should stand free of that revolution instead of sending troops. He said that "[a] revolution isn't exported," alluding to claims by administration officials that the Soviet Union, Cuba, and Nicaragua have instigated the guerrilla revolt with arms and technology. "Revolution comes out of the soil of injustice and misrule and that it is precisely what is happening in El Salvador."[140]

He accused Reagan of being unable to forge an effective foreign policy and was highly critical of the "overblown and wasteful" defense budget, "ill-advised" tax cuts, and budget cuts that "savaged programs of education, transportation, alternative energy, agriculture and drug abuse." "Reagan also is blind to the greatest threat . . . the possible human extinction due to the nuclear arms race."[141]

Pleased by the clear-cut repudiation of the New Right in the 1982 elections, McGovern now turned his attention to building discussion of public issues by citizen groups. He spoke out in favor of a "'Second Chance G.I. Bill' similar to the one that educated and trained millions of veterans after World War II." Such a bill would provide long-term, low-interest loans for citizens who wanted "to fit themselves for tomorrow's needs and job opportunities. For dollars spent, the nation would receive higher dividends in productivity, revenues and citizenship from education, rather than from any other public investment." McGovern spoke out against the Reagan military expenditures that he believed weakened our country and increased our deficits. In short, McGovern remained an unrepentant New

Deal Democrat. "A central weakness of Reagan and some other American presidents is that they have not had a vision of what people can accomplish in using government as a great tool for progress. These presidents have dulled our public vision by describing government as the enemy rather than as the servant of the people."[142]

By mid-1983, McGovern had been encouraged by the reception of the ideas he had been advancing for the past year and a half, and he began thinking seriously about seeking the Democratic nomination later that year.

CHAPTER TWO

The Decision to Run:
Quixotic or Common Sense?

None but he knows what he can do, nor does he know until he has tried.

—Ralph Waldo Emerson

George McGovern's decision to run for president again, for the second or third time, depending on how you count it, seemed to defy not only reason and logic, but also common sense. To be certain, there had been other politicians who seemingly rose from the dead—George Bush, who in 1988 trailed Michael Dukakis by seventeen points before the August GOP Convention; Abraham Lincoln, who in August 1864 himself believed that he would be defeated; and Richard Nixon, who returned from the political wasteland in 1968 after losing bitterly for governor of California in 1962. Perhaps the greatest political comeback was Harry S Truman's victory over Thomas Dewey in the 1948 election.[1] Yet even that unexpected turn of events would be dwarfed in the annals of spectacular comebacks from political oblivion had George McGovern managed to secure the Democratic Party nomination and election to the presidency in 1984.

To understand what drew McGovern to run in 1984, despite his losses, we must first try to understand the man's views of politics and the political process. One key factor to grasp is that he was driven by a fundamental conviction that politics is an instrument of responsibility and morality. He possessed a firm belief that politics was not an end in itself, but rather a vehicle through which he could "bear witness to the values that should endure among our people."[2] His intellectual conviction and psychological suitability thrust him into the political arena time after time, as he overcame seemingly insurmountable odds. For McGovern, losing a political campaign was not seen as failure; rather, he saw his entire career as a part of a process that allowed the triumphs of the past to overshadow the failures.[3]

George McGovern was a political animal who thoroughly enjoyed public service and the contests for public office since he began organizing a grassroots political movement in South Dakota in the early 1950s. Together with his beloved wife, Eleanor, who well understood and supported him, he drew much satisfaction from those many years of service. McGovern had great difficulty in 1976 and 1980 being on the sidelines and watching others less experienced and less qualified struggle for the party's nomination. He honestly believed that he owed it to the country to be in the struggle, and he understood that he possessed the sense of issues, debate, presentation, judgment, and style that come from long years of experience and grace under pressure. America had given George McGovern a marvelous education and a sense of history, vast experience in public office and international travel, as well as a deep sense of the country's greatness that he did not recognize in many of the announced candidates.[4]

According to George Cunningham, McGovern's longtime friend and aide, although the senator's primary purpose was "always to win, in 1984 he also wanted to influence the Democratic platform and the viewpoints adopted by the ultimate nominee. The '84 race was one way to bring his positions to the public's attention." If there had been a great outcry in '84 against the military budget as there had been against Vietnam in 1972, his candidacy could very well have been propelled to the forefront of the debate.[5]

During the two and a half years that McGovern was on the lecture circuit, he found overwhelming support among a variety of constituencies who urged him to run. According to Mary McGovern, his campaign manager for fund-raising and finance, "although this was obviously unofficial, he reacted to it."[6] Throughout 1982 McGovern hinted at college campuses that the crowd might well be hearing from him again soon.[7] In the spring of that year, McGovern talked privately about a "special kind of presidential bid in '84" which, due to his lack of holding office and the odds against him, would allow him to be free from pollsters and political consultants.[8] Also, he would have the luxury of speaking out on the issues as directly and candidly as possible.[9] There is something intriguing about this prospect. In the fall of 1982, the *New York Daily News* reported that the former senator was discussing making another stab at the White House in 1984.[10] Although McGovern was not actively seeking support, he was not shy about letting his intentions be public.

On April 7, 1983, McGovern wrote to a friend:

> I wanted you to know that I am now giving very serious thought to getting into the Presidential competition myself, about Labor Day. I am going to wait and see how all the other contenders do this Spring and Summer, but

so far it is my judgment that they haven't set anybody on fire, including me. If things are looking about the same by September 1st, I think I am going to get into the race and wage a very special candid, courageous campaign on the issues that I think need to be most discussed. Whether or not I can prevail, of course, only time will tell, but I think the right kind of campaign will be worthwhile whether I win or lose. Naturally, I would be greatly honored if you saw fit to support me.[11]

In a July 1983 interview with *The Los Angeles Times*, McGovern talked candidly about the man to whom he lost the 1972 election, praising President Nixon's foreign and defense policies. The praise was in sharp contrast to McGovern's comments on the policies of the Reagan administration, and the interview helped give an indication of what was on his mind that summer.[12]

"Nixon was right on track in the last years of his administration when he was working toward détente with the Soviet Union," McGovern told *The Los Angeles Times*.[13] He was seriously considering entering the 1984 race because the other Democratic contenders failed to adequately raise issues he considered vital: defense spending, the federal deficit, deteriorating relations with the Soviet Union, and increased U.S. involvement in Central America.[14]

"I'm going to spend more time thinking about it," McGovern said of his possible run for the Democratic presidential nomination. "I'm taking the month of August off. Sometime after Labor Day I'll decide to do it or to support one of the other candidates."[15] The six active contenders were former Vice President Walter Mondale of Minnesota, Senator John Glenn of Ohio, Senator Alan Cranston of California, Senator Gary Hart of Colorado, Senator Ernest Hollings of South Carolina, and former Florida Governor Reubin Askew. McGovern said that all six "[were] running for the nomination with essentially the same views and are not really ready to take head-on the question of military involvement in Central America."[16] McGovern, who opposed such involvement, said "someone has to speak out."[17] Although McGovern believed at the time that the six Democratic contenders were not adequately addressing the issues, he added that "if any one of the six candidates wins the nomination, I would have no trouble campaigning for him. I think they are all pretty good men."[18]

For McGovern, President Ronald Reagan's policies toward El Salvador and Nicaragua would inevitably lead to the commitment of U.S. troops in the region. McGovern's praise for Nixon's Soviet policies was in sharp contrast to the criticism he levied at the Reagan administration's hostile attitude toward the Soviet Union. "They are not willing to face the fact that the Soviets are sending all kinds of signals that they are ready for an agreement, not only on arms control, but that they want to get along with us in a number of areas, including trade," McGovern said.[19] He added that his attitude toward Nixon mellowed due to his distress over Reagan's foreign and domestic policies. Although he remained critical of Nixon's role in the Watergate scandal, he acknowledged that Nixon had recently sent a copy of his new book to him. McGovern returned a thank you letter to his old rival, telling the former president that "you have done the best job of any president since World War II in achieving détente with the Soviet Union." Nixon wrote McGovern back that although the two of them had been intense rivals, he was "glad to know we shared some important views."[20]

Although McGovern was receiving a warm response from audiences, the press reaction was one of confusion and negativity. For example, *The Washington Post* ran an editorial in early September 1983 indicating that another McGovern candidacy would be hopelessly doomed. In this editorial, which was a response to an interview McGovern gave to reporter T.R. Reid, the *Post* mocked McGovern's opinion that his 1972 campaign was mostly a success because he won the nomination beating "some really top guys" and "the campaign treasury ended in the black."[21] McGovern's notion that he felt fully vindicated by history was entirely erroneous, according to the *Post* editorial. The winners of the election were ultimately humiliated (Nixon resigned in disgrace, and several of his top aides were jailed), the editorial stated, but for reasons that had nothing at all to do with the judgment Americans made in 1972 about McGovern's politics.[22]

The *Post* editorial went on to attack McGovern on several other points. One was a criticism of McGovern's 1972 theme, "Come Home, America," charging that it was an invitation to isolationism and irresponsibility. Another was a criticism of McGovern's effort to change the Democrats' rules for delegate selection by creating a system that, by its own excesses, had held the party up to ridicule and diminished its chances in general elections. The editorial also stated that McGovern evidently failed to understand that the fundamental programs and policies he came to be identified with made his candidacy unacceptable to most voters. According to the *Post*, McGovern's fuzziness of vision from 1972 clearly still existed in 1983, and McGovern's comments to Reid about the Soviet Union were labeled grotesque. In the interview, McGovern had said of the Soviet Union that "we ought to be very thankful that this man Andropov seems to be a reasonable guy and somewhat restrained because certainly the Reagan-Weinberger approach is one of intense confrontation. It's almost as if they were spoiling for a military showdown." Thus, according to the *Post*, McGovern was nominated in 1972 because "at one moment in history his vision coincided with that of a critical mass of Democratic activists," and that would unlikely happen again.[23] This was a sentiment obviously not shared by McGovern, however.

In October 1983, Patrick Caddell, the former McGovern poll taker, wrote a privately circulated paper, "The State of American Politics," urging a Democratic candidacy of fresh blood and new ideas. Caddell concluded that it was not too late either organizationally or financially for a major candidacy to be successfully mounted. Caddell shared McGovern's conclusion that there seemed to be little enthusiasm evidenced for the current field of Democratic candidates. Caddell saw a widespread perception that the Democratic Party was moribund politically and intellectually and that it needed to be more than an alternative available to replace Ronald Reagan. As McGovern had written earlier that year, none of the contenders stirred any real excitement or generated a message capable of beating Reagan, and all had serious liabilities.[24] For McGovern, that left open the possibility that lightning could strike twice.

McGovern observed that, in a recent nationally televised interview, Pat Caddell said he had asked a large audience of active Democrats how many of them had been involved in previous Democratic presidential nominating contests. Ninety percent of those present raised their hands. However, when he asked how many were involved in one of the six current presidential campaigns, only about 10 percent indicated involvement. On the same program, political commentator and longtime political activist Mark Shields, and Hodding Carter, a former Carter administration official from Mississippi, reported on the lack of enthusiasm among rank-and-file Democrats. McGovern had traveled and lectured extensively across the country in the past year, observing that the apathy and noncommittal attitude of Democrats was a serious problem needing to be addressed if the Democrats were to have any hope of defeating Reagan.[25]

Despite observing that the six candidates had a broad background of political experience, McGovern felt that the party had not clearly defined its stance on the major issues before the country since suffering the crushing defeat of 1980. It seemed to him that, with the exception of Cranston's elevation of the nuclear war issue, Hart's writings on industrial policy and defense reform, and Hollings's call for a federal spending freeze, there was really not much attention being paid to the Democratic contenders.[26] Reagan, on the other hand, came to Washington on an appeal for "getting the government off our backs" in domestic policy and promised to greatly expand our military forces abroad.[27] For McGovern, Reagan's policies were a prescription for disaster that weakened the country both at home and abroad. He was frustrated that Reagan was able to arouse a large constituency and be perceived as a leader who knew where he wanted to lead the nation, which seemed to contrast with the public's view of the Democrats. As McGovern had said time and again on the lecture circuit, the Democrats needed to spell out a clear alternative. In discussions with people around the country, he believed that 80 or 90 percent of the Democratic voters were uncommitted to any candidate. He had the distinct impression that they were sitting on the sidelines waiting for someone to say something that would get them excited; he hoped to accomplish that. McGovern concluded that the current lack of enthusiasm within the Democratic Party was not only a serious political handicap, but stemmed from "the lack of any compelling Democratic vision of where America ought to be heading in the years ahead."[28] He was not timid in discussing his 1972 defeat and was quick to point out that he helped to galvanize millions of Americans around what was the transcendent issue before the nation: "the seemingly endless involvement in the misguided Vietnam War."[29] McGovern alleged that his rejection was due in large measure to the Nixon campaign's heavy investment in distortion and deception. Troubled at the onset by the Eagleton problem, coupled with the shooting of Governor George Wallace, which permitted Nixon to combine the Republican vote with the Wallace vote in the South, McGovern alleged that was the real formula for the Nixon landslide and he rejected the conventional wisdom that he lost by being "too far out." This misperception that "in order to win you must stand in the center," was suspected by McGovern as being one of the reasons for the Democrats' timidity and their fear of falling victim to the kind of defeat he suffered in 1972. McGovern warned his fellow Democrats to have an alternative message and a clear sense of where they wanted the nation to go. "Where there is no vision, the people perish," he said.[30]

As the prospects of a 1984 candidacy began to look more likely, lifelong friends called McGovern and said, "[P]lease, please don't do this, you're going to end up hurt and looking like a dang fool idiot." He received a postcard from Mitchell, South Dakota, from a former supporter who used to raise money for his campaigns. On it were just two words: "FORGET IT!"[31]

"That's okay," McGovern said. "I know what she was trying to tell me. I still love her dearly." It wasn't the need for fame or the TV cameras that was driving him back, McGovern insisted. He had had his fill of all that and had made a nice living on the lecture circuit. It was the issues, the country, and his conscience. And when he convinced his family of this, they acquiesced. However, it took McGovern a month of convincing them during the summer of 1983 during a retreat in the Smoky Mountains. His five children, all of whom were grown, came down "in installments." Two of them were ready to go, but the other three asked him to reconsider.[32]

"I decided that we needed a month. I couldn't say, 'I'm going to run and the hell with what you think.' I had to have a month, to talk it out with each of them. And I think I got all of them to accept it graciously," said McGovern. "Maybe it wasn't the thing they wanted me to do, but at least they could see it was the thing I had to do: to be a public man again, to weigh in on the public issues." He added, "I think they all saw the logic of it, but I don't think they could see my willingness to take the . . . risk."[33] The entire McGovern family had been crippled and emotionally drained by the overwhelming defeat by Nixon that was further complicated by the Eagleton affair.[34]

Veteran Washington political writers, however, did not see the logic in McGovern's interest in another try for the nomination. Several months prior to his announcement he met with them and asked candidly about his chances. Their reply was not encouraging. They advised McGovern that the reason he was perceived as a big loser was that he not only lost a race for the presidency, but also lost his own Senate seat. They were pretty much in agreement too that he was coming into the race too late. They prepared McGovern for the almost certain attacks that were to come. Some of the attacks were old and predictable, but others were new and sobering. The reporters envisioned new attacks on McGovern's sense of fair play for what he would be doing to the chances of nomination for his old campaign manager, Gary Hart.[35]

Several Washington insiders privately speculated that the true reason McGovern was in the race was not because he believed he had any real chance of getting the nomination, but because it would enhance his business and marketing and get him to receive some network coverage, which had been virtually nonexistent in recent years.[36] However, one of the things McGovern had to do in becoming a candidate for president was to cancel out about $75,000 in lecture fees.[37]

"Look, I am not trying to vindicate my place in history, or get even for my '72 defeat, or inflate my ego," explained McGovern.[38] And while there was no deafening swell of voices pressing or encouraging him to run, George McGovern was encouraged from a scattered and growing number of people who voiced approval for his maverick candidacy.[39] McGovern hoped that his candidacy would help compel Democrats to address seriously the issues set forth in his platform, particularly the need for "more sensible relations between the United States and the Soviet Union," as he put it.[40]

"When I lost in 1972 they said I was ten years ahead of my time," McGovern said when he disclosed he was thinking about running. "Well, it's ten years later," he said.[41] "To be frank with you, one thing I worry about is looking ridiculous," McGovern told a reporter. "But the more and more I come to the conclusion that it isn't very important. . . . I just find it impossible to sit on the sidelines any longer."[42]

As if to signal a return to the grassroots in his long-shot try for the presidency, McGovern waited at a printer's counter for 250 copies of his four-page announcement at a cost of $60. Thus it was on September 13, 1983, that George McGovern announced his candidacy for president at George Washington University. The sixty-one-year-old former Democratic senator pledged to run under a liberal banner of peaceful coexistence with the

Russians, improved relations with Cuba, and an end to U.S. military involvement in Central America. McGovern would push for full employment and arms control. He announced his candidacy before a cheering college audience on a platform of "realism and common sense."[43]

In announcing his candidacy, George McGovern declared that his purpose was "to help mobilize a realistic alternative to the Reagan policies and to set a clearer, more hopeful vision of the American future."[44] Observing that millions of Americans were concerned about the course of our nation but had not yet been activated, he hoped that his candidacy would enlist many of those citizens then on the sidelines. McGovern envisioned a Democratic Party that faced the future with faith and imagination while drawing upon and firmly opposing the wholly unrealistic policies of the Reagan administration. He accused Reagan of being "tragically ill-informed about the world around us and about the potential promise of the coming age."[45] The issue of 1984, he said, was reality versus fantasy. Our country should elect a president "who has the most realistic vision of the future," McGovern said.[46]

McGovern repeated his pledge of 1972 "to offer the American people a choice—not between parties or ideologies, not between liberal and conservative or right or left. The choice is whether our civilization can serve the freedom and happiness of every citizen."[47]

McGovern then added, "We will not be helped to understanding by leadership built on image-making or television commercials; by those who seek power by back-room deals, coalitions of self-interest, or a continued effort to adjust their policies and beliefs to every seeming shift in public sentiment. . . . For my part, I make one pledge above all others—to seek and speak the truth." He also added these words from 1972: "I shall seek to call America home to those principles which gave us birth. I have found no better blueprint for healing our troubled land than is found in the Declaration of Independence, the Constitution and the Bill of Rights." On the back of the copy of his announcement, McGovern penned his vision of America as immortalized by Woody Guthrie in "This Land Is Your Land."[48]

"You have to do what you have to do, and I have to do this," McGovern said.[49] He called the issues of the day "far more grave" than in 1972, and pledged changes in U.S. foreign policy from Central America to the Middle East. McGovern broke with the Democratic Party's 1980 platform on Israel and told his audience that the time had come "to tell the warring parties of the Middle East that there will be no more American aid and no more American soldiers unless Arabs and Israelites [*sic*] and Palestinians get to the conference table and begin at long last serious negotiations for peace."[50] In a question-and-answer session with reporters, McGovern was asked if he was proposing a change in the relationship between the United States and Israel. McGovern replied, "[O]nly in the sense that they will be treated the same as the other countries of the Middle East if I became convinced that Israel was blocking reasonable negotiations for a settlement."[51] He vowed an even-handed policy in the Middle East and pledged to significantly cut military aid to Israel or any country in the region that refused to negotiate in good faith. "We should not reserve any influence and power that we have in bringing the warring parties to the conference table," he said.[52] "It's the only way we can exert any effective leverage." McGovern's stand on the issue was a break from the Democratic Party's 1980 platform, which stated that the United States would not use aid to Israel as a bargaining tool.[53]

McGovern also vowed to end all U.S. military involvement in Central America and begin a "new day" in foreign relations with Cuba, a country he had visited numerous times. He called for a substantial reduction in military spending after ratification of "a verifiable arms control agreement" with the Soviet Union.[54] According to McGovern, the recent incident in which a South Korean airliner with 269 people aboard strayed off course and was shot down by a Soviet fighter off Siberia "underscores the folly of the present Cold War tension."[55]

On the domestic front, McGovern proposed increased federal spending for education and job training, and a private partnership to create jobs that would build "the finest railway system in the world."[56] As he began to outline his views of what policy changes needed to be made, it seemed that McGovern was comfortably slipping back into the role of the political campaigner, yet this time around, the campaign would be a little bit different.[57]

McGovern's wife Eleanor told reporters prior to her husband's announcement that although she supported his decision, she would not become actively involved in his campaign.[58] "I am reluctant to return to the road. And at this point, I won't," Mrs. McGovern said.[59] "I'm not enthusiastic," she said. But she would wait and see how the campaign progressed.[60] Her husband, meanwhile, was just starting to build momentum.

"I believe I am ready now as at no previous time in my life to lead this nation toward justice, honor, and peace," McGovern said.[61] He called his 1972 defeat "honorable" compared with the "shameful behavior" of Richard Nixon. He told reporters that he had become "increasingly restless on the sidelines" and hoped to "take advantage of that great forum" of presidential politics to help shape the national debate. McGovern noted that the performance of the six Democratic rivals had nothing to do with his decision, and he complimented Gary Hart on the way Hart had challenged old assumptions about military spending.[62]

McGovern and his aides said that he had intended to campaign strongly against Reagan's foreign policy and the "unfairness" of his economic policies. His longtime adviser and fund-raiser, Henry L. Kimelman, stated that McGovern believes "we have no alternative but to live peacefully and to co-exist with the Russians. He will project himself as the kind of man who will sit down with them."[63] McGovern spokesman Mark Kaminsky conceded that the campaign started off months behind the field.[64] McGovern campaign chairman George Cunningham looked at it this way: "With the complex federal and party rules, candidates must be prepared to possibly move in and out of federal matching fund eligibility as the primary season unfolds." Cunningham saw the current field of candidates making it possible to project a Mondale-Glenn-McGovern contest in later primaries with McGovern having sole position of the left wing of the party.[65]

During the first weeks of the campaign, McGovern collected more than $30,000 in unsolicited funds, according to Mary McGovern, who left her job at the United Nations to join her father's campaign.[66] Her immediate job after the announcement was trying to find bigger offices for the national headquarters in Washington, D.C. "I am surprised at how little of it does hurt me, the attacks on him, the abuse. The way I look at it, when people write stupid things about my father, untrue things, they're the ones who have to live with it. His profession is public life. His profession is politics," Mary McGovern explained.[67]

"I'm going to go into every state. I'll be in Iowa and New Hampshire, but I made a commitment to my family this time. I won't drop out of life. I am very sensitive to knowing some of the damage it did to my family before," George McGovern said.[68] Mary McGovern, a true believer in her father's cause, claimed that "George McGovern has a fighting chance to win the nomination and the election."[69]

CHAPTER THREE

This Land Is Your Land: The Press Reaction

Each time a man stands up for an ideal, or acts to improve the lot of others, or strikes out against injustice, he sends forth a tiny ripple of hope, and crossing each other from a million different centers of energy and daring those ripples build a current which can sweep down the mightiest walls of oppression and resistance.

—U.S. Senator Robert F. Kennedy

If the press reaction to George McGovern's candidacy was anything, it was predictable. Few journalists yearned for McGovern's honest style where politics as usual was never the norm. However, even his most ardent critics could not dispute that he possessed the qualities that Arthur Schlesinger Jr. had advocated in the 1984 nominee, namely, McGovern had an instinct for remedies, and he possessed both a conviction about a new course of direction for the country, and a capacity to convey that vision to the American people. Despite this fact, most columnists did not share Schlesinger's view at the start of the campaign, choosing instead to write about McGovern as a washed-up politician making one last, misguided run.

The *Chicago Tribune*, in an editorial titled "Candidate George McStassen," was among the first to equate George McGovern with Harold Stassen, a Republican who had become something of a political punch line due to his numerous failed presidential bids. In this editorial, The *Tribune* declared that McGovern had fallen prey to the "Harold Stassen Syndrome," which they defined as a strange, wholly unsupported conviction among some political has-beens that millions of people were waiting for a chance to put them back into office. The *Tribune* argued that McGovern's candidacy would bleed away some primary votes from the other liberal candidates—Mondale, Cranston, and Hart—making them look marginally weaker than they already were. To the people at the *Tribune*, McGovern was an inept, preachy candidate whose ultraliberal views were outside the mainstream of the American electorate.[1] Another newspaper ran an editorial titled "Not George, Again," ridiculing McGovern as someone who was both unrealistic and unthinking.[2] The political cartoons were no less biting and cruel.[3]

McGovern saw his career and Stassen's as very different. McGovern had only one serious bid for the presidency and was nominated. By contrast, Stassen had run numerous times since 1944 and was never a serious contender.[4]

A day after the *Tribune* editorial, McGovern, in an interview with *The Village Voice*, commented:

> It's really a cruel, nasty editorial. It's not the kind of thing that is going to destroy you, but it is almost hysterical. The truth of the matter is that if you were to take two politicians whose careers were different in terms of what actually has happened to them, it would be Stassen and me. I ran for the Presidency once before in a serious bid and I was nominated. Stassen has run every time since 1944 and I don't know whether he has ever carried a primary.[5]

The only time on the campaign trail that the gentle, mild-mannered George McGovern would become decidedly ungentle and angry was when a reporter asked him about Stassen. McGovern replied, "Mr. Stassen was never the nominee of his party. He never served in the U.S. Senate. He never. . . ."[6] The comparison that McGovern preferred, which was proposed by admirer Richard Parker, a Harvard Law School professor, was to Barry Goldwater, who was the esteemed senior statesman of Republican conservatism. "I think that's a fair parallel," McGovern said. McGovern believed that Goldwater had a clearly enunciated set of viewpoints, and people respected him for stating his position. Additionally, Goldwater's views eventually became adopted by the Republican Party, which was a hope McGovern had for his own party.[7]

Although McGovern might have preferred the Goldwater comparison, the media was still caught up in the more vitriolic McGovern-Stassen comparison, with various columnists pontificating on what McGovern's true motives for running must be. Columnist James Reston offered an explanation for the Stassen-McGovern Syndrome. He explained that presidential ambition is an addiction, as powerful as sex or booze. "Once they have gone through all those bowling halls, they dream about it in the night. Somehow they forget all the agony—the demeaning scramble for money, the vicious charges of their opponents, the unfeeling and often frivolous criticism of the press, and the endless plane and bus rides."[8] R. Emmett

Tyrell Jr., another syndicated columnist, declared that McGovern was right at home with fanatics and liberal extremists and that he had encouraged the fanatics who afflicted the Democratic Party. For Tyrell, McGovern's very name was synonymous with Democratic fanaticism. Did McGovern, as he declared, stand for "realism and common sense," or was he advancing radicalized liberalism? Tyrell concluded that the reason behind McGovern's run for the presidency was quite simple: McGovern was running because he had celebrity, and that was quite enough to be thought of as qualified to seek Lincoln's house.[9]

The New Republic was not any kinder, reporting that George McGovern had nothing better to do, and thus was running just for the sake of running for president. *The New Republic* saw McGovern's candidacy as "a sad spectacle" and charged that he was more likely to become an object of derision, since any success he achieved would come at the expense of Alan Cranston or Gary Hart. It reported that McGovern had no money, no staff, and a wife who was against campaigning. Of his platform, *The New Republic* reported that it remained one of isolationism and national guilt, and the only way his candidacy could serve a public purpose would be if he took his platform down to defeat with him.[10]

The reaction by the national press to McGovern's campaign was by and large openly biased, and was based only tangentially on historical fact. Just as people continue to lament presidential politics today, in 1984 the national press was content to report on electing a president based on theatrics rather than upon substance. On the very day McGovern announced his candidacy, Dan Rather reported for the *CBS Evening News* that McGovern had run previously in 1972. Next it was reported that McGovern's nickname had been "McGoo," and on the screen appeared the words "nickname: McGoo." *Newsweek* reported that McGovern wanted another chance to "cavort" in the limelight. And in Boston, a reporter compared him with an adolescent trying, once too often, to gain attention by "belching" loudly at a social event. As McGovern knew quite well, in the degenerate state of our political culture, defeat tends to eclipse everything else, and the media focus in 1984 was to ignore the quality of the candidate and his ideas and to focus on his potential for victory.[11]

The news was not all bad, though. On October 9, 1983, George Gallup, one of America's leading pollsters, reported that George McGovern's entry into the contest had catapulted him into third place.[12] *The Atlanta Journal* reported on October 10 that 16 percent of the nearly 3,000 Iowa Democrats who heard the seven candidates thought McGovern was a more effective speaker than the candidate they personally backed.[13] And in South Dakota, *The Sioux Falls Argus-Leader* reported on October 12 that the South Dakota Democratic Party leaders had passed a resolution urging people to support George McGovern. The resolution was passed unanimously.[14] As he began to make his platform known, press reaction tilted, and journalists were not so quick to get on the McGovern-bashing bandwagon. *The Philadelphia Daily News* reported that McGovern's platform was as clear as one was likely to hear, and if that was crazy, one had to wonder how sanity was being defined.[15]

Those who knew McGovern best realized that he was driven by the fundamental conviction that politics is an instrument of responsibility and morality, not an end in itself. McGovern held a strong belief that to lose a political contest did not forever seal a pact with failure. According to *American Politics*, this combination of intellectual conviction and psychological suitability for the game thrust McGovern, time after time, into the political arena.[16]

The Iowa City *Daily Iowan* asserted in its endorsement that McGovern was as qualified to be president as any candidate. Equally important, the *Iowan* said, were "[his] deeply humanitarian convictions, which lead him to advocate policies that would promote opportunity for those without privilege, help for those in need and peace for a nation whose military bureaucracy has for too long gone unchallenged." McGovern, in short, would "shift the country's priorities back where they belong—to the provision of basic necessities to all Americans."[17]

On November 13, 1983, Senator McGovern appeared as a guest on the NBC program *Meet the Press*. In response to the first question by Bill Monroe of NBC News on why the Democrats should consider nominating someone who led the party to an overwhelming defeat twelve years earlier, McGovern responded:

> I'm in this race for one thing: I want to say some things that I think are very important that need to be said, in terms of the needs of the country, right now. I have no idea where the voter's at. I don't know whether I am going to be any better received in 1984 than I was in 1972. I do know that I don't want to sit on the sidelines and see this country pursuing policies both at home and abroad that I think are not in the national interest.
>
> Let me say, that although your point is right, that we have seven other candidates in the field, I've been around the country enough to know that probably eight or nine of ten Democratic voters are still not committed. They're still out there on the sidelines waiting for somebody to say something that will get them excited and into this campaign, and I hope I can play a role in doing that.[18]

In early October, *The Des Moines Register* reported that, now that McGovern had been seen and heard in his first foray into Iowa, it seemed that McGovern would actually perform a valuable service. What was lacking in the Democratic race was a candidate who could force the party to think hard about its stance as an effective alternative to Ronald Reagan.[19] After all, that is what the 1984 election was all about.

The McGovern campaign began using slogans such as "George McGovern: This time . . . let's listen" and "George McGovern: There IS a difference." The campaign's theme began to develop around the notion that McGovern offered the clearest alternative to Ronald Reagan.[20] With the central theme coming together, and with people gaining more perspective on why McGovern was running again, the journalistic naysayers began to die down. Bill Peterson of *The Washington Post* even reported that McGovern had certainly not become a Democratic Harold Stassen. Away from the cynicism of Washington, McGovern was being treated as a serious candidate and was saying things that none of the other Democratic candidates were saying. He was finding that his message still resonated with a large and enthusiastic audience, and he appeared smoother and more relaxed than he did in 1972. Realizing in 1984 that his campaign was not a life-or-death matter, he started telling people what he thought, not what his advisers and staff told him was politic to say. He was therefore becoming one of the most interesting candidates in the crowded Democratic field, and, unlike the other hopefuls, he remained an unabashed New Dealer unwilling to be moved away by any conservative tide.[21]

With his smoother, more confident campaign, McGovern began receiving favorable write-ups in the nation's Op-Ed columns. David Nyhan of *The Boston Globe* went so far as to say that McGovern's campaign was beginning to rise "Phoenix-like." It was clear that McGovern offered the starkest alternative to Ronald Reagan, and his platform was simpler and bolder than what the other Democrats were saying.[22] Although McGovern realized quite well that the chances of his being nominated by the Democratic Party were very remote at best, in a wishful corner of his mind he still imagined that a popular groundswell could somehow stun the nominating process the way it did for him back in 1972. Regardless of the outcome, though, it was clear that the main reason George McGovern was running again was that he wanted to talk, and he wanted people to listen. The mass media was much more porous than it was in 1972, and the Washington press no longer controlled the dialogue exclusively. McGovern knew that he would have ample exposure on radio and television shows, as well as in candidate forums. He fully expected to garner respectable vote tallies in the primaries, and with expectations so low, he expected to do respectably well enough to surprise his detractors. With the loss of his Senate seat in 1980 costing him his public platform, McGovern realized that the lack of political pressure from holding office freed him to say exactly what he thought. McGovern was drawn into the 1984 race by the need to disprove what he believed was the wrong lesson drawn from 1980.[23]

They saw Carter go down to defeat, and they thought, "Gee that's because he's not strong in handling the Russians." Carter got a bad rap from you

guys in the press; then they saw all the liberals knocked off in the Senate—
Church, Bayh, Culver, Nelson, myself—and I think it frightened people in
Congress. They thought, "My God, these guys have been out on the cutting
edge of liberalism, so it must not be too popular anymore. So let's not get
too far away from the Reagan position."[24]

McGovern believed that this political analysis was wrong and that
Ronald Reagan's presidency was a disaster. Although McGovern viewed
Reagan as a lightweight intellectually and predicted that his stature would
diminish in time, he was aware that Reagan controlled the political debate
primarily because Democrats were unwilling to confront the president
fully.[25] "Reagan isn't all that nimble," McGovern said. "If the Democrats
were really going after him with intelligent criticism, I don't know how
effective he'd be." William Greider of *Rolling Stone* observed that
McGovern possessed a practical, urgently needed vision that did not rely
on bristling militarism and Cold War myopia.[26]

Steven Pearlstein, editor of *The Boston Observer*, in endorsing
McGovern's candidacy, attacked the hypocrisy of the cognoscenti who
gathered at places like the Kennedy School, running up expense accounts
while complaining that "the presidential campaign is too long, that candidates are too much creatures of their staffs, and that the path to the
White House is paved with the fool's gold of political action funds."[27]
These people were the same elitists who declared that McGovern's entry
into the race was too late and that his plain speaking and hard-hitting
positions were the luxury of a dark horse. What was needed to defeat
Ronald Reagan, according to Pearlstein, was a "Democrat who would not
let Reagan set the terms of the debate or concede him traditional American symbols and values."[28] Reagan's political strength, Pearlstein observed, lay not in his inflated Pentagon budgets and his supply-side
economics, but "in his skill at manipulating simple themes that resonate
with common anxieties and aspirations. He is the genuinely likeable, sincere fellow who appears to have temporarily captured the high moral
ground. He speaks for old-fashioned frontier values of independence, freedom, self-sufficiency, and strength, and he leaves to subordinates the
messy, unpopular task of translating these into policies most Americans
deplore." In all these aspects, Pearlstein argued, McGovern was the only
Democrat who was Reagan's match: a liberal who brought a moral perspective to government, not against it. McGovern, he said defiantly, was
the "loyal opposition, the clear alternative, the genuine liberal, the real
Democrat."[29]

Steven Stark, Jimmy Carter's issue coordinator for the 1976 primary
campaign, and a lecturer at Harvard Law School, wrote that McGovern,
as a peace candidate, had some surprising strengths. Since McGovern was
widely known as being strongly identified with policies critical of the

defense establishment, held no office, and was given virtually no chance of winning, he had the opportunity to speak more boldly about nuclear-arms cutbacks than such candidates as Mondale, Cranston, or Hart, who tried to walk the line of being acceptable to a majority of the electorate, while protecting their home base. Stark recognized that as a former nominee, most voters knew what McGovern stood for, and advertising would be of little use to him in the primary campaign. While an organization undoubtedly helps a candidate, McGovern's voters were thought to be those highly motivated activists who tended to show up at the polls without a reminder. Stark recognized that although McGovern would not likely be the Democratic Party's nominee, he called on the media not to repeat the mistake of 1972 by writing him off completely. Just as the pendulum eventually swung Ronald Reagan's way after decades of derision, it was possible that it might swing McGovern's way and change the future of the discussion of issues during the campaign.[30]

CHAPTER FOUR

On the Road Again: Hoping Lightning Strikes Twice

Getting the ideas out is what's important now. If I can do that, then at least I'll know in 1984 that I did something; I will have discharged a duty to myself not to be silent.

—George McGovern

At age sixty-one George McGovern was back again on the campaign trail in pursuit of a Democratic electorate that would listen to his ideas, grant him a fair shot, and seriously consider making him the Democratic nominee, and he was enjoying every minute of it. Although his Democratic opponents were spending more and had campaigns that were much better organized, McGovern was absolutely convinced that this journey was the "right thing to do."[1] He was taking things slowly and on a small scale, traveling without the usual entourage associated with a presidential campaign, flying tourist-fare on commercial flights, or riding in the backseat of a volunteer's small car; nevertheless he was a contented man. He no longer had much of a staff, and of the fourteen people working in his Washington headquarters, two were his daughters, Mary and Ann, who were both deputy campaign managers.[2] Mary McGovern made many of the daily operational decisions in the campaign. She acted as a trouble-shooter for everything that went on—finances, personnel, strategy, schedules. The major decisions were made with the approval of the senator himself.[3]

Since many of the best campaign professionals were with other campaigns by the time McGovern announced, his staff consisted largely of people with limited campaign experience, many of whom were not recruited but who came into the campaign on their own. Several staff workers, due to necessity, were elevated to policy positions and positions of responsibility sometimes beyond their previous experiences.[4]

Despite his entry into the race, McGovern had no illusions about his chances, and realized that he would not be nominated by the Democratic Party again "unless lightning strikes." Still, McGovern felt that "there [were] things worse than losing," and having no political seat to lose, he felt completely free to tell people exactly what he thought about each issue.[5] This candid attitude made people take notice of his presidential campaign, and it also helped make him one of the most interesting candidates in the crowded Democratic field. Despite this, there was a long, uphill road in front of him.

Longtime aide George Cunningham, who initially advised McGovern against running, joined the campaign temporarily as general chairman, stating that McGovern "reminded me we had marched together in so many campaigns."[6] Cunningham, who had served as McGovern's administrative assistant in the Senate for eighteen years, already had made plans to run for the U.S. Senate in South Dakota in 1984.[7] Later on in the campaign, Cunningham was replaced by Paul Sullivan, a veteran of a number of campaigns, including 1972. Sullivan's strength, according to McGovern, was his relationship with the people who had been actively involved in 1972.[8]

One of the main hurdles Cunningham had to help McGovern overcome was that McGovern lacked the image of a winner. After being defeated for the presidency in 1972 and losing his Senate seat in 1980, he bore the stigma of being one of the biggest losers in American politics. Keeping modest goals, McGovern insisted that he would not judge his own campaign on the basis of victory or defeat.[9]

"If, at the end of all this, people say, 'Well, George made a lot of sense,' that's all I want," McGovern said.[10] It was impossible for McGovern to sit on the sidelines and see the country pursuing policies both at home and abroad that he believed were not in the national interest. Although there were a half dozen candidates in the field, McGovern believed that 80 or 90 percent of the Democratic voters remained uncommitted and were waiting on the sidelines for someone to say something that would get them excited and into the campaign. He believed he had some qualities that set him apart from the pack, qualities that might catch on with the voters.[11] For example, unlike the other Democratic hopefuls, McGovern remained an unabashed dove and New Dealer, unwilling to be moved by the Reagan tide. McGovern's strong, unapologetic liberal convictions were just one of the qualities that he felt offered Democratic voters a choice.[12]

McGovern often received an affectionate and emotional reception to his reappearance on the national political scene, and he found that many Democrats still harbored a fond regard for him because he motivated them, back in 1972, to become involved in politics with his pledge to end the Vietnam War.[13]

"They all come up to me wearing buttons for Mondale, Glenn, Hart and all the others and tell me they are glad to see I haven't given up," McGovern said. "They say I'm the reason they got into politics back in 1972. It's a good feeling."[14] McGovern's positions in 1984 did not mark him as an out-of-step ideologue, as some viewed him in his 1972 bid. In addition to being one of the few outspoken liberals in the race, McGovern had another quality that was soon picked up on: He was conducting a gentleman's campaign. While the other candidates were taking chunks out of each other, McGovern spoke only well of his competitors. Speaking to New Hampshire Democrats at a dinner in October, McGovern had something nice to say about each of his opponents. When McGovern was introduced on stage, sitting next to the other candidates, the hall erupted with applause and cheers, and he began his speech in a most gentlemanly fashion. He praised Cranston for raising arms control so forcefully in the campaign, and John Glenn for demonstrating "long ago he had the right stuff." He called Gary Hart a "great campaign manager," and Hollings a brilliant senator. And McGovern mentioned that both Askew and Mondale had been approached to be his running mate in 1972. His speech was regarded as one of the most gracious speeches ever delivered by a presidential candidate, and it was warmly received by the audience and his fellow contenders. By any measure, he was the emotional favorite of the event.[15]

Emotional favorite or not, McGovern had set some basic points on what was needed to run a legitimate, realistic campaign. Operating under the knowledge that he was already behind front-runners Mondale and Glenn, he planned to concentrate until mid-March on the Iowa caucuses and the New Hampshire and Massachusetts primaries. If he did not rank among the top four finishers in these states, he would probably get out of the race. "If I were to come in fifth in Iowa, I'd probably quit right then," McGovern said. "Certainly in the following week, if I came in fifth in New Hampshire, I would quit." He said he would also have to finish among the top three contenders in Massachusetts in order to attract the press attention, the support, and the money necessary to stay in the race past the March 13 primary.[16]

The early McGovern strategy rested in part on the chance that Mondale would stumble, thus not locking up the nomination. According to George Cunningham, if Mondale had not locked up the nomination by March 13, either because Jesse Jackson drew away black votes or because Glenn won the many southern primaries, the race would be opened up again. In order to keep himself in the running, however, McGovern still had to deal with his image problems.[17]

Cunningham believed that McGovern's image as a fuzzy-headed liberal persisted to some degree, believing "that can be overturned; not with ease, but it can be overturned." Of more concern to McGovern's staff was the rumor that not even McGovern's wife supported him.[18] To rectify this, McGovern's staff had Eleanor endorse her husband at the opening of his headquarters in Des Moines.[19] She was, in fact, quite surprised at the reaction to her decision not to actively campaign, and said there was nothing in her statement about not supporting what George was doing.[20]

"He knows how I feel about it. He knows I support what he is doing and he respects my decision not to get involved," Eleanor said in Sioux Falls, South Dakota. Commenting on the progress of the current campaign, Mrs. McGovern appeared satisfied as her husband began to win the kind of respect that most journalists and Democrats denied him after his announcement. "He feels good about it. I feel good about it. It's something he deserves," she said.[21]

Around the time that Eleanor was endorsing her husband, *The Des Moines Register* welcomed him into the race as a Democrat representing controversial and even unpopular ideas that might force his party to think hard about effective alternatives to Reaganism.[22] Despite this, Cunningham once remarked about the campaign: "This borders on fantasy. I look in the mirror and say 'George, what am I doing here?'"[23]

According to William Keyserling, an independent political consultant, as well as the national campaign director of the Hollings for President campaign, McGovern had a major handicap in the national media. The media would essentially "defeat" any candidate who held a vision transcending political interests, or who saw the party and the nation as more than the sum of its parts. Any candidate wishing to present such a vision to the average Democrat was doomed to either be neglected by the media outright, or dismissed by them, and would never have a chance to be judged on his merits by the public at large. Another major problem was that the media automatically gave much more coverage to the candidates who were presumed to have the most likelihood of winning from the start, thus robbing all other candidates of valuable press, and feeding the public the notion that a vote for any of these poorly covered candidates would be wasted.[24] The media had already settled, in early 1983, on what Theodore H. White described as a dramatic, two-man contest between Mondale and Glenn, with Jackson as an unusual sidebar who would receive a little notice. Two of the networks, ABC and NBC, announced plans that the top three Democratic candidates would get most of the coverage, dealing a severe blow to the candidates that the networks felt didn't stand a chance. *The Washington Post* carried a piece in 1983 declaring that Mondale had the nomination wrapped up, and in early December, *The New Republic*'s cover story featured Mondale, asking, "Has He Won?" *Business Week*, on August 1, outlined the candidates' positions and limited it to candidates Glenn and Mondale. *Time* magazine, October 10, featured a five-page review of the candidates in which it devoted a total of three paragraphs to Cranston, Hart, Hollings, Askew, and McGovern. *The*

New Yorker, in a lengthy "Political Journal," written by Elizabeth Drew on November 21, glibly analyzed the "other candidates" out of the race.[25]

Keyserling argued that, due to the way the media shaped the coverage, the other five men contesting the nomination were whittled out of the process before the first caucus delegate or primary voter had cast a vote. A decade before, a presidential candidate could sell himself hand-by-hand through civic clubs, living rooms, and plant gates. Before the Iowa caucuses of 1976, "Jimmy Who?" played the "consummate retail political trader" while the opinion leaders of the national media refused to recognize his campaign. Keyserling contended that retailing was made possible by reforms of the early 1970s that were designed to put an end to the domination by the political bosses.[26] By 1983, however, there existed a political supermarket managed by an alliance of the news media and the party infrastructure. "Conventional wisdom" prevented genuine dark horses from emerging as they had repeatedly in American history.[27] By January 1984, before the first primary or caucus, Askew, Cranston, Hart, and Hollings spent as much time in the race as Jimmy Carter had at that point eight years earlier, yet all that they had accomplished, according to Keyserling, was managing to get written off. All but Askew had run up debts averaging roughly a half million dollars.[28]

There is a reason for this downward shift in fortune for the potential dark horse. The new Democratic Party rules, devised by a commission chaired by Governor Jim Hunt of North Carolina, created a system that was heavily "front loaded." Nearly 40 percent of the pledged delegates were selected from within the first month of primaries and caucuses.[29] Under these circumstances, a candidate would need to begin with heavy support and hold it through the first month of primaries and caucuses. Any candidate with a vision transcending the interests of the party bosses, the large special interests, or the perception of the media was doomed and would never have a chance to be judged by the rank and file. Thus, Democratic organizations were essentially incapable of treating the candidates in an equitable manner. Once the front-runners had been established, they would naturally receive more attention from the party and the press. Each state party chair was eager to use the leading candidates as centerpieces for fund-raising, and, with the exception of New York Governor Mario Cuomo, no state organization ventured to provide fair exposure for all the Democratic presidential contenders in the fall of 1983.[30]

Things were quite different in McGovern's previous presidential run. In the fall of 1971, polls showed that Senator Edward M. Kennedy had the support of 26 percent of the registered Democrats, Senator Edmund Muskie had 22 percent, and George McGovern had just 6 percent. Similarly, in November 1975, Senator Hubert H. Humphrey had 30 percent, Governor George Wallace 20 percent, and Jimmy Carter had just 2 percent.[31] If those campaigns had been held a decade later, McGovern and

Carter, the two eventual party nominees, would almost certainly have been trampled out of the race long before their campaigns could ever gain the momentum that eventually would sweep them to the party's nomination.[32]

Another media concern was covered in an interview given by Hal Bruno, political director for ABC News, who said that it was difficult to cover issues in a twenty-two-minute evening news show. Other editors and producers argued that many issues were just too complex to deal with in the coverage of a political campaign.[33] This led to the media taking the easy way out, reporting on fluff items and rumors, rather than tackling the substantive issues in an informative way. In 1984, this trend led to the coverage of such things as rumors plaguing the Hart campaign and other such gossip, rather than how each candidate would deal with the issues of the day.[34]

Regardless of the media problems, McGovern was gratified that what he was saying was getting out to the people at all. Looking back on the 1972 campaign, McGovern felt that his real message did not get out; it was buried in a blizzard of negative advertising and bad press. This time around, McGovern felt good about his campaign largely because he began receiving serious and respectful treatment in the press.[35]

"At first start, I was afraid of ridicule," he said. "And that fear was pretty well justified in the first two weeks or so. The press knocked the hell out of me. But then, all of a sudden, the coverage turned, and it's been pretty good." Particularly satisfying for McGovern was the freedom he felt to just expound on what he believed about every issue, without condition or compromise. "If the voters agree with me, that's great, but if they don't, I'm not going to pull back," he said. "It never feels good, and I don't think it helps anybody, either. Every time I trimmed or modified in '72, I lost ground."[36]

On October 6, 1983, all seven of the announced Democratic presidential candidates appeared together for the first time in the 1984 campaign. It was held at New York City's Town Hall, where each of the candidates took turns accusing President Reagan of running the economy into the ground, took good-humored swipes at each other, and sought to spell out their strategies for nuclear arms reduction. McGovern accused the Reagan administration of "closing its eyes" to human rights violations abroad. The New York State Democratic Committee Forum was organized by Governor Mario Cuomo and U.S. Senator Daniel Patrick Moynihan. Questions came from the candidates themselves and from a panel composed of former U.S. Representative Barbara Jordan, author Theodore H. White, and Duke University Political Science Professor James David Barber.[37]

The next week, on October 13 in Cambridge, Massachusetts, the seven Democratic candidates clashed in an hourlong debate at Harvard University. The program, cosponsored by the Massachusetts Coalition for Arms

Control and Harvard University's Institute of Politics, was hailed as one of the premier events of the 1984 presidential campaign, and seven of the Democratic presidential hopefuls debated arms control issues in their first confrontation in Massachusetts. The Forum was broadcast live locally and shown in twenty-four other cities throughout the United States. Thirty-five percent of America's television viewers had an opportunity to gain firsthand insight into the candidates' attitudes toward critical nuclear arms issues. The candidates addressed audience questions on the proposed nuclear weapons freeze, the MX missile system, and other timely policy issues.[38] While it produced no clear winners, it was, for the most part, a well-mannered, intellectually challenging exchange. Robert Pear, in a *New York Times* article, reported that Senator Alan Cranston impressed many in the audience of arms control advocates with his passionate, single-minded emphasis on the dangers of nuclear war. The high point of the debate, according to some observers, came when Senator Glenn posed a multipart question to Mondale regarding the sale of F-15s to Saudi Arabia, the grain embargo, and nuclear fuel sale to India. Glenn also asked about the MX missile, challenging Mondale's private disagreements with the Carter administration's decision to develop and deploy the MX missile. All the candidates but Askew expressed support for mutual and verifiable freeze on the testing, production and further deployment of nuclear warheads, missiles, and other delivery systems by the United States and the Soviet Union.[39]

In this debate, McGovern challenged the conventional wisdom that considered military spending as a way of strengthening the country. He quoted President Dwight D. Eisenhower, the only five-star general ever to serve as president, who once said that if the military spends too much, it actually weakens the country by depriving it of other sources of national strength. McGovern declared that the United States was now at the level where military spending of an excessive nature would not only threaten the survival of the race, but would also weaken America. The excessive spending was bankrupting the national treasury, contributing to a $200 billion federal deficit, and undermining funds that the United States needed for education, health care, the environment, and other important sources of national power. McGovern was the only candidate recommending a 25 percent cut in the Reagan $275 billion 1984 military budget. That would still leave the United States as the strongest military power on earth, but would free $75 billion to build up America.[40] He also favored a unilateral nuclear weapons freeze and would not put any definite time limit on it. McGovern said that the country could well afford, in its own interest, to follow the example of President Kennedy, who nudged the United States on a path toward the nuclear test ban agreement by announcing that, without reference to the Soviet Union, the United States would be halting the testing of nuclear weapons and that the country would not resume if the Soviets followed suit. They did follow suit, and the United States got the limited test ban treaty as a result. McGovern advocated the same type of initiative, then, at a time when the United States had the capacity to destroy the Soviet Union several times over without building any additional nuclear weapons. McGovern said the United States should stop producing such weapons, even if the Soviet Union continued to build them.[41] "We could always resume the building of nuclear weapons" if the Soviet Union did not follow America's example, he said, adding:

> I think the one central fact we have to keep in mind is that there is no practical purpose for nuclear weapons other than deterrence. And once each side achieved the capability of utterly destroying the other one, no matter who hit first, everything since that day has been wasted on redundancy and surplus that adds nothing at all to the security of either side.[42]

Around this time, George Gallup announced that McGovern's mid-September entry into the contest for the Democratic nomination had two immediate effects. First, it catapulted McGovern into third place with 9 percent of the Democrats' votes, right behind leading contenders Mondale and Glenn, and ahead of would-be nominees Cranston, Askew, Hart, and Hollings.[43]

Second, by drawing Democrats' votes away from the six original contenders, especially Mondale, McGovern's presence in the race narrowed the once-considerable gap between Mondale and Glenn. In the Gallup survey, Mondale had 37 percent of the Democrats' support, compared with 26 percent for Glenn. However, in surveys conducted during June and July, before McGovern entered the race, Mondale had led Glenn by as much as 17 percent. Although Mondale's lead over Glenn among Democrats shrank since McGovern's entry, the two leaders remained virtually deadlocked for the nomination among Independents, who not only constituted almost one-third of the electorate but also many of them would vote in the Democratic primaries in 1984. When Jackson's name was included, he received 8 percent of the votes, placing him in a dead tie with McGovern.[44]

While McGovern was basking in the serious treatment he was receiving from the press and his fellow candidates, his campaign was still considered quite a long shot. By mid-October, in fact, it was looking like the race for the 1984 Democratic nomination might be locked up. One harsh blow to the McGovern campaign came when Governor Cuomo became the sixth Democratic governor and Senator Moynihan became the seventh U.S. senator to endorse Walter Mondale for the Democratic presidential nomination. "Of all the candidates, Walter Mondale will be the best President because of his ideals, his ideas, and his experience," the governor said.[45] (Another difficult blow would come two months later, when the National Organization for Women, the AFL-CIO, and the National Education Association, all powerful Democratic supporters in the past, would also throw their support behind Mondale.)[46]

However, the McGovern campaign took the knocks and pushed on. By December 1983, the McGovern campaign established its New Hampshire headquarters in Nashua, recruiting Woody Woodland to be McGovern's New Hampshire coordinator. Woodland, a Presbyterian minister, newsman, and talk show host for WSMN in Nashua, commented that it was "kind of silly to give up a job, but I've always thought you should try to do what you believe in."[47] Richard Maiman, professor of political science at the University of Southern Maine, came aboard as the campaign's coordinator for the state of Maine.[48] And Judy Wilson, chairwoman of the Polk County Iowa Democratic Central Committee, was named acting state coordinator in Iowa. She commented to *The Washington Post*:

> None of the other candidates stimulated me. I kept waiting for one of them to break from the pack, but none of them did. Then, I heard McGovern and his ten-point plan. I'm an issues Democrat. . . . People like me had no place to go but with McGovern.[49]

Additional endorsements came in from Peter Clarke, chairman of the Essex County Young Democrats and a member of the Georgetown Town Committee, and Dr. Richard Saltman of the Marblehead Democratic Town Committee in Massachusetts. As the endorsements rolled in, the pace of the campaign began to pick up, as well.[50]

On Monday, December 5, the candidates clasped hands and heard themselves referred to as "the next President of the United States" at a $1,000-a-plate dinner opening their drive for money and party unity. A schedule later that week included a fund-raising breakfast in Chicago, a breakfast in Atlanta, and a meeting with western governors in Albuquerque. A Democratic Party spokesman said the goal for the presidential sweep was $1.5 million. Former Governor Reubin Askew of Florida dropped out of the tour at the last minute after a death in his family, and Senator Alan Cranston refused to participate, boycotting the tour as a show of support for party officials in Iowa and New Hampshire who were embroiled in a dispute with national party officials over the primary and caucus schedule. Iowa wanted to hold its caucuses February 20 instead of February 27, the date set by the national party. New Hampshire, likewise, was determined to have its primary on February 28 rather than on March 6.[51]

December was proving to be quite the hectic month for McGovern. On December 14, he made his first trip into Wisconsin and held a press conference on arrival at Madison Airport. On the 15th, he kicked off a three-day swing through Iowa with a press conference in Cedar Rapids, after which he was going on to Iowa City, Mucatine, and Davenport. From there, he would head to Clinton and Dubuque, and then depart from Waterloo on the 17th, returning to New Hampshire on the 20th.[52] He also found time to address the National Organization for Women's annual conference in Washington.[53]

As McGovern worked tirelessly throughout December, he received some favorable press. The *New York Times* reported on December 7 that "Mr. McGovern refused to speak ill of either Chicago Democrats or his opponents in the presidential campaign. Instead, he focused his remarks on Reagan's foreign policies, saying those policies are 'leading us into war.'"[54] *Time* magazine reported on December 19 that only one candidate, McGovern, chose not to "twit" his competitors. Instead, he directly addressed issues such as poverty and hunger in America and worldwide, the current administration's excessive military spending, and what approaches the Democrats would take to solve these problems.[55]

In addition to making personal appearances, McGovern also took some time in December to speak out on the issues. In San Francisco on the 10th, reacting to remarks made by White House Counselor Edwin Meese concerning hunger in America, McGovern said:

> If we ever needed proof that Ronald Reagan's heart beats for the rich rather than the poor and the hungry, it is here in the comments of Edwin Meese, his closest advisor. . . . This nation is being governed by men who would rather deny than resolve the problems that their disastrous policies have created. Their contempt for the poor only adds to the misery caused by their politics of selfishness. . . . Any person who has traveled the country as I have knows that there are millions of men, women and children who are not getting enough to eat—while this Administration pays our farmers not to produce. Just as Mr. Reagan does not see hunger in America, he is blind to the millions of people overseas who need American food far more than American weapons.[56]

On December 12, when again asked, "Why run?" McGovern answered:

> I want to be President of the United States. . . . It isn't the fun of running, although that can be exciting and enjoyable. It isn't only to sharpen debate on the issues that I think need to be addressed—although the Presidential race offers a greater forum than almost any other for an informative discussion of policy options before this nation. I'm running because, however unlikely it may seem to some, there is a real chance that I may win the nomination and go on to be President of the United States. I hope it doesn't sound too boastful to say that if I were able to make it, I think I'd be a whale of a good President. My whole life, in a sense, has been a preparation for the office and I think the proposals I am making to the country are based on

more experience and more thought than those being made by the other candidates.[57]

On December 14 in Madison, Wisconsin, McGovern was asked what emphasis "President McGovern" would place on human rights in his foreign policy. He responded by saying:

I don't see how any decent American can quarrel with the United States raising the banner of human rights all over the world. I am sick and tired of seeing American armaments and American military advisors wrapped around these miserable military dictators in places like El Salvador; the embrace of Marcos in the Philippines, Pinochet in Chile, and other places. We are weakening our stance in the world and opening doors for the Communists by throwing our arms around some of the most odious military dictators on the face of the earth.[58]

Visiting with senior citizens in Iowa City, McGovern was asked why, as a decorated World War II combat pilot, he chose not to play up his military background when Reagan, whose military experience ran to having starred in *Hellcats of the Navy*, was identified as a strong man. McGovern responded by saying:

Well, I don't go around boasting about my military record because there were millions of people who signed up for service. . . . I flew a full string of combat missions against Nazi Germany. I would do the same thing again under similar circumstances. There isn't anybody running for President this year who has had any more first-hand experience with bloody combat than I have had, so I know what war is all about, and I am for a strong national defense. But I would prefer a more cooperative approach to the world and less of this interventionism and confrontation that we've had in the last couple of years. There is a certain amount of insecurity on the part of those who feed on some kind of a macho display—sort of a neighborhood bully mentality. It makes them feel tougher if they can push people around. I have never held to that view. I think that anyone who has a quiet confidence in the integrity and the soundness of American institutions and the American way of life is not always boiling for a fight with somebody else.[59]

McGovern's remarks did not fall on deaf ears. John Patrick Hunter reported in *The Capitol Times* on December 15, "[E]nthusiastic listeners braved a traffic-disrupting snow storm . . . to cheer [McGovern] when he called President Reagan 'the most dangerous man ever to occupy the White House.'" A standing-room-only audience at the University of Wisconsin gave McGovern a stirring response.[60]

As McGovern spread his ideas throughout December, the national press continued analyzing what his presence added to the race. Curtis Wilkie reported in *The Boston Globe* that McGovern descended on the presidential campaign like a prophet, and was the most outspoken candidate, Jesse Jackson notwithstanding.[61] Tom Wicker reported in the *New York Times* on December 26 that George McGovern had been making the most sense out of all of the candidates. He added that the front-runners, no doubt feeling a need to protect their positions by avoiding taking controversial stands against Reagan, were acting out of self-preservation, not leadership.[62]

"The Democrats in the nation don't need and won't elect a mere well-known name or a collector of endorsements," Wicker wrote. "They need a leader with the right stuff to stand up and challenge Ronald Reagan, to make the opposition case and offer a change."[63] Ellen Goodman wrote in *The Washington Post* on December 31 that the column she'd most like to issue a recall on was published back in September, when George McGovern threw his hat in the ring. She had pronounced his candidacy "embarrassing" in that now-lamented column, and wrote that she had a correction: "He's got a lot of class."[64]

The widely held belief that Mondale enjoyed a commanding, if not insurmountable, lead in the race for the nomination was based on the polls. Polls at such an early stage of a campaign measured name recognition, media coverage, and, of course, money. More and more in presidential politics, however, polls were becoming events in themselves.[65]

Success in preprimary polls became the measure of a presidential campaign's success or failure. Polls did not take on an exaggerated importance, despite what many politicians believed. Since only a small number of delegates were at stake in Iowa and New Hampshire, these early contests were seen as crucial because they generated money and publicity for the winning candidates. However, prior to the primaries, polls served that function.[66]

As 1983 turned into 1984, the campaign grind became even more intense. McGovern, who enjoyed traveling alone, received Secret Service protection on January 14 while he made rounds through New England.[67] On the 16th, McGovern met with nuclear freeze activists in Boston, and early on the 17th, he had one of his most memorable campaign stops at Friendly House. "What a nice name for a place that feeds the hungry," said McGovern. He enjoyed a creamed-chicken lunch with about one hundred elderly poor folks on Grafton Hill in Worcester, Massachusetts. "These programs," he said, "are right out of the Judeo-Christian teachings of our country: 'Feed the hungry.' You can't read the Bible and not come to the conclusion that programs like this are what we're here for. Social Security, education, housing, Medicare: they're all extremely valuable programs, but none have done more good for the money invested than WIC [Women, Infants, and Children], food stamps, and school lunches." McGovern later told the reporter who had accompanied him:

When you get hold of one of those grizzled hands and those faces that are just hungry for attention, you know why you're doing it. Almost without exception every one of those hands really gripped mine. Lots of them cling. I've never gotten to the point where it becomes a drag. The joining of hands is a meaningful experience in that it identifies people with a national figure who makes them feel closer to the political process. It lets the candidate feel he belongs to the country—that he's not just out there trying to manipulate public opinion. I really find myself being carried along. It may be after years of interacting with people that this was one of the things that made me feel dissatisfied on the sidelines. Two and half years out and I felt I was coasting. I'd made more money in two and a half years than in the previous ten, but I was missing something. It wasn't the same as being at the center of the national political debate.[68]

Another memorable campaign stop was the last of the day before the New Hampshire Committee on National Security Forum at St. Anselm College in Manchester, New Hampshire. Moderator Tom Gerber chided McGovern for "straying from 'security' issues to speak of acid rain and the erosion of Iowa topsoil at rates as high as ten tons per acre per year." McGovern responded:

I'll have to insist on my own definitions. We tend to assume the only danger we face is physical attack from the enemy, when we are also threatened by things we're doing to ourselves. Our food supply is every bit as important to our national security as our military forces are.

It includes the strength of our economy. It includes the effectiveness, fairness, and believability of our political system. It includes the vision of our public officials and the health and educational well-being of our citizenry. And of course it includes the preparedness of our military forces. I would never shortchange the essential defense needs of our country, but the strength of our country depends at least as much on our economy . . . our compassion. . . . It is still true that where there is no vision the people perish. That is the truth, a literal truth, in a national security sense.[69]

The next day, he met with the Human Services Coalition in Concord, New Hampshire, spoke at New England College in Manchester, and opened the campaign's New Hampshire headquarters in Nashua.[70]

On January 19, McGovern paired up with Bob Shrum to debate William F. Buckley and George Will on the topic: "Resolved: Ronald Reagan should be re-elected in 1984." Shrum, Senator Edward M. Kennedy's press secretary since September of 1980, had been McGovern's speech writer from 1972 through 1975. The debate, which was preceded by a press reception and occurred at Yale University in New Haven, offered a perfect forum for McGovern to really let loose and talk about what he felt was wrong with the current administration.[71] To begin with, McGovern charged that Reagan felt the American people "should feel good merely because he is working to resolve problems he himself has made worse."[72] McGovern went on to say that any success that Reagan might claim for his so-called domestic recovery stemmed from his excessive and distorted use of Keynesian economics, which he campaigned against in 1980. According to McGovern, the heavy government spending sufficient to create a $193 billion deficit in the last fiscal year, together with ill-advised major tax reductions, was a classic textbook approach not of priming the economic pump, but of flooding the pump with red ink. For true fiscal conservatives, McGovern alleged, the use of deficit spending to pull out of recession must bring them little joy. Yet, he was critical of many of the same voices raised against Democratic "big spenders" who had fallen "strangely silent" in the deep pit of the Reagan-created federal deficits.[73]

McGovern argued against Will's implication that any arms strategist with a new weapons proposal was "entitled to have it produced regardless of whether it is functionally, strategically, or militarily sound."[74] Reagan's military build-up may have been designed to prompt greater U.S. success in arms control negotiations, but, according to McGovern, it actually contributed to the collapse of those negotiations. McGovern advocated not exchanging any category of American military power for the Soviet counterpart, and believed that U.S. air power, naval power, and strategic nuclear power were all superior to Russia's.[75]

Another point of contention that McGovern argued was the Reagan administration's support for every "tin-pot dictator" who sought to qualify as a recipient of the country's military largess by "waiving an anti-Communist banner." McGovern saw totalitarianism of either the right or the left as unacceptable and proposed that the answer to the problems the United States faced in Third World countries was not to be found in crushing revolutions. He felt that the United States should stand militarily clear of these revolutionary movements and U.S. involvement should be limited to diplomacy, trade, and economic assistance.[76]

The last major point that McGovern took Will to task for was the assertion that Reagan's budget adequately provided for the poor. McGovern claimed that 34 million American citizens were at or below the poverty line, 3.5 million American children did not have an adequate diet, nearly 10 million Americans were unemployed, and 5 million were underemployed. McGovern advocated that the federal government take constructive efforts to resolve these serious problems. At the end of the debate, the vote clearly gave the victory to Shrum and McGovern.[77]

On February 1, 1984, George Will titled his newspaper column "McGovern's Politics Quixotic." Will's article was written about the Yale University debate over Reagan's reelection. He mocked McGovern's message as "Come Home, America, Part II." He charged that McGovern took Orwell's axiom "too much to heart" and that McGovern advocated "the quickest way to end a war is to lose it."[78]

According to Will, McGovern's theory was that "Soviet military spending is reactive and emulative—that it is provoked by ours—so U.S. restraint would be reciprocated." In his article, he was highly critical of McGovern for calling for defense cuts of 25 percent and for contrasting defense spending with spending on "human needs." Will acknowledged, however, that the vote at the end of the debate did go against them and in favor of Shrum and McGovern. Will also conceded that more domestic spending was needed and prudent.[79]

McGovern countered in an editorial article published about two weeks later in newspapers throughout the country. He argued that he was unable to recognize the debate as it was described in Will's column and alleged that neither Buckley nor Will responded to his basic allegations. He was critical of Buckley and Will for cavalierly dismissing the vote at the end of the debate that gave the victory to McGovern and Shrum. "This does not surprise me," McGovern wrote. "Those with the philosophy of Will and Buckley have been all too willing in the past to dismiss the insights and idealism of the young both at home and abroad."[80]

With his warm reception at debates, his favorable press coverage, and his poll numbers, McGovern seemed to be in a good position at this point of the campaign, compared with his last presidential run. In January 1972, candidate McGovern had the backing of only 3 percent of Democrats for the party's nomination, compared with 1984, when he was in third place with 11 percent of the vote. In 1972, McGovern's support increased only marginally, until it shot up to 17 percent that April. By May of 1972, he was even with his key rivals, winning 25 percent of the support of Democrats. (George Wallace and Hubert Humphrey each had 26 percent.) By late June, as the 1972 Democratic Convention neared, he moved ahead of his opponents, winning 30 percent of the vote to Humphrey's 27 percent and Wallace's 25 percent.[81]

Now, in the 1984 campaign, McGovern's early polling numbers seemed downright rosy in comparison. The *New York Times*'s CBS News poll (taken just before the AFL-CIO endorsement in mid-December) gave Mondale 34 percent of the vote, Glenn 29 percent, and McGovern 11 percent.[82] Another nationwide poll conducted in December, this time by *The Los Angeles Times*, also put McGovern solidly in third place. Gallup showed that support for McGovern in the Midwest had more than doubled in a month, leaping from 7 to 15 percent. The Gallup results also indicated that McGovern was favored by almost three times as many women as men.[83]

"I have good news," McGovern told volunteers in New Hampshire one day in January 1984. "I'm twice as high in the polls as I was at this point in 1972." Breaking down the numbers for analysis, we can see that, in New York, a September statewide poll by the Marist Institute of Public Opinion showed that McGovern was the choice of 6.8 percent of the Democratic voters, compared with Hart's 2 percent and Cranston's 1.8 percent.

McGovern was by far the most identifiable liberal in the poll, and, next to McGovern, front-running Mondale appeared to be more of a moderate and thus harder for Glenn to catch. That was bad news for Glenn, trailing Mondale 39.8 percent to 21.1 percent. Glenn's strategists predicted that McGovern's name recognition would pass Hart and Cranston in the polls.[84]

On January 31, 1984, seven Democratic candidates attended the foreign policy debate sponsored by Harvard University's Kennedy School of Government and *The Boston Globe*. Only Florida Governor Reubin Askew passed up the ninety-minute debate. It was the third debate for the Democratic field, and it differed markedly from the eight-way confrontation held in Hanover, New Hampshire, when front-runners Mondale and Glenn engaged in heated exchanges over their proposals for trimming deficit spending. This time, Glenn and Mondale sparred briefly over the Salt II treaty, which was negotiated under the Carter administration, and was opposed by Glenn. Unlike the last time, no voices were raised, no fingers pointed. Rather, the compliments were flying in the debate between the two candidates. McGovern said he favored cuts "on the order of 25 percent," while Hart said he wanted to trim Reagan's build-up by about $100 billion over the next two or three years. McGovern also said Lebanon was "almost the same cycle" as Vietnam.[85] James Reston wrote in an article in the *New York Times* that it was interesting in the Democratic Party debates that the most enthusiastic applause went to George McGovern and Jesse Jackson when they said, "Come on, let's begin to talk to the Russians about the control of nuclear weapons and the reduction of military budgets, and think about the poverty and suffering of the human race."[86]

From the very start of his campaign, McGovern had been putting a greater emphasis on criticizing the Reagan administration's military campaigns and excessive military spending than had any other candidate. McGovern's call for more than $50 billion in cuts in Reagan's defense budget, a ban on new deployment of U.S. nuclear missiles, and an immediate resumption of diplomatic relations with Cuba made McGovern the first contender to support a "unilateral freeze." Back in September, McGovern had said, "If the Russians want to keep wasting money piling those things (nuclear weapons) up, I would say go for it," adding that "it's no more a threat to us than what they have now." In an interview that same month, just before embarking on his first campaign tour, with visits in Maine, Iowa, and New Hampshire, McGovern said he had more freedom to stake out liberal positions on issues since he lost his Senate seat and was no longer accountable to constituents. "It's a little harder for me to call for a 20 percent or a 25 percent cut in the overall Pentagon budget when I am representing a state with a Strategic Air Command Base in it," admitted McGovern. He suggested that Cranston "wouldn't have to cling to that B-1 bomber if he weren't a Senator from California."

Cranston made arms control the central theme of his campaign, but supported the B-1 bomber, which was important to the aerospace industry
of California.[87]

It was history repeating itself, as American military involvement overseas was again the centerpiece of a McGovern presidential campaign. For
months before President Reagan decided to move Marines offshore in
Lebanon, McGovern was calling for their immediate withdrawal, as well
as for an end to U.S. support for guerrilla fighting in Central America.
Back in mid-November, McGovern had strongly rebuked fellow Democrats who supported the U.S. invasion of Grenada. "I hope they'll come
to their senses," he said. He labeled the invasion "shameful" and said
Democrats should use the episode to criticize the administration's excessive reliance on military force.[88]

> It's almost an unwritten rule that, no matter how outlandish a military ad-
> venture might be, people will rally around for about thirty days. That even-
> tually will change. I'm convinced that history will not treat us kindly.[89]

McGovern believed some Democrats probably were supporting the
invasion, or had muted their criticism because they thought it was unpopular with voters. He was disturbed by opinion polls showing strong
public approval of the invasion. "If that's true, I think this country is in
bad shape," he said. "All we've really proved is that one of the most
powerful countries in the world can easily overrun one of the tiniest."[90]
Even with an overwhelming military advantage, however, the U.S. forces
suffered a "lot of military screw-ups," McGovern alleged. He charged that
many U.S. and civilian casualties were caused by the military's careless-
ness and poor planning. "I'm beginning to think the military is so concerned about landing those big contracts for military hardware that they
have forgotten how to conduct a military exercise," he said defiantly.[91]
McGovern was troubled with reports from Grenada about the American
military screening the civilian population to see who was loyal to the
government of Grenada. "What kind of function is that for the American
military? They ought to come home," McGovern insisted.[92]

Appearing on *Meet the Press* back in November, McGovern had told
Marvin Kalb of *NBC News*:

> I don't mind U.S. intervention of the right kind. But instead of intervening
> with U.S. Rangers and Marines in Grenada, I wish last spring, when Maurice
> Bishop was here in Washington, trying to work out an accommodation with
> the President and with the Secretary of State, trying to work out some more
> friendly and cooperative relationship, we had accepted that and offered to
> send in some doctors, some teachers, some construction workers. I would
> even have been willing to help them with that runway. I notice that
> Governor Scoon has said that he thinks that it ought to be completed, that

Grenada does depend on the tourist trade. That's the real reason the British and the French were helping out on that runway. Why do we wait until the Cubans and the Russians move into these areas and then after it's too late in the day, we rush in with the Marines? I think we arrived about six months late with the wrong method.[93]

A month later, on December 4, McGovern had criticized the Reagan administration for U.S. air strikes on Syrian positions in Lebanon. He reacted to the air strikes and the killing of eight Marines in Beirut by saying that "step by step the United States is approaching war with Syria. . . . Ronald Reagan is compounding his mistakes in Lebanon rather than facing his original mistake of assigning Marines to a sitting-duck role at the Beirut Airport." McGovern alleged that Reagan virtually consigned the Marines as hostages of the Arab-Israeli conflict and declared that "those who have survived should be brought home immediately before they fall victim to President Reagan's mishandling of American policy in that region."[94]

McGovern first called for bringing the Marines home in September and predicted Marine casualties "will grow as strikes and counter-strikes escalate."[95]

Lebanon wasn't the only situation in which McGovern was willing to stick his neck out. New York Mayor Ed Koch circulated an issues questionnaire to the Democratic presidential candidates asking whether they would use tactical nuclear weapons to halt a Soviet invasion of Western Europe. According to elementary deterrence theory and three decades of NATO defense policy, the only responsible public answer to Koch's question would be an unequivocal "yes." However, only McGovern, the longest of the long shots, could bring himself to speak honestly about it. "Yes, I would use tactical weapons if they were the only way to prevent a Soviet takeover," McGovern said.[96]

By mid-January, this hard-hitting stance McGovern had adopted had allowed him to remain in third place, with his prospects for gaining ground no longer looking quite so outlandish. The prospects of unseating the current president were looking up, as George Gallup announced that President Reagan was in a dead heat with both leading Democratic contenders, Walter Mondale and John Glenn. Reagan and Mondale were tied, with 45 percent of the vote each, and the poll showed that Reagan was also tied with Glenn by the same percentage. Mondale was seen as far stronger than Glenn for the Democratic nomination, 68 percent to 24 percent, but fared no better than Glenn in a test race against Reagan because of Glenn's greater appeal to voters outside of the Democratic Party. The finding, according to Gallup, represented a leveling out of the slight rise in support recorded for Reagan in test elections against Mondale and Glenn in November and December. However, Reagan continued to run far ahead of Jackson, 65 percent to 23 percent, and McGovern, 56 percent to 32 percent.[97]

On January 22, 1984, the McGovern campaign ran a full-page ad in the *New York Times* titled "George McGovern Makes the Most Sense." Included in the ad were McGovern's ten-point program and numerous quotes from national newspapers. This ad was one of the ways the campaign hoped to add momentum and jump-start enthusiasm.[98]

The enthusiasm in McGovern's own camp needed no such shot in the arm. On January 23, the McGovern campaign's national headquarters moved to more spacious quarters at 1612 20th Street, N.W., in Washington, D.C. While the campaign headquarters was being reestablished, so too were the strategies.[99] Brian Best became director of political outreach at the beginning of January, and he began laying the groundwork for working relationships between the national campaign and organizations whose agendas were similar to McGovern's. The organizations Best intended to focus on dealt with Central American concerns, the peace movement, the gay and lesbian community, the environmentalists, the antihunger communities, the Hispanic community, the black community, and a few other groups. Best's primary focus for outreach efforts was to the two organizations who were most likely to be interested in supporting McGovern: the peace movement and Central American groups. Clearly, no other candidate had a better record or stronger positions on either of these issues than McGovern. Best felt, however, that McGovern did have some obstacles to overcome. For example, it was becoming clear that members of the peace community were either nominally supporting Cranston, or were frustrated with the process of electoral politics. Many Cranston supporters jumped on his bandwagon in a major way at first, and were slowly backing off as they considered his B-1 support and his approach to the nuclear freeze.[100] The major hurdle in gaining the support of the peace community was in convincing them that George McGovern had a chance of winning. A poll taken by the Nuclear Arms Educational Service in Stanford, California, indicated that of the 319 peace leaders who responded, 50 percent said that McGovern was the ideal candidate, but only 17 percent said that they would recommend that people vote for him. The rest recommended voting for someone else whom they felt had a better shot at winning the White House.[101]

Best was finding that McGovern's positions on the other issues were fairly similar to that of the other candidates. Almost all had good environmental positions, and almost all shared similar positions on women's issues. Jackson's "Rainbow Coalition" and Cranston's concentration on the gay and lesbian community locked McGovern out on those issues. McGovern was still in the race, though, appealing to the environmentalists and the peace community in significant ways.[102] McGovern had a long history in championing environmental causes, and, certainly, McGovern's label as a peace-seeking politician was a just one. In early February, for example, McGovern agreed to sign a petition put out by the new National Campaign for Peace in Central America. The four points in the petition were (1) to oppose U.S. military aid to El Salvador, Guatemala, Honduras, and Costa Rica; (2) to halt CIA-supported attacks against Nicaragua; (3) to oppose direct U.S. military intervention in El Salvador or Nicaragua; and (4) to oppose the deportation of Salvadorian and Guatemalan refugees from the United States. Only Jackson joined McGovern in signing the petition.[103]

By mid-January, Jeff Biggers, the national field director of the McGovern campaign, announced official and unofficial state coordinators in thirty-two states.[104] One reason for naming all these coordinators, certainly, was to raise funds for the campaign war chest. As at any time prior or since, one of the biggest campaign worries for any presidential hopeful was raising enough money to sustain a long and far-reaching campaign. McGovern hit a significant point in the campaign back in December when his campaign qualified for receipt of federal matching funds. The campaign sent out a request to enroll at least 20,000 citizen friends who would make financial commitments to the campaign on a monthly basis.[105] On December 30, Deputy Campaign Manager Mary McGovern reported that the campaign would file for its matching funds within the week, having raised a quarter of a million dollars thus far. According to McGovern's press secretary, Mark Kaminsky, part of that money would go toward a media campaign in Iowa, New Hampshire, and Massachusetts.[106]

Compared with his opponents, McGovern was operating on a very small amount of money. President Reagan did not make his candidacy official until January 29, but documents filed with the Federal Election Commission (FEC) on January 31 showed that his campaign committee raised nearly $3.6 million from October 17 through December 31. The Reagan-Bush Committee spent $1.7 million in 1983 and ended the year with nearly $2.1 million in cash on hand.[107]

Over in the Democratic camp, Mondale reported total 1983 contributions of $9.4 million, but he had spent $3.6 million in the fourth quarter and nearly $9.6 million for the year. By December 31, he had less than $400,000 in cash and debts of almost $800,000. His chief rival, John Glenn, raised $1.6 million for the last quarter and a little less than $5.8 million for the year. Glenn's campaign had only about $100,000 in cash on hand, and it owed more than $1 million by the end of 1983. In addition, by the end of the year, Glenn's campaign reported difficulty in generating contributions.[108]

The McGovern campaign was far behind the pack in money and had collected just over $200,000 in contributions since September. McGovern raised nearly $218,000 and spent $147,793. That left him with $102,034 in cash in the bank and debts of $44,857, including a $30,000 loan from the candidate.[109] The money came from many of the usual sources, with a large percentage coming from the direct mail solicitations.[110]

In mid-January 1984, the McGovern campaign applied to the FEC for matching funds. It had, by that date, raised $250,000, and the campaign money was being put to good use. There were now operating campaign offices in five states, with a goal of having ten state offices operative by April 1.[111] In addition, awarding-winning filmmaker Saul Landau had joined the McGovern network in December as media consultant. "Fortunately," Kaminsky said, "name recognition is not a problem, and our media can deal strictly and frankly with the candidate's positions on the issues."[112]

CHAPTER FIVE

The McGovern Platform: Realism and Common Sense

I'm an unabashed New Deal Democrat.

—George McGovern

George McGovern saw the critical task before the Democratic Party in 1984 as being the need to provide a clear alternative to the policies of President Reagan. The Democrats had to offer the American people a set of values and priorities to replace the politics of confrontation abroad and injustice at home. McGovern proposed a ten-point program to enable the Democrats to do more than defeat Ronald Reagan in 1984; it was a program fashioned out of American tradition, and it was a vision for the future.[1] McGovern's ten-point program had, as its highest priority, the halting of the arms race. McGovern felt that there would be no real security and no sustained economic recovery as long as America geared up for nuclear war. The militarization of foreign policy, the absurd prospect of winning a nuclear war, and support for dictatorial regimes defied the national interest. As a great world power, the United States must lead away from nuclear peril to peaceful coexistence, he believed. America, according to McGovern, should abandon wasteful military spending in order to fight the enemies from within: unemployment, crime, hunger, deteriorating education and infrastructure, and a despoiled natural environment. The next American president had the challenge of showing the world what Americans truly cherished.[2]

Actually, the concept of the ten-point program was nothing new for George McGovern, who proposed a different one to eradicate world famine in his 1964 book, *War Against Want*.[3] The McGovern program of 1984, however, dealt with a wider range of topics. For his ten-point program, McGovern advocated:

1. The United States should begin the nuclear freeze immediately. The MX missile and the B-1 bomber should be discontinued, and no new missiles should be deployed in Western Europe. U.S. military procurement practices and weapons testing practices should be reexamined. Military spending should be cut in the range of 20 to 25 percent below the $275 billion requested by the Reagan administration for fiscal year 1984.
2. The United States should terminate all military operations in Central America immediately.
3. The United States must bring the Marines home from Lebanon as soon as a cease-fire permits.
4. The federal government should put unemployed Americans back to work rebuilding and conserving America, including creating the world's finest rail system by the year 2000.
5. The federal government should restore the dream of home ownership and revive the construction industry with one-time government-backed mortgage loans of not more than 10 percent.
6. The complicated, loophole-ridden tax code should be simplified by adopting the Bradley-Gephardt fair tax bill.
7. Low-cost government loans should be provided to every American who seeks additional education and job training through a "Second Chance GI Bill of Rights."
8. The federal government should stop paying farmers not to produce, and instead should begin paying them fairly for their production to win the battle against hunger in America and abroad.
9. The equal rights of all Americans, especially the majority of whom are women, should be guaranteed.
10. The states should be relieved of the burden of welfare and Medicaid costs by full federal responsibility for these services, and free state funds to permit greater support for education and crime control.

Each of these points is elaborated upon in this chapter, and we start by examining point one, which deals with the nuclear arms race, national security, military practices, and the military budget. This will be broken into three different segments: the arms race with the Soviet Union, McGovern's proposed military policies, and his proposal for a financial overhaul of the military. As we have seen in earlier chapters, McGovern felt that Reagan's military budget was excessive, his decisions to send U.S. troops to foreign lands were ill-advised, and his treatment of the Soviet Union was downright dangerous. By constantly blaming the Soviets for the problems of the world, and by taking a tough, macho stance at every turn when it would be much more productive to have frank discussions with Moscow, Reagan seemed to be taking the United States on a path toward war.[4]

1. The United States should begin the nuclear freeze immediately. The MX missile and the B-1 bomber should be discontinued, and no new missiles should be deployed in Western Europe. U.S. military procurement practices and weapons testing practices should be reexamined. Military spending should be cut in the range of 20 to 25 percent below the $275 billion requested by the Reagan Administration for fiscal year 1984.

At the dawn of the Reagan administration, relations between the United States and the Soviet Union quickly deteriorated. At the same time as relations were worsening, each country continued to stockpile nuclear weapons, and George McGovern was worried that this combination could very easily lead to a nuclear war. He simply could not keep silent as the two countries were going through the worst relations in two decades, and the specter of nuclear holocaust hung in the air. In order to halt the arms race, McGovern wanted to unilaterally freeze the production and deployment of all U.S. nuclear weapons for at least one year. He believed that international stability would be threatened if the United States continued to build more nuclear weapons. Moreover, McGovern was convinced that if the United States froze production and deployment, the Soviets would do likewise, as they did following President Kennedy's unilateral cessation of atmospheric testing of nuclear bombs in 1963.[5]

Speaking on the NBC program *Meet the Press* on November 13, 1983, McGovern articulated his views on the arms race, stating that "nuclear superiority" is a nonsense term:

> Once each side has the capacity to utterly pulverize the other one, no matter who strikes first, it doesn't make a nickel's worth of difference which one is ahead at that point. They're both going to die anyway. I shouldn't use that word, a "nickel's worth of difference," because what he's talking about is going to cost us tens of billions of dollars that will be added on a deficit that's already running around $200 billion a year. So, far from blaming the Soviet Union for the absence of a nuclear arms agreement, I think we ought to go back to what really happened.[6]

McGovern felt that Reagan, more than anyone else, was responsible for the fact that the superpowers did not have an arms control agreement with the Soviet Union in 1983.[7] In 1980, candidate Reagan bitterly assailed the Salt II Treaty, which had been proposed by both President Ford and by President Carter. McGovern recognized that the Soviets had, in fact, demonstrated more willingness to agree to arms control than the United States, and he took a great deal of criticism for pointing this out.[8] McGovern believed that the Russians were probably as confused as he was as to what was going on.[9] He attributed the complete absence of an arms limitation dialogue between the two superpowers partially to the Reagan administration's unwillingness to impose a moratorium on the deployment of

Persian II and Cruise Missiles. These missiles were protecting no one, all the while straining the precarious balance between the two superpowers. According to McGovern, their deployment had resulted in the termination of negotiations on intermediate-range weapons, as well as the suspension of strategic arms talks.[10] Ultimately, although the Soviet Union signed off on the Salt II Treaty twice, it died in the U.S. Senate under domestic, irrational political pressures that were not in the interest of the United States.[11]

In many ways, it seemed as if Reagan were only halfheartedly trying to lead the United States and the Soviet Union toward any real arms agreement in 1983. In fact, McGovern believed that the Reagan administration was still trying to go for nuclear superiority, and that was the true purpose of the MX missile and the B-1 bomber. McGovern, still hopeful that a treaty could be worked out with the Soviet Union, recommended that the United States link intermediate range talks in Europe, on so-called Persian II and ground launch cruise missiles, with the Strategic Arms Limitation Talks, and then provide at least a one-year moratorium before the United States deployed any further nuclear weapons at all in Western Europe. That was the reasonable way to arrive at an arms agreement, as opposed to the threats that Reagan was uttering.[12] While Reagan was busy playing tough guy, McGovern had other, more constructive ideas.

McGovern's philosophy on Soviet relations descended from the policies of Presidents Eisenhower and Nixon, both of whom had a realistic assessment of the Soviet Union. The Eisenhower and Nixon administrations took the path of practical accommodation, Eisenhower calling his policy "coexistence" and Nixon calling his "détente." In both cases, neither president was under any illusions that the Soviets agreed with the United States ideologically, or that they were always going to take the same view of Third World problems as the United States did. Both men realized that, despite these differences, in order to avoid an unending series of wars, some common ground was going to have to be found, and the differences would just have to be lived with.[13]

McGovern believed that peaceful coexistence with the Soviet Union was the only rational option in an age when both countries had more than enough nuclear weapons to completely obliterate each other. In speech after speech, McGovern charged that avoiding nuclear war had more to do with avoiding needless confrontation with the Soviet Union in places like Lebanon and El Salvador than it did with catchy-sounding schemes for missile reduction. McGovern saw no conceivable scenario in which a tactical war between the United States and the USSR would not escalate into nuclear war. McGovern's views on the military, the Soviet Union, and national security often brought him into debate with the other Democratic candidates.[14]

One of the main topics of disagreement between McGovern and the other candidates was how much money was needed for the defense of the country. McGovern and Hart, for example, clashed on industrial policy and the military budget. Hart's build-down theory called for strengthening tactical weapons, while downplaying the nuclear rhetoric. McGovern believed that tactical weapons were not going to be of any help to national security, and this belief naturally led him to feel that Hart's plan was ill-conceived. McGovern criticized Mondale as well, for not calling for cuts in the military budget.[15] He felt that Mondale, as well as Glenn, differed only in degree from Reagan in the amount of wasteful money they would toss at the military, and he noted that the United States "should be cutting the wasteful, bloated monster that is devouring our national substance and fueling an open-ended arms race."[16] And, although McGovern and Alan Cranston were the only two who focused on peace as their central issue, McGovern was the only person who advocated no new weapons deployment or testing of further weapons. Ultimately, no other candidate came close to McGovern's position in cutting the entire military budget.[17]

Overall, McGovern was the one Democratic candidate who was critical of the Reagan administration's priorities as reflected in the gigantic military budget, which he saw as both wasteful and dangerous. McGovern recognized that simply pouring money into the military was not going to solve all of America's problems, and some problems would actually be worsened. As he stated over and over during the campaign, he believed that the $250 billion defense budget threatened to bankrupt the Treasury and retard the nation's economic growth, without buying national security. "The military budget could be easily reduced by at least 25 percent with absolutely no risk to our national security,"[18] McGovern said, adding:

Aside from being dangerous, unrestrained defense spending is, and should be seen as, a drain on our economy. It contributes to inflation by channeling money into the economy in the form of wages without producing goods and services that can be bought with these funds.[19]

Useless and dangerous weapons such as the MX, the B-1, and the Cruise Missile could be eliminated, freeing up money and resources. Under McGovern's plan, the military procurement system, which often paid outrageous prices for spare parts and weapons that were not even operable, was to be overhauled, ridding it of the fraud and waste it was currently operating under. U.S. overseas forces were to be reduced, transferring more of the legitimate military costs to the country's allies, and an immediate freeze on production and deployment of all nuclear weapons was to be instituted. By reducing U.S. military force levels, the personnel costs, which account for more than half of the military budget, would lower dramatically.[20]

McGovern, a combat veteran of World War II, was the one political leader who spoke out on military spending as a drain on the national economy rather than as a source of jobs and stimulus to growth.[21] In McGovern's view, military products have no economic value, being neither consumed nor having any investment value. Although they produce jobs and generate income, they are a steady, heavy drain on the economy. Additionally, McGovern stated that military production contributed to inflation by channeling money in the form of wages into the economy without producing goods and services that could be bought with these funds. Therefore, he strongly advocated converting the economy from a military orientation to a peaceful one.[22] Meanwhile, the leftover money that had previously been needlessly spent would now be channeled toward more productive venues, such as paying for the vital resources needed to improve the standard of living for all people on earth.[23]

The financial overhauls of the military were also to be applied to the federal government. Although Reagan came to power promising to root out every cause of waste and fraud in federal spending, he gave the Pentagon a blank check and free rein. The result, McGovern said, was that mismanagement, inefficiencies, and poorly conceived weapons had become more of a drain on the national economy. Even the Office of Management and Budget (O.M.B.), in 1981, estimated that there might be $25 billion in sheer waste stemming from sweetheart deals and poor contracting, which could be eliminated. McGovern advocated instituting an independent accounting, testing, and contracting agency to allow the careful and honest analysis of procurement decisions. Such analysis was currently lacking in the system, which was riddled with conflicts of interest.[24]

On the domestic front, McGovern saw the federal deficit as one of the greatest economic challenges facing the next president, and this tied in directly with the military budget. He believed that, with the direction of so much of the federal budget going to the bloated Defense Department, the United States would get little of the stimulative virtues of a deficit, especially compared with the more beneficial results of spending in the social services sector of the economy. McGovern planned to attack the financial problems of the country in three ways. First, his plan of slashing the military budget by 25 percent would free up $62 billion in Fiscal Year 1984, which could be used to fight the size of the deficit. Second, McGovern had a commitment to full employment, which would result in a net savings by putting people on the tax rolls and reducing the number of people receiving unemployment compensation. And third, McGovern wanted a thorough overhaul of the tax systems.[25]

And how did McGovern's military budget proposals resonate with the public at large? An answer may be found in a story that ran in *The Boston Globe* in the fall of 1983. The *Globe*, in speculating that certain candidates might move upward in the polls if they could get their message out to the public, pointed to McGovern as an example. The *Globe* reported that when people were told that McGovern was the only candidate to recommend a 25 percent cut in military spending; increased expenditures for rebuilding roads, highways, bridges, and railroads; and withdrawal of U.S. troops from the Mideast and Central America, McGovern picked up 12 points among likely Democratic voters in a poll. Clearly, then, McGovern was not alone in his thinking.[26]

2. The United States should terminate all military operations in Central America immediately.

The second step of the ten-point program called for the disengagement, entirely, from military operations in Central America. McGovern felt that Reagan's policy of military intervention against the revolutions convulsing Central America flew in the face of history. The effort on the part of the United States to overthrow or undermine the legitimate revolutionary government of Nicaragua, and to crush the revolution in El Salvador, was a repudiation of the revolutionary history and the tradition of self-determination of the United States. He believed that the United States had no business interfering in Central America's problems and that Reagan held the mistaken notion that Russia and Cuba were behind the revolutions in that region. McGovern recognized the situation for what it truly was. Even if every Russian and Cuban disappeared, there would still be a revolution in El Salvador, and the Sandinistas would still be in Nicaragua, because those revolutions did not come from Moscow or Havana. They came about due to the unacceptable conditions of life in those countries. McGovern knew that one does not export revolution like one would export a bale of cotton. Revolution comes out of deep-seated dissatisfaction with conditions that people find intolerable, and that was the case here.[27]

Historically, in El Salvador, a ruling cabal exploited the impoverished people of that country. Nicaragua, likewise, was a country governed by a dictator who exploited the people and stole everything in sight, and who should have been thrown out of office. It was true that the Cubans were sympathetic to the revolutionary forces and assisted them, but neither the Cubans nor the Russians caused or controlled the revolutions in Nicaragua or El Salvador. Although Reagan took a tough stance and said that he would not permit those revolutions to succeed, he did not make much progress in this area. The insurgents in El Salvador were far stronger in 1983 than they were when Reagan first came to office. The Sandinista government in Nicaragua was consolidating its power and its progress despite the 10,000-man army the United States had "covertly" trained and equipped in Honduras.[28]

McGovern was critical of Democrats such as Glenn and Mondale for supporting the U.S. intervention in Grenada, saying that "history is not going to deal kindly with this invasion."[29] His most outspoken comments, of course, were directed firmly at the president himself. The problem was that Reagan seemed to think that if he just confronted the Russians at every turn and accused them of stirring up revolutionary currents in Central America, then somehow he was doing his job as leader of the United States and the Western World. In all actuality, he was merely compounding all of the problems both for the United States and for the developing world. In accusing the Russians of all of the problems in Central America, Reagan not only refused to deal with that situation appropriately, but also aggravated relations with Moscow.[30] If Reagan's policies in Central America had succeeded, they would have placed the United States in league with the most reactionary and brutal forces in the region, undercutting the superpower's position in the eyes of its Latin American neighbors. Certainly, the brutish behavior of the United States made it easier for the rest of the world to view the country as the bad guy in these situations, which would then, of course, unwittingly make the communists seem somewhat more sympathetic than they actually were.[31]

The more fundamental issue for the United States, according to McGovern, was which side was the nation going to be on? Would the country side with military dictators oppressing their own people, simply because they declared they were anticommunist? Or, was the United States going to stand clear of those revolutionary upheavals and let them work their own course? McGovern supported a policy that would not be in opposition to those revolutionary nationalistic forces. Rather than using military force, the United States should seek to influence those countries in a constructive direction and toward a cooperative relationship through the use of diplomacy, trade, and assistance. The lesson in Vietnam, McGovern said, was not to rely on military solutions to political problems and not to militarize American foreign policy. Instead of military advisers, guns, and Marines, the United States should be sending surplus food for the hungry, teachers for the illiterate, health care and sanitation workers for the poor and sick.[32]

McGovern believed that, historically, the United States had not treated the countries in Latin America and the Caribbean basin in a way that would permit them to develop their own democratic institutions. Instead, the United States tended over the years to support the established group of landowners and corporate businesses while ignoring the plight of the people. As a result, the United States had ended up on the side of the right-wing dictatorships, opposing any and all major movements for sound change. The obvious impact of this self-centered foreign policy was obvious, as death squads roamed the streets in the countryside of El Salvador and Contras indiscriminately killed women, men, and children who for the first time in their lives had access to free medical care and education.[33]

A McGovern administration would support the Contadora peace plan unconditionally and call for its immediate implementation; call for the immediate resumption of diplomatic and trade relations with Cuba; work with Latin American countries to allow significant change to occur peacefully, ending centuries of oppression and exploitation; and use U.S. resources to wipe out poverty and hunger instead of "subversives." The United States, McGovern said, stood on the principal of improving the standard of living of all people:

> Our principal war must be the one against poverty; our principal weapon must be development aide that frees people from dependency on others, including dependency on the United States.[34]

The path to peace in Central America was clear to George McGovern. The Contadora group, in their September 1983 Cancun declaration, called for negotiations, respect for each nation's sovereignty, and the withdrawal of all outside military personnel. Only the Reagan administration was an obstacle to peace in this region; instead of working with the countries of Central America, Reagan sought a military solution.[35]

McGovern opposed the recommendations of the Kissinger Commission, which called for increased military assistance to the governments of Central America. He viewed the report of the Kissinger Commission as an insult to the citizens of the region and to the efforts of the leaders of the Contadora group, and saw the clearest way to bring peace and stability to the region was for the United States to fully support the efforts of the Contadora countries.[36]

McGovern put forward a series of proposals designed to bring peace to the Central American region and to stabilize relations between the United States and that area. The basic underlying concept was to replace all military aid with financial and diplomatic aid. For starters, McGovern wanted to end all military aid, both overt and covert, to the Contras, who were seeking to undermine the government of Nicaragua. He wanted to recall all U.S. military advisers and trainers from El Salvador, Honduras, and elsewhere in the region, and to dismantle the bases being built in Honduras. The shipments of arms and military equipment to all nations within the region were to end, for McGovern hoped to encourage and support regional diplomatic efforts to reach peaceful solutions to the various conflicts. In place of using guns and force to solve problems, McGovern wanted to work with the countries in the region to develop programs of economic and social aid, which would encourage the emergence of self-reliant, independent local economies. He also felt these countries needed help to develop emergency aid programs to meet the massive problems of hunger, malnutrition, and disease, especially among refugees from the fighting. McGovern wanted to respect existing UN and O.A.S. (Organization of the American States) Treaty obligations regarding the sovereignty of member nations. And McGovern also felt that the time was right to establish diplomatic relations with Cuba.[37]

McGovern believed in the above ideas because he recognized that the violent, military "solutions" that had been tried for decades didn't accomplish anything positive. Actually, they had been counterproductive. By trying to stem the tide of change, the U.S. policies often created anti-American sentiment. McGovern realized that military intervention could do nothing to stop the tumultuous upheaval spawned by the legacy of poverty, oligarchy, and repression that the United States itself had helped to create in Central America. He was critical of U.S. policy which undermined its own political position by seeking military solutions to social and economic problems. McGovern was often critical of U.S. policy which was all too ready to embrace military dictators regardless of their abuses of human rights, provided they proclaimed themselves to be anticommunist. He maintained that the United States made a fundamental mistake by thinking that the continued existence of corrupt, antidemocratic oligarchies in Central America was in the national interest of the United States. McGovern felt that the United States should realize that its own interests were intertwined with the best interests of the Central American citizens, and these would be better served by working to eliminate extreme inequalities and wealth, widespread hunger, malnutrition and disease, poor living conditions, and the lack of social opportunity. McGovern fervently believed that it was this social inequity, and not communist guns and agitation, that bred civil war. McGovern said that Ronald Reagan's belligerent response to the problems of the region had made the job of guerrilla recruiters much easier, because Reagan's policies could easily be construed as living up to the stereotype of the ugly American. And it was the responsibility of the United States to encourage the process of the Contadora group in every way possible.[38] As McGovern stated:

> I would neither back the Government in El Salvador nor back the revolution, but let it run its course and then try to come to terms with what I think will be a revolutionary victory there.[39]

McGovern advocated taking this same commonsense approach to other troubled spots. In Grenada, McGovern would not have invaded the country, but would have tried to come to terms with Maurice Bishop in working out an accommodation. He advocated the same course the United States followed thirty-five years earlier with Yugoslavia, which he believed was a model for dealing with revolutionary or marxist governments. Instead of trying to boycott them or overturn them, the United States should try to work out a diplomatic and economic relationship that would at least be partially satisfactory.[40] McGovern did not understand the rationalization for the invasion of Grenada and did not believe that the American students enrolled at St. George's University were in any danger. He decried the consequence of that invasion, which left eighteen young Marines and some forty or fifty Grenada citizens dead. Additionally, a mental hospital was accidentally bombed, killing a number of mentally ill patients, as well as some Cuban construction workers.[41] Again, instead of military attacks, the United States should have offered doctors, teachers, construction workers, and assistance in building a runway. The British and French were already helping out on that runway because Grenada depended on the tourist trade. In McGovern's mind, the United States arrived about six months late with the wrong method.[42]

In summation, the Reagan administration had taken the United States away from arms negotiations and diplomacy, and toward a reckless spending binge that was jeopardizing both the peace of the world and the financial solvency of the U.S. government. American military forces were tied down in dangerous and ill-advised missions in Lebanon, El Salvador, Nicaragua, Honduras, and Grenada. In addition, terrorism and guerrilla warfare were becoming the new weapons of the developing Third World. The United States, due to Reagan's policies, was increasingly a likely target of the terrorism of these nations. Ultimately, McGovern saw Reagan's confrontational approach to the Third World as isolating the United States from much of the rest of the world.[43] Clearly, McGovern had many issues with Reagan's approach to many important matters concerning budgets, national security, and the country's relationship with the rest of the world, and he had some alternative ideas that he wanted to try.

3. The United States must bring the Marines home from Lebanon as soon as a cease-fire permits.

Long before any Marines were killed in Lebanon, McGovern urged that they be brought home. Two hundred and sixty-five Marines needlessly died in that ill-conceived attempt to substitute Marines for diplomacy, according to McGovern. The sacrifice of those Marines should have been regarded as a shocking failure of presidential leadership. Instead, Reagan attempted to divert attention from his diplomatic failure by attempting a Hollywood-style invasion of the little island of Grenada.[44]

McGovern alleged that Reagan placed 1,600 Marines as hostages in a recklessly exposed position at the Beirut airport, and 265 of them paid with their lives. He asserted that never again should any American president send American boys abroad without a clearly defined mission and without the procedural safeguards of the U.S. Constitution.[45]

McGovern accused the Reagan administration of following policies that produced more terrorism, more militarism, and more isolation of the United States from friend and foe alike and called on Reagan to immediately withdraw all U.S. Marines from Beirut.[46]

4. The federal government should put unemployed Americans back to work rebuilding and conserving America, including creating the world's finest rail system by the year 2000.

To restore the American economy, help reduce the country's deficits, and restore equity in the country's economic system, McGovern advocated full employment and called for imaginative public sector job creation. "I believe we could put many unemployed Americans back to work rebuilding roads, sewers, and bridges, and building the finest railway/mass transit system in the world. This would create jobs, contribute to economic growth, and meet the desperate need for reinvestment in the infrastructure of our economy," McGovern said. Although this would mean some new federal expenditures involved in funding such programs, he believed that there would be a net savings as the government reduced the unemployment and welfare roles and increased the number of people paying income taxes.[47]

5. The federal government should restore the dream of home ownership and revive the construction industry with one-time government-backed mortgage loans of not more than 10 percent.

McGovern was troubled by the shortage of affordable mortgages and the low rate of new home construction. He called upon the federal government to guarantee the availability of mortgage credit, at reasonable interest rates, for a one-time purchase of a house by families who might otherwise not be able to afford one. He believed this program would also stimulate the construction of new homes, thereby reducing the high unemployment rate in the construction industry.[48]

According to McGovern, the current crises in mortgage markets stemmed from unprecedented high interest rates in all financial markets due to the Reagan administration's gigantic deficits. This was exacerbated by the tight monetary policy pursued by Reagan and the Federal Reserve Board. The high interest rates, as well as the downturn in the economy, led home builders to construct fewer new homes than were built in the early 1970s. As a result, fewer and fewer Americans could afford to buy a home in 1983. Since the 1930s, the federal government had played the leading role in assuring that a strong and stable market existed for mortgage financing of home ownership. "The federal government must step in to provide adequate mortgage capital for first-time home buyers," McGovern said. His solution called for a federal mortgage bank to be established to make direct mortgage loans to home buyers at effective interest rates of not more than 10 percent. The bank would initially be

funded through direct tax revenues and through the sale of federally in-
sured bonds to private investors. Once the bank was established, it would
be close to self-funding as the mortgages were amortized over time.[49]

**6. The complicated, loophole-ridden tax code should be simplified
by adopting the Bradley-Gephardt fair tax bill.**

High on McGovern's list of economic priorities was tax reform. He was
critical of the tax cuts by the Reagan administration and called for their
repeal.[50] McGovern felt that supply-side theory, which forecast an increase
in tax revenue following a reduction in tax rates, was a fraud. This theory,
in practice, caused a severe reduction in government revenues. That,
combined with extravagant defense spending, caused the existing deficit
problem.[51]

One major sticking point for McGovern was that the existing tax code
was simply too complex. He believed that many people either cheated or
resented the loopholes available to the affluent, and he found that there
was a flourishing underground economy in this country. Commonly,
McGovern said, goods and services were being bartered to avoid payment
of taxes, as workers, professionals, and businesspeople "do favors" for
each other in order to duck federal, state, and local taxes. According to
IRS estimates, the underground economy involved $20 billion per year.
In order to restore fairness and end most of the deductions and loopholes
in the tax code, he called for the elimination of tax shelters, which would
result in lower taxes for most individuals. In setting the highest tax rate
at about 30 percent, McGovern called for preserving a progressive rate below that level and raising the threshold of the minimum taxable income.
McGovern was opposed to a constitutional amendment requiring a balanced budget.[52]

Another issue was that McGovern saw the existing tax policy as doing a poor job of directing investment toward desirable goals, creating
incentives for nonproductive investments, and allowing the affluent to
avoid the bulk of their tax obligation. He found it so cumbersome that
many people were in technical violation of the tax code without even being aware of it. McGovern said that the Economic Recovery Act of 1981
severely retarded the degree of progressiveness in personal income tax
rates and all but eliminated the corporate income tax.[53]

McGovern felt that the inefficiency of the tax system stemmed from
Congress's growing use of the tax code to try to direct investments from
various deductions and exemptions rather than as a means of raising revenue. A more efficient means of directing investment would be for Congress to collect taxes and then appropriate funds as it saw fit.[54] McGovern
also called upon reforming the tax code in order to bring fairness to the
system. "Over the last decade, we have slowly moved away from the idea
of progressive taxes. Yet, a tax system from which most tax deductions

have been removed, with moderate levels of taxation, would actually result in lower taxes for most individuals while increasing revenues," McGovern said. He sought to encourage those who currently spent their time thinking of ways to shelter their income to direct some of their creativity toward solving pressing economic problems:[55]

> I think the deficit is a deadly serious matter. It's the first time in the nearly 30 years I've been in politics that I've really worried all that much about the federal deficit, because it's always seemed to me in the past that it was manageable. It's sometimes been substantial, but never just wildly out of control like it is now.[56]

In supporting the repeal of the 1981 tax law, McGovern advocated replacing it with something like the Bradley-Gephardt fair tax bill. He also called for canceling most of the tax write-offs. He would leave the home mortgage interest write-off and philanthropic giving, but virtually everything else would be canceled. He also called for lowering the overall tax maximum, but not more than 30 percent. In looking over the situation, McGovern criticized Reagan's contribution to the situation.[57]

"Reagan's tax policies have been shown to be little more than a means of shifting the burden of taxes from those most able to pay to moderate and low income citizens," McGovern said. "Even in cases where the tax deductions represent the general interest, these deductions are, in essence, expenditures from the Treasury," he explained.[58] Clearly, the system had much room for improvement.

7. Low-cost government loans should be provided to every American who seeks additional education and job training through a "Second Chance GI Bill of Rights."

McGovern, being a teacher himself, supported the wisdom of investing in human resources through improved education. Back in 1958, as a freshman Congressman, McGovern served as a member of the House Committee on Education and Labor. He played a significant role in drafting the National Defense Education Act, broadening that legislation to extend financial assistance to students seeking higher education regardless of their major area of study. In 1967 and again in 1974, McGovern steered through the Senate amendments authorizing and then requiring advance funding of federal programs for elementary and secondary schools, thus enabling administrators to better plan for the coming school year on the basis of expected federal aid. In 1978, Senator McGovern co-sponsored the Middle Income Student Assistance Act, which expanded assistance programs to include more families in the middle income brackets and increase the level of grants to students. His proposals in the 1980s, then, were merely a continuation of his established ideas.[59]

McGovern found that sustained economic and social growth was impossible without sustained investment in human resources. "Economic growth and development is closely related to the amount and diffusion of knowledge throughout a society," McGovern explained.[60] He recognized that the federal government has an important, though not exclusive, role to play in fostering the widest possible access to quality education for all Americans. McGovern accused the Reagan administration of wielding "a clumsy sledgehammer, cutting many effective federal programs, and threatening local funding of public schools" by supporting tuition tax credits for private and parochial schools. McGovern said that the federal government's main role in primary and secondary education had been to ensure equal educational opportunities for the poor, the handicapped, and minority groups. As president, McGovern would restore funding for the many effective programs cut by Reagan. McGovern said that it was "too much to expect state legislatures, which are required to annually balance their budgets, to adequately fund all of the important programs, given their limited financial resources." He believed that basic decisions about primary and secondary education should be made at the local level. In order to get more money into the hands of state and local school boards, McGovern proposed that the federal government assume the burden of welfare and Medicaid costs, targeting the money made available to the states by this for education. He proposed that a new federal loan program, modeled on the GI Bill, but open to all, be created. Students seeking college or graduate education, and workers seeking retraining for jobs in industries requiring new skills and knowledge, would be eligible for low-interest government loans. Those loans would be paid back through a special withholding system administered by the IRS. "A better-educated work force will mean a stronger, more productive economy. More importantly, each person's feeling of self-worth will be enhanced by exposure to the wonders of education," McGovern said.[61]

8. The federal government should stop paying farmers not to produce, and instead should begin paying them fairly for their production to win the battle against hunger in America and abroad.

One of McGovern's ambitions, from the time he first entered the political arena, was to see that as many people as possible would be well nourished. In 1984, this meant that McGovern desired to expand the food stamp program and the school lunch program, as well as other nutritional programs. "They're not all that expensive, in any event, and they're consuming things that are in surplus here in the United States," he said.[62]

McGovern's record on this area stretched back to before he was even a senator. In the early 1960s, he served as President Kennedy's Food for Peace director, seeking not only to feed hungry people, but also to aid the stability of Third World nations, promote their economic development, and create new commercial markets for American agricultural goods. During his eighteen years in the Senate, McGovern served on the Agriculture, Nutrition, and Forestry Committee, and chaired the Senate Select Committee on Nutrition and Human Needs. Among the books he authored on the subject were *War Against Want* and *Agricultural Thought in the Twentieth Century*.[63] During his tenure as a senator, he pioneered the concept of setting prices for commodities above the value of price support loans, devised countercyclical restrictions on meat imports according to levels of domestic production, and sponsored disaster assistance to defray drought-related expenses and losses. He also urged cooperation with other wheat-exporting countries to develop a viable plan for marketing wheat at an adequate price for farm producers. Two of his special concerns were (and are) to give young people the opportunity to farm their own land and to keep corporate interests from squeezing out the family farmer.[64]

In his presidential campaign, McGovern proposed expanding the Food for Peace programs as well as the distribution of food surpluses to those in need in the United States. "While we must maintain a fully adequate food reserve, there is no sound reason to have surpluses rotting in federal warehouses when there is hunger in the land." McGovern would pursue "an aggressive domestic nutritional program and expand it overseas."[65] The focus of McGovern's farm program would be to advance the cause of the family farmer. He regarded the family farm as the most cost-effective and efficient unit for agricultural production, as well as an important part of societal stability in rural America. McGovern firmly believed that "American farm production can do more to dry up the areas of despair and hunger which feed Communism than all the military hardware we've shipped all over the world."[66]

In 1984, McGovern supported a return to the 90 percent parity concept as a base for a combined target/loan price. "The goal," he said, "is to insure that farmers at least have a price support foundation that will equal their cost of production. Anything less than that is unacceptable." He believed that the nation needed a system of reasonable and low-cost credit for farm purchase and operational loans "enabling younger farmers to get into agriculture and family farm operations to continue in business during the lean years. I would propose an immediate freeze on all farm foreclosures until the new farm credit system is in place."[67]

9. The equal rights of all Americans, especially the majority of whom are women, should be guaranteed.

George McGovern was an idealist in many ways, in that he felt that every American citizen should be treated exactly the same, regardless of race, creed, religion, or gender. In reality, of course, there were often discrepancies in how people were treated, either by the law, by other citizens, or by the government. In seeking the presidency, McGovern sought to enforce this idealism across the board.

One issue McGovern had always championed was that of women's rights. Women's rights had been a large political minefield for decades, and, even though the vocal feminist movement of the 1970s had quieted some, McGovern was still very sensitive to this issue.[68] Swimming against the conservative tide of the early 1980s, he was an outspoken supporter of a woman's reproductive rights, and he opposed any and all attempts at undermining a woman's right to fully exercise those rights. McGovern said that "the decision to have an abortion is a deeply personal choice which a woman must be free to make up on her own after seeking whatever counsel she desires from her family, clergy, and friends. It is not the place of the federal government to impose itself in this decision."[69] He added:

> As long as abortion is declared legal by the courts and by the government, it has to be available to the poor as well as to the rich. I'm not very sympathetic to abortion, but I think there are extenuating circumstances where a parent might reach the conclusion that an abortion is the best solution. I think it's a judgment that should be made very carefully and painstakingly by the mother, along with medical consultation. I don't consider it something that 100 aging Senators ought to be deciding for the rest of the people in the country.[70]

McGovern was also not happy with the way many conservatives were attempting to mix church and state. As one who studied for the ministry, and as the son of a minister, he was often offended by the cynical use of school prayer by politicians such as Ronald Reagan. He saw the separation of church and state as a basic American value, and he noted a particular irony: it seemed that the people who sought to increase the responsibility of families for the raising of children were the very same people who were anxious to move the prayer out of the family's den and into the public schoolhouse. "Families are the proper institution to teach children the value of prayer, not the school," McGovern said.[71]

Many conservatives, in addition to attempting to mix church and state, were also quite antagonistic to homosexuals. McGovern recognized that prejudice runs deep in the United States, and much of that prejudice is based upon one's sexual orientation. "We must put an end to anti-gay discrimination in the social, political, professional, economic, and religious life of the nation," said McGovern. He strongly supported gay Americans' demand for equal protection under the law, which he saw as their right, not a privilege. Thus, McGovern was willing to take what could be an unpopular stand on various issues to ensure that the U.S. Constitution was upheld fully and free of prejudice.[72]

10. The states should be relieved of the burden of welfare and Medicaid costs by full federal responsibility for these services, and free state funds to permit greater support for education and crime control.

McGovern's ten-point program was indeed a detailed, well-considered plan for dealing with the various problems that the nation faced in the early 1980s. However, not even McGovern was going to claim that this plan was all-inclusive or that it alone was going to solve all of America's problems; indeed, there were certain issues that the program did not address or only briefly touched upon. Despite the fact that his ten-point program did not list or emphasize these items, they were just as important to McGovern, and he did recognize, both in public and in private, several of these issues that needed to be addressed.

One such area that needed McGovern's attention was the state of the U.S. economy in 1983. By the early 1980s, the U.S. economy was becoming increasingly subject to the influence of the international economy, thereby making U.S. trade policy a major political issue. In 1970, merchandise exports accounted for 4.3 percent of the Gross National Product (GNP), and imports accounted for about 4 percent. By 1982, however, exports accounted for 8 percent of the GNP, and imports accounted for about 9 percent, the first time that this relationship had shifted towards imported goods. Increasingly, American farmers, workers, and industries depended on the export market for their economic survival. This was clear evidence to McGovern of the growing importance of international trade and the need to formulate an American trade policy that encompassed the mutual interests of the United States and its allies. A sustained recovery of the U.S. economy was dependent on a revival of world trade and vice versa. The fundamental threat to such a revival of trade was the unprecedented high real interest rates in the United States and inordinately high value of the American dollar in the international currency markets. McGovern hoped his financial proposals (mainly the ones dealing with slashing the military budget) would free up enough money and leverage to undercut this threat.[73]

Additionally, McGovern believed that the United States should work toward upgrading the equitable facets of trade with its GATT (General Agreement on Tariffs and Trade) partners and allies. McGovern advocated reversing the Reagan administration's mercurial support in making longstanding commitments to existing international fora such as the World Bank, the International Monetary Fund (IMF), and the International Development Association (IDA).[74]

McGovern believed that U.S. trade policy must be consistent with the country's long-term national interests, and the United States should promote development of new industries at home, while resisting the temptation to engage in simple protectionism, which usually caused more problems than it solved. McGovern felt that protectionism devices are detrimental in the long run, creating unemployment in other sectors, spurring inflation, and obstructing the effective allocation of trade within international markets. They have a way of becoming habit forming, while providing little incentive to attain the proclaimed goal of allowing new investment by the protected firms. Instead, McGovern advocated more positive and direct steps to accomplish the goal of stimulating needed investment. As the economy began to profit from such reinvestment, the American worker would have the tools to produce higher quality goods and services to be exchanged on the open market.[75]

Another point that McGovern made was that the United States should avoid wild swings in trade policy, spurred all too often by domestic politics. The American government should not fail to consider the positions of its allies in the world economy before using trade as a weapon to accomplish geopolitical goals. McGovern believed that history has shown that trade sanctions are effective only when they were truly multilateral, that is, when all competing suppliers were included in the sanctions and when the countries involved were willing to keep sanctions in place for extended periods of time. In most instances, however, trade sanctions are counterproductive because they merely stiffen the resolve of the sanctioned country and backfire economically for the imposing country.[76]

Also significantly, McGovern pressed for a conversion of the country's war economy into a peace economy. In 1963, in his first year in the U.S. Senate, McGovern introduced the National Economic Conversion Act, which would have set up planning mechanisms to assist in this transition from war to peaceful production. It did not pass then, however, and nothing similar had passed since. The military-industrial complex, of which President Eisenhower warned the nation, continued to grow fat and powerful on misspent funds, and McGovern remained convinced that the country's economic orientation must change as the huge military budget was slowly dragging the economy down, channeling more and more capital into the production of goods and services with no economic value.[77]

Another area not mentioned in the ten-point program, but which McGovern was certainly thinking about, was the relationship between the United States and Israel. The ever-conflicted Middle East was just as unstable in 1983 as it had been for the past several decades, and there were few encouraging signs that pointed towards any improvement. Aware that the United States was the most powerful, outspoken ally of Israel, McGovern wondered whether it was possible for an American politician to take issue with specific Israeli policies without alienating American Jews as voters, contributors, and influential citizens. He saw that in American politics, a candidate who frankly stated a position against the policies of a particular Israeli administration was flirting with political disaster. During his twenty-two years in the U.S. Congress, McGovern consistently supported every request for military and economic aid to Israel. As president, he would regard the independence and survival of Israel as a vital

U.S. interest. Nevertheless, there were a few times when he raised questions either about U.S. or Israeli policy in the Middle East. In 1975, when he was the chairman of the Senate Foreign Relations Subcommittee of the Middle East, McGovern visited briefly with PLO leader Yasser Arafat. On another occasion, he accepted the judgment of Carter administration Middle East experts that Egypt and Saudi Arabia should be included with Israel in a package transfer of American military planes. He also protested the Begin-Sharon policies that included an invasion of Lebanon in 1982 and an aggressive settlement policy in the disputed West Bank area. In each instance where McGovern questioned the official Israeli position, he found himself charged with being "anti-Israel," sometimes by lobbyists for Israeli support organizations, sometimes by Jewish journals, and sometimes by longtime Jewish friends. He found it politically risky for an American politician to recognize that the Palestinians had a legitimacy to some of their claims and that it was safer for an American politician to criticize U.S. policy than it was to criticize Israeli policy.[78]

At this time, Reagan was pushing for a military and economic compact with Israel that would cost U.S. taxpayers billions of dollars. None of the eight men seeking the Democratic presidential nomination believed that the expansion of Israeli settlements on the West Bank represented wise policy. But when McGovern offered dissent on the issue, one longtime Israeli lobbyist cited his dissent as proof that he could not really be "serious" in seeking the presidency.[79] As president, McGovern felt that he would have to take a more even-handed approach, and he would not have given Israel a blank check unless Israel made more of an effort on compromising on the West Bank and keeping open the door to eventual settlement of that area by the Palestinians. He felt that the United States had to be fair and deal with Israel as it would with any other nation, and did not have a special obligation to make sure that Israel survived. Still, McGovern would have been willing to enter into a defensive arrangement with Israel that would promise instant aid (including U.S. troops, if necessary) to the country if it were attacked.[80]

He saw the Palestinian claim to a homeland as legitimate but, at the same time, would insist that as a condition of dealing with that problem seriously, the Palestinians must recognize not only the existence of Israel but also her right to live permanently as an independent Jewish state.[81] McGovern advocated support for an international peacekeeping mission for the next fifteen to twenty years if the Israelis, Palestinians, and Arabs came together in some kind of agreement on a homeland for the Palestinians.[82] In contrast to Reagan's ideas, McGovern preached that America's role should not be an isolationist one. "We have interests in the Middle East to protect and we have rivals to be dealt with. But Mr. Reagan has approached this delicate situation with his fist when he should have used his head," McGovern said.[83] McGovern thought that it was a great mistake to draw peacekeeping soldiers from any country that had a heavy economic or political interest in the Middle East. He advocated that the better solution was to have soldiers from countries without any deep emotional or economic interest in the Middle East.[84]

The final issue is McGovern's stance on the environment. While this too was not emphasized in the ten-point program, environmental policies had long been an issue close to McGovern's heart. Looking over his senatorial record, we can see that McGovern had quite a long history in championing environmental concerns. He either authored or sponsored all of the significant environmental legislation enacted over the previous fifteen years, including the Environmental Policy Act of 1969, the Clean Water Act, the Clean Air Act, the Environmental Protection Act of 1972, the Endangered Species Protection Act, stringent strip mining regulations, and the legislation establishing the Occupational Safety and Health Administration (OSHA). As a member of the Senate Agriculture Committee, McGovern introduced legislation to expand federal support for soil conservation programs and the establishment of greenbelt wind shelters. An early supporter of efforts to expand research support into alternative energy sources, McGovern sponsored legislation for this purpose back in 1973. In a survey of 1984 presidential candidates by Environmental Action, McGovern received top ranking. It was no surprise, then, that he was outspoken on Reagan's track record on the environmental issue.[85]

"Environmental policy during the first years of the Reagan presidency has been an unmitigated disaster," McGovern insisted.[86] Although Reagan claimed to be a true conservative, his energy and environmental policies were anything but. Reagan's appointees consistently ignored or stretched rules and regulations duly enacted by Congress. McGovern advocated that the most effective means of protecting the environment was "simply to enforce the rules and laws which already exist."[87] He was troubled by acid rain and called for a 50 percent reduction in national sulfur dioxide emissions in ten years, coupled with a Canadian commitment to match the reduction in the United States. He was equally troubled with "nonpoint" sources of water pollution—water runoff from farms, city streets, and construction sites, and observed that attempts at resolving these problems through unfunded voluntary efforts and self-motivated land management practices have been unsuccessful. He called upon enlisting the farmers of America in a new civilian conservation program to save the country's precious topsoil. He also supported the enactment of legislation to place ground water under the jurisdiction of the Clean Water Act and place smaller polluters under the Environmental Protection Agency (EPA) regulations.[88]

In the field of energy policy, McGovern advocated the revival of the search for alternatives to dependence on imported oil. He also called for improved conservation and pursuing research into alternative sources of energy such as solar, biomas, geothermal, hydro, and more efficient and cleaner burning of wood and coal. McGovern called the nuclear power industry, a once promising area, a dead-end that must finally be written off. He believed that the preservation of the environment and economic growth were compatible goals, but not within the framework of the Reagan administration. "The costs of a clean and safe environment are slight in comparison with the price of a despoiled one," McGovern said. He alleged that the people appointed by Reagan, the positions his Justice Department had taken, and the ugly rhetoric emanating from the administration had voided the guarantees of protections for the natural world.[89]

The McGovern program of 1984 may seem very new to people. It is a sad fact that the program was never fully discussed by the public at large as it should have been. Whatever criticism could be levied on George McGovern, one could not argue that his positions over the years were inconsistent, vague, or poorly thought out. When one studies his long political career, in fact, it is remarkable how consistent those ideals were for over four decades. The greatest and most fair criticism is that his positions were never truly debated by the American electorate.

On February 13, 1980, Senator George McGovern announced his intention to seek reelection at a rally at the Corn Palace in Mitchell, South Dakota. The guest speaker (above) was Senate Majority Leader Robert Byrd of West Virginia. (Courtesy of Senator George S. McGovern Collection, Layne Library, Dokota Wesleyan University, Mitchell, South Dakota.)

Senator George McGovern chatting with Israeli Prime Minister Menachem Begin at the Senate Foreign Relations Committee Coffee on April 16, 1980. (U.S. Senate photograph.) (Courtesy of Senator George S. McGovern Collection, Layne Library, Dakota Wesleyan University, Mitchell, South Dakota.)

After his Senate defeat in 1980, McGovern went out on the lecture circuit speaking at college campuses across the country. On March 2, 1982, he spoke at an event sponsored by the Fairfield University Young Democrats on the topic, "Reagan and the Liberal Alternative." (Courtesy of Richard M. Marano Collection.)

In 1982, George McGovern attended a fund-raising event in Westport, Connecticut, in support of Congressman Toby Moffett. McGovern endorsed Moffett in his bid to unseat incumbent Connecticut Senator Lowell Weicker. Also attending in support of Moffett was singer-songwriter Carly Simon. (Courtesy of Richard M. Marano Collection.)

Former Vice President Walter F. Mondale, the 1984 Democratic nominee for president, with whom Senator McGovern shared many views. (Courtesy of Senator George S. McGovern Collection, Layne Library, Dakota Wesleyan University, Mitchell, South Dakota.)

U.S. Senator Gary Hart came close to upsetting Mondale for the Democratic Party nomination. Hart, McGovern's close friend and former campaign manager, nearly carried his "new ideas" theme to victory. (Courtesy of Senator George S. McGovern Collection, Layne Library, Dakota Wesleyan University, Mitchell, South Dakota.)

Senator George McGovern with his longtime friend and supporter, actress Shirley MacLaine. (Courtesy of Senator George S. McGovern Collection, Layne Library, Dakota Wesleyan University, Mitchell, South Dakota.)

Three old friends and colleagues, Gary Hart, George McGovern, and Walter Mondale, competed head-to-head in the 1984 Massachusetts Democratic Primary. (Courtesy of Senator George S. McGovern Collection, Layne Library, Dakota Wesleyan University, Mitchell, South Dakota.)

Enjoying a light moment with George McGovern at a 1984 cocktail reception in New York City was cohost Arthur Schlesinger Jr. (Courtesy of Richard M. Marano Collection.)

George McGovern held his last political rally at noon on March 12, 1984, at Copley Square in Boston. He assured the crowd that he was in the race to win, but if he failed to finish first or second in the Massachusetts primary, he would withdraw from the campaign. On March 13, after finishing third behind Hart and Mondale, he withdrew as an active candidate. (Courtesy of Richard M. Marano Collection.)

"You blasted idiot! I keep telling you I'm feeling fine!"

Ed Stein. Reprinted with permission of the *Denver Rocky Mountain News*.

Bob Englehart, *The Hartford Courant*. Reprinted with permisson.

"McGovern for president! Stop the war! Bring the troops home!
Give everybody a free thousand bucks! Waddayasay?"

Reprinted with permission of Dana Summers and *The Orlando Sentinel.*

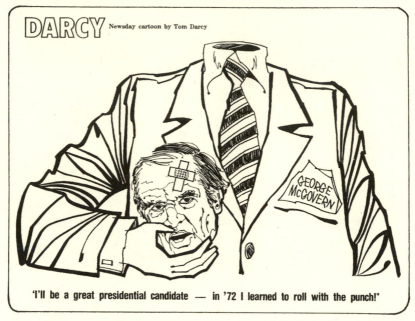

Reprinted with permission of CP Houston and *The Houston Chronicle*.

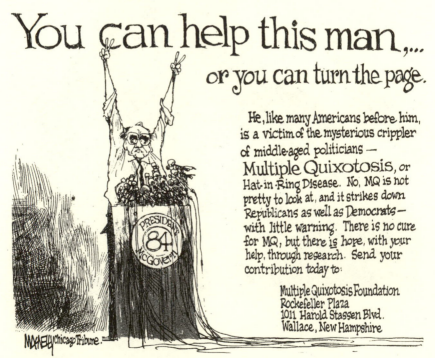

Reprinted with permission of Jeff MacNelly.

Reprinted with permisson of Jeff MacNelly.

Reprinted with permission of CP Houston and *The Houston Chronicle*.

Where Democratic Presidential Candidates Stand on Defense Issues

	Mutual nuclear freeze	MX missile	B1 Bomber	Chemical/ biological weapons production	Nuclear aircraft carriers	Military draft	SALT II treaty	Increase/ defense budget **
Askew	against	against	against	against	undecided	against	for	+ 5 %
Cranston	for	against	for	against	against	against	for	+ 4 %
Glenn	for	against	for	for	for	against	for	+ 6 %
Hart	for	against	against	against	against	against	for	+ 4.5 %
Hollings	for	against	against	for	for	for	against	+ 3 %
Jackson	for	against	against	against	against	against	for	freeze
McGOVERN	FOR	AGAINST	AGAINST	AGAINST	AGAINST	AGAINST	FOR	− 25 %
Mondale	for	against	against	against	against	against	for	* increase

*Unspecified amount

**Increases are after inflation

Source: New York Times, December 26, 1983 and The Boston Globe, December 29, 1983.

CHAPTER SIX

This Land Is My Land: Iowa

Never doubt that a small group of thoughtful, committed citizens can change the world; indeed, it is the only thing that ever has!
—Margaret Mead

Even as early as five months before the Iowa caucuses took place, all eyes were on them in February, the first major battle ground of the presidential season. In October 1983, those important caucuses were months away, but the intensive campaigning in that state was already underway. McGovern knew that, in order for his campaign to gain any credibility, he would have to perform well in Iowa. On October 8, he spoke at the Jefferson-Jackson Day Dinner in Des Moines, with a speech that was received so warmly as to suggest that people were willing to take his candidacy seriously. He drew first place in the speaking order and began by suggesting that the one thing all seven candidates agreed upon was that Iowa and the nation needed Tom Harkin in the U.S. Senate, which would help redeem the loss of two of the greatest senators—Dick Clark and John Culver. He also took the time to outline his ten-point program, and he said that he did not blame Reagan for all of the economic problems that faced the country. The economy, McGovern observed, was in trouble before the present administration came into power. "But, I am equally sure that the Reagan prescription is not the cure for our economic illness. His supply-side tax plan will cost the government an average of $125 billion annually in lost revenues, with very little benefit to the average taxpayer."[1]

McGovern also blasted the Reagan program on military spending and called it a "wasteful binge" that threatened the very "vitality of our economy." He noted that until 1965, it cost less than $100 billion to run the entire United States government and that current arms spending had pushed military outlays alone beyond $200 billion a year. "The man who promised a balanced budget has combined an unworkable tax scheme with a foolishly conceived arms spending explosion to produce a $200 billion annual federal deficit," McGovern said. He also noted that the Reagan administration was responsible for 41 percent of the total national debt that had accumulated since the days of George Washington. "By any test," the former teacher explained, "Mr. Reagan is the most reckless deficit spender in American history." He challenged the Iowa Democrats to convert the arms race into a peace race and to stop the waste at the Pentagon and begin the revival of America.[2]

The auditorium erupted into applause and cheers, as McGovern reeled off his concise platform, and, to the astonishment of many, his positions were not too politically risky for the "serious" candidates.[3] He carried the crowd that night with repeated applause and a warm response and was thereafter convinced that he was on the right track, never doubting the essential soundness of that agenda from that night on.[4] The Des Moines speech was later regarded as a turning point to the question of why was George running.[5]

Galvanized by the enthusiastic reception, McGovern set up a headquarters in Des Moines within a month. He recruited Judy Wilson, the Democratic chairwoman of Polk County, and had begun campaigning on Iowa campuses.[6] Wilson explained her commitment to McGovern by saying that "none of the other candidates stimulated me. I kept waiting for one of them to break from the pack, but none of them did. Then, I heard McGovern and his ten-point plan. I am an issues Democrat. I've never based my decision on any candidate on whether he would win or lose. People like me had no place to go but with McGovern." It did not take long for McGovern's campaign to take effect in Iowa.[7]

Wilson, the state coordinator, was experienced and tough. Despite not having sufficient help, Wilson ran the schedule, made contacts with the press and politicians, and oversaw the organization. McGovern's late start in Iowa robbed his campaign of many probable supporters who had signed on with other campaigns. Her schedules for McGovern were "man-killers" but, as a result, he moved throughout Iowa and harvested more local press than any other candidate. Considering what she had to work with, including having only 812 caucus leaders for the 2,496 Iowa precincts, she did a truly remarkable job.[8]

Senator Alan Cranston, who initially took the lead among Iowa peace groups, began to feel his support waning as McGovern was getting support from these groups too. These shifting currents underscored the potential fluidity of support among Iowans. "At this stage of the game, everybody's support is soft," observed Jim Riodan, a former candidate for Agriculture Commissioner who was uncommitted in the presidential race.

"People say now they're for Mondale, but when they go to the caucus, they may not go that way."[9]

By mid-October, McGovern was only getting started in the Iowa campaign. He arrived at the campus of the University of Iowa, accompanied by his two assistants, to deliver a speech and to put a local campaign in place. Despite the short notice, he filled the auditorium with students who could barely remember his first presidential campaign twelve years earlier.[10]

McGovern was jubilant. He boasted about his 1972 campaign, saying, "It was a campaign of candor, compassion and common sense. It is history's verdict that our opponents waged perhaps the most shameful campaign in American history."[11] When the speech was over, two dozen or so students accepted his invitation to meet in a room in the student union in order to organize a local campaign committee. One of McGovern's aides, William Kaplan, tried to urge people to step forward and sign up. But those in attendance did not step forward. McGovern then looked around the room and singled out the most mature looking man in the room, whispered a few words to him, and then announced the appointment of his local campaign chairman.[12]

McGovern explained that he delayed his announcement hoping that one of the other candidates would catch fire. "But, I don't think there's been a roar of approval for anybody. The so-called liberals are sort of bored by the candidates. People who are pretty well informed aren't really ready to make up their minds. I'd like to see if I can't add a little more passion to what's going on."[13]

When asked whether he thought his late entry would handicap his campaign, McGovern responded, "I don't have the name-recognition problem now that I had in 1971." However, he added, "that may be a handicap, the way some people recognize my name." An ABC News–*Washington Post* poll showed Mondale at 41 percent among registered Democrats, with a 13-point lead over Senator Glenn, a 31-point lead over McGovern, a 37-point lead over Cranston, and a 40-point lead over Hart, Hollings, and Askew. McGovern, who insisted he intended to win the nomination, was faced with the dilemma of cutting deepest into Mondale's support.[14] He defended his campaign as a full-fledged proposition, though, stating, "I'm not running just for the exercise. I want to be on the cutting edge."[15]

On November 15, Mondale and Glenn clashed in separate appearances at a policy forum in Washington sponsored by the Coalition for a Democratic Majority. Glenn accused Mondale of "a fundamental lack of support for an adequate defense." Mondale replied that Glenn was "out-of-step with the Democratic Party" and was offering the Pentagon a "blank check."[16] The next day, McGovern thrust himself into the debate. In his response, he lumped Reagan, Glenn, and Mondale together, saying that all three advocated increased defense spending "when we should be cutting the wasteful, bloated monster that it is devouring our national substance and fueling an open-ended arms race." He told a gathering of peace activists that "if you want a 10 percent increase in military spending every year, vote for Ronald Reagan. If you want a 7 percent increase, vote for Glenn. If you want a 5 percent increase, vote for Walter Mondale. But if you want a 25 percent decrease, vote for George McGovern."[17]

Speaking before a crowd of clergymen and peace activists, McGovern said that his rivals were making a mistake to appear before such a group that "wants to open the entire Treasury" to the Pentagon. "I doubt if the Coalition has ever seen a weapons system it didn't like, or an arms control treaty it did like," he said.[18] McGovern also blasted the two frontrunners for supporting the U.S. intervention in Grenada, saying that "history is not going to deal kindly with this invasion. If the American people and their leaders feel upbeat about the invasion, I urge the clergy to redouble its prayers for the soul of the country."[19]

That speech, which was well received, came at the start of a four-day campaign tour through the Midwest in which he appeared before student and peace groups.[20] The tour continued to attract large crowds of students in speeches at Drake University, DePaul University in Chicago, and at his alma mater, Northwestern University. "There are worse things than losing," he told students at Northwestern. "That landslide, victorious team of '72 spent a total of 180 years in prison, and the President resigned in disgrace. I want you to know I didn't even have to check in with a probation officer before I came here today. I didn't come before you as a humiliated candidate, but as a vindicated one."[21]

McGovern's greatest obstacle was that most Democrats were looking for a winner. And after being defeated for the presidency in 1972 and his 1980 bid for reelection to the Senate, McGovern bore the stigma of being one of the biggest losers in American politics. He insisted that he was not going to judge his campaign on the basis of victory or defeat, however. "If at the end of all this, people say, 'Well, George made a lot of sense,' that's all I want."[22]

Two and a half months into the race, the McGovern campaign arrived at a symbolic milestone of sorts: Eleanor McGovern came on board as a full participant in her husband's campaign. McGovern's staff treated it like a major media event, decorating their Iowa headquarters with crepe paper and balloons. It had been widely reported that Eleanor was unsupportive of her husband's presidential run. She didn't seem to understand all the fuss. She'd actually been with him from the beginning. "I was really stunned by the volley of charges that I wasn't supporting him. That simply wasn't true. I just wasn't wholeheartedly enthusiastic. I didn't want to see him hurt. I was afraid the press would belittle him," Eleanor said.[23]

McGovern returned to the campaign trail in earnest in his quest for his party's nomination. On a wearying two-day swing through northwestern Iowa, his fourth trip to the state, he stumped in seventeen towns, shook hands at the gate of a meatpacking plant, addressed an audience of college freshmen, spoke to groups of people ranging in size from eight to one hundred, and gave interviews to as many radio, television, and newspaper reporters as his staff could find. Despite the hectic pace, it was all done in a relaxed fashion that was hard to reconcile as a typical political campaign. McGovern continued to speak well of the front-runner, Walter Mondale. He also said, "I'm having a better time than in any other campaign." He acknowledged that he had less worry and frustration now than he did in any previous campaign. McGovern hoped to place among the top three or four finishers in the Iowa caucuses in order to demonstrate credibility and strength. He had to overcome the earlier campaign starts, more extensive campaign organizations, and the memory of his landslide loss to Nixon.[24]

By mid-January, McGovern was finding that many voters still had not made up their minds, and in this he found hope. On January 21, McGovern found a receptive audience when he participated in a forum organized by a coalition of farm groups and allied associations that had been demanding farm aid programs. The event was broadcast statewide on public television and included a live audience. The only Democrats not appearing were Senator John Glenn and Rev. Jesse Jackson. The forum was sponsored by the Iowa Farm Unity Coalition (FUC), made up of several farm organizations, including the AAM of Iowa, an outgrowth of the American Agriculture Movement, which organized "tractorcades" to promote a farm strike in the 1970s. The guiding force of the coalition was Rural America Incorporated, an advocacy group that helped troubled farmers with counseling and organized protests when they faced foreclosures. The issue about which they had been most outspoken was demanding parity prices for agricultural products.[25]

Many of the Democratic candidates addressed some of the farmers' concerns, indicating they would seek to reduce the budget deficit and interest rates, urge credit policies to reduce or forestall foreclosures, and support increased incentives for soil conservation. But only McGovern specifically addressed the idea of parity pricing for all farmers. In a position paper, McGovern said he would "support a return to the 90 percent parity concept," for the income-support programs.[26]

Senator Gary Hart also advanced the parity concept in a position paper, but only as part of a "tiered" program "targeted toward small and moderate family-sized operations." Mondale advocated a variety of measures to aid rural development and expand exports, but his overall agricultural policy statement offered no specifics on policies designed to support farm prices except to say that he would "put in place a reliable, multi-year program" that would control acreage, boost consumption and bring production in line with demand.[27] McGovern and Hart appeared to score most heavily with support for increased farm-income supports that would be based on an index for "parity" prices. The index was based on a relationship between prices and costs that existed seventy years earlier. At the parity index level, prices would be much higher than those farmers were then getting.[28]

McGovern advocated "a strong price support and target price system that secures enough compliance to keep production within reasonable limits and assists the family farmer." McGovern added that "the federal farm program should be geared primarily to the small and medium-size farm." Additionally, all six candidates backed temporary moratoriums on farm foreclosures, saying hard-pressed farmers needed time to recover.[29]

McGovern and Hart gained ground among farmers after the forum. Of the two, McGovern appeared to score the most points, although both men promised to back sharp increases in farm income support programs. McGovern joined Mondale in evoking a fear that present national policies could lead to armed conflict. McGovern's hopes of finding converts at his speeches were beginning to pay off. Richard Meyers, a farmer from the nearby village of Maxwell, said, "I went there favoring Mondale and I came away favoring McGovern." James Milligan, of southern Illinois, said, "For me it would be pretty close between McGovern and Hart. I guess if I had to choose right now, I'd give the edge to McGovern." Senator Hart's strategy was to get enough supportive farmers out to Iowa's precinct caucuses in order to make inroads into Mondale's heavy support among union members and urban consumers.[30]

Judging by the applause, it appeared that McGovern was the hands-down favorite of the more than 1,500 farmers who had gathered from a dozen states for the event. Among the candidates, only McGovern appeared to use the words the farmers most wanted to hear. McGovern promised to support farm prices and income at sharply higher levels, though Senator Hart vied with him for attention on the income-support promises. "What's wrong with going from $3.50 a bushel to $6 for our wheat in commercial sales in international markets?" McGovern asked. The cheers that greeted his question were thunderous.[31]

While McGovern gained ground in the speeches, other candidates saw their ratings take a dip. Senator Glenn appeared to have done extensive damage to his campaign by his absence. There was a note pinned to a conference door explaining that Senator Glenn had a prior commitment. "This tells me one of two things," said Gary Lamb, a farmer who was on the panel that questioned the candidates at the Iowa State University auditorium. "Either Glenn doesn't consider farm problems a major issue, or he doesn't feel well versed enough to talk about them."[32] *The Des Moines Register* ran a cartoon focusing attention on Glenn's absence. It showed the former astronaut in a spacesuit staring in apparent wonder at a steer.[33] Glenn wasn't the only one hurting, though. Alan Cranston was jeered when he suggested that a formula favored by many for measuring the fairness of farm prices was so outmoded that most growers paid no attention to it.[34] Rev. Jesse Jackson was the only other major candidate who did not appear at the forum (which drew farmers from as far away as Texas), and the caucus results were predictable.[35]

The people of Iowa weren't concerned only with farming issues, of course. An Iowa poll, published by *The Des Moines Register* on January 23, indicated that 65 percent of 1,003 Iowans interviewed said they feared that President Reagan's foreign and military policies had increased chances of involvement in a war in the Middle East or Central America.[36]

While the six Democratic presidential candidates discussed farm issues, they also spent much of their time hearing differences over domestic content legislation aimed at protecting U.S. auto workers. All six pledged their efforts to strengthen family farms and to bolster American agricultural exports, but were divided over whether the domestic content bill that failed to pass Congress in 1983 would work against the best interests of farmers. While the six participants aimed most of their fire at the current administration's farm policy in opening statements, Hart and Askew set the tone for what was to follow by sharply criticizing the domestic content legislation favored by the other four Democrats on the panel. Hart, for instance, said the legislation would be a disaster for farmers because it would prompt other countries to put up trade barriers against U.S. farm exports. Askew, the U.S. trade representative in the Carter administration, argued that the legislation "would invite retaliation against corn, soy beans and other exports" of crops grown in Iowa.[37]

Former Senator McGovern advocated "a strong price support and target price system that secures enough compliance to keep production within reasonable limits and assist the family farmer." McGovern added that "the federal farm program should be geared primarily to the small and medium-size farm." Additionally, Mondale, Cranston, Hollings, McGovern, and Hart backed temporary moratoriums on farm foreclosures, saying hard-pressed farmers needed time to recover.[38]

On January 25, a *New York Times*/CBS poll found strong national support for Reagan. The poll was based on telephone interviews conducted January 14 through January 21 with adults around the United States. The *Times*-CBS survey showed a sixteen-point gap between Reagan and Mondale and a twenty-two-point gap between Reagan and Glenn, in direct presidential matchups among the public at large. The president's lead narrowed significantly among those who said they had been paying close attention to presidential politics. In that group, Reagan led Mondale by five points, and Glenn by just one point, margins similar to a Gallup survey released a week earlier. The five Democrats trailing Mondale, Glenn, and Jackson were McGovern with 4 percent, Askew with 3 percent, Cranston and Hart with 2 percent each, and Hollings with 1 percent.[39]

As the campaign rolled into early February, Walter Mondale and John Glenn were arguing over taxes. Mondale charged that Glenn's proposal to defer tax indexing and to impose a 10 percent surtax on personal income would perpetuate the unfairness of Reaganomics. "I think he's flat wrong," decried Glenn, campaigning in Iowa. "Once again, Mr. Mondale is using cooked numbers," said Glenn campaign aide Michael McCurry. "We reject his estimates altogether, but at the same time we do not deny that there would be sacrifices in reducing the Reagan deficits." Mondale continued to criticize Glenn for having supported Reaganomics.[40]

While Glenn and Mondale sparred over taxes, McGovern was accusing President Reagan of using religion for political gain. Speaking on February 9 at a Roman Catholic college in Davenport, Iowa, McGovern noted that Reagan "seldom seems to attend church, yet he demands state-operated prayer sessions in public schools in violation of constitutional separation of church and state." McGovern charged that Reagan "repeatedly and cynically exploited the religious sentiments of the American public for personal political gains." Reagan "ignores the Judeo-Christian mandate to feed the hungry and minister to the poor, yet he repeatedly invoked the name of Jesus in the recent kick-off to his campaign before the Christian broadcasters in Washington," McGovern said. "It is an abomination of religious faith the way the President has been manipulating it for his re-election campaign." As in other stops on the campaign trail, McGovern also talked about Reagan's foreign policy while he was in Iowa.[41]

On February 10, George McGovern challenged the direction of U.S. foreign policy in the Middle East, asking: "Why is it in the interest of the United States or Lebanon or peace in the Middle East for us to be taking sides militarily in the Lebanese conflict?" Speaking at Iowa Wesleyan College in Mount Pleasant, McGovern wondered "if the shelling of Moslem and Druze positions in Lebanon by the U.S. Navy, and the delay in withdrawing our Marines, means that Mr. Reagan has taken leave of his senses."[42]

McGovern continued on:

> We have no reason to be against the Druze or the Moslems or any other faction in Lebanon. It is the most incredible kind of nonsense that we are lobbying [*sic*] 16-inch shells against the people with whom we have no quarrel. The collapsing Gemayel government has the support of perhaps 15 percent of the Lebanese people. Why do our leaders want to shell and bomb the positions of those representing the majority of the Lebanese people? We should put our Marines on board ships today and then head the ships for the U.S.A.[43]

On February 11, just nine days before the all-important Iowa caucuses, the eight Democratic candidates appeared at a debate in Des Moines that was televised live by CNN and shown on PBS. The candidates took questions from one another, and from James Risser of *The Des Moines Register*'s Washington bureau. They also responded to several Iowans. In this important event, they criticized Reagan's foreign and domestic policies. McGovern repeated his call to "put the Marines on the ships today and start those ships back to the U.S.A."[44] He called it a "modern tragedy" that Reagan had never met with Soviet President Yuri Andropov, who ruled for fifteen months before his death. Most of the candidates, Mondale and McGovern included, called for Reagan to attend Andropov's funeral, but Reagan chose to send Vice President George Bush in his place.[45]

In addition to criticizing Reagan, the candidates also sought to depict front-runner Walter Mondale as the anointed choice of power brokers, special interests, and the party establishment. During the two-and-one-half-hour debate, the candidates took occasional jabs at Mondale, but it was at the very end of the event, when the candidates were allowed to question each other, that his rivals truly unleashed on him. Surveys were showing many Iowa Democrats remained undecided, and the contenders took their chance to make an impression.[46] John Glenn said to the Iowa Democrats, "You're not on a leash. Big organizations come in and tell you it's all over. I don't buy that at all. Iowa is not for sale." Gary Hart asked Mondale whether he had ever disagreed with organized labor? Mondale, on the defensive, responded that he was his own person and was not running for president of the AFL-CIO. He said that the Federation was endorsing his policies, not the other way around.[47]

Of all the candidates, McGovern was the least visceral when it came time to answer to his colleagues. When he was asked by Alan Cranston what lessons he learned from being the Democratic standard-bearer for president, McGovern responded that "there are some things that can happen to you in politics that are even worse than losing an election. I wouldn't change places with the man who won in 1972. Having said that, let me give all of you a little practical advice. Work hard, but don't work so hard that you get fatigued to the point where your judgment becomes clouded. Most of the mistakes that are made in presidential campaigns are made because of fatigue . . .," McGovern said. He further called upon his colleagues to say what they really believed and not watch those changing and unpredictable public-opinion polls too much. He then challenged his colleagues to lay out the weaknesses of the present administration as clearly as possible without "knocking each other over the head."[48]

Of Mondale, McGovern only said, "I don't think he's got it locked up." He added that many Iowans had told him they support him on the issues but "don't want to throw away their votes" on a candidate who can't win. McGovern evoked the greatest response of the debate when he scorned those who said Democrats should pick their nominee for president on the basis of his electability in November rather than what he believes.[49] McGovern said,

> I've encountered three different kinds of voters here in Iowa over the last few months. One group are the kind of people who agree with me on the issues on which I've taken a stand, and I would say to them simply, "Thanks a lot and congratulations on your superior wisdom."
>
> There is another group of voters who tell me that they disagree with me on one or more of the positions I've taken, and that they can't vote for me on grounds of conscience and to those people I'll pray that their understanding will be enlarged.
>
> But there's a third group of voters that I've encountered all over this state who tell me they agree with what I've said, that they think I'm right on the issues, but they're not going to vote for me because in their view, I can't be nominated and they don't want to throw away their votes, as they put it.
>
> Now that's the group I want to talk to for just a moment. Let's assume that that judgment is right, that somebody else has this nomination locked up. We'll just say for the purposes of discussion it's Fritz over here. If that's true, and he wins, he knows I'm going to be out campaigning for him. I don't think he's got it locked up, but let me say this:
>
> If you really believe that I'm the closest to your views on the issues before this country, you owe me that vote for this reason: It's the only way you're going to be able to send a message to whoever you think is the nominee of the direction in which you want that man to move. If you want military spending cut rather than increased, and you're convinced I can't be the nominee, vote for me anyway and the bigger that McGovern vote is, the more this eventual nominee is going to move in the direction that you think we ought to go. Don't throw away your conscience.[50]

That last remark produced the longest and loudest applause of the debate. McGovern made many people feel guilty about supporting the front-runner, and many of them were thrilled to be challenged. He received over thirty seconds of applause after he made his statement, and the applause would have continued had the moderator not cut people off. In contrast, the other candidates received no more than ten seconds of applause each. His aides agreed that he made an "impressive" showing as he urged Iowans who agreed with him politically, but thought he could not win, to vote their consciences.[51] He also warned his rivals that they were hurting the party's chances of regaining the presidency by attacking one another rather than President Reagan, a peacemaking note he continued to sound.[52]

"The Democrats simply cannot beat the incumbent if the nominee is cannibalized in advance by his own party," McGovern warned. "Each of us, myself included, wants to be the nominee of the Democratic Party as I was twelve years ago. But the nomination will be greatly diminished if the nominee has been riddled by potshots and slashes from his fellow Democratic contenders."[53]

Energized by assessments of his showing in the debate, McGovern was pressed to win over the large number of uncommitted Democratic voters. "This nomination hasn't been decided," he declared at a livestock auction on February 15. "The eyes of the whole country are going to be upon Iowa next Monday. Most Americans still don't know who they are going to support in 1984 and they are going to be watching to see what Iowa does."[54] McGovern began his final effort with his fortieth visit to Iowa since announcing his candidacy.[55]

McGovern campaigned in Tama, Marengo, and Waterloo, in an effort to get out the vote. His visits were considered critical since his campaign did not spend much money for radio or television advertising. McGovern sought a coalition of farmers, peace advocates, liberals, and students for the caucuses that could place him in the top half of the field of eight. He stressed his rural background and his eighteen years on the Senate Agriculture Committee.[56] The hectic campaigning schedule, however, was beginning to catch up to him. At one point, he was bitterly worn out from several weeks of walking pneumonia. McGovern asked Judy Wilson to cancel a couple of Sunday events so that he would have a chance to rest up a bit (and perhaps even escape to Tampa, Florida, to see the Redskins play in the Superbowl). Wilson gambled on the theory that McGovern would eventually make his way to the scheduled events, and did not cancel. Wilson's gamble was poorly placed, however, and as a result, McGovern left a small band of Iowa City Unitarians feeling that they had been stood up. The resulting flap provided McGovern's chief news coverage for days. To make matters worse, the Redskins lost the Superbowl, despite McGovern's sacrificial presence there.[57]

The real problem for McGovern, however, was that some voters continued to be concerned that by voting for him, they could be taking away votes from candidates with similar positions. Senators Hart and Cranston were frequently mentioned. When asked why it took him so long to announce, McGovern responded that none of the other candidates then in the field were raising the issues that he had since he announced. "I urged that we should get out of Lebanon right now, that we should put a nuclear freeze in effect right now and that the military budget should be reduced from 20–25 percent right now," he said. "Those were bombshells. I mean I saw those guys and they thought I was crazy. Then they began to watch the audience reaction and pretty soon the whole debate began to turn around."[58]

In mid-February, Dr. Helen Caldicott, president emeritus of Physicians for Social Responsibility, asked McGovern to appear on a platform with her for a talk she was giving in Iowa just prior to the Iowa caucuses.[59] In her prepared statement she said,

While I don't propose to endorse any candidate before the Democratic Convention, I think it is important for all of us to read the position statements of George McGovern on nuclear weapons, the defense budget, Lebanon and Central America. He injects a note of statesmanship and quiet common sense into the debate, and the ideas he promotes must become an integral part of the Democratic debate and Democratic platform.[60]

As the Iowa caucuses approached, the Op-Ed pages of the nation's newspapers were offering a reassessment of McGovern's campaign. David Broder reported in the *Washington Post* that McGovern had been more relaxed, good-natured, and persuasive than ever before. McGovern, he observed, had been stating his views with such candor, and offering himself with such self-deprecating charm, that he had gained what seemed far beyond his grasp last fall.[61] In an interview with *CBS News*, Broder said that up to this point, no one had really attacked McGovern's positions.

I think it's partly that he's out of office and I think it's also partly that he's had the advantage so far of not coming quite high enough in the polls so that anybody else has really sort of asked hard and skeptical questions about those positions. I remember the first time I heard him say that the military budget could be reduced 25 percent and I thought, uh oh, here we go. But those propositions of his really haven't been terribly well examined so far.[62]

In a *Philadelphia Daily News* editorial published on February 17, titled "The Sage," it was reported that the other Democratic candidates were, for the most part, playing it safe and were missing the strong, consistent positions McGovern was offering. As the candidates debate and campaign, the editorial stated, McGovern stood "out more and more."[63]

McGovern is neither mincing words nor backing away from his positions until an election is safely over. He's offering the choice that our political system was intended to give us, not some sanitized, limp version designed to impress people snoozing in front of their TV sets. Whether you like his positions or don't, you know what they are. His ten-point platform is a totally clear political document. . . . He's the one candidate willing to speak out rather than simply try to create an "image." He's become the conscience of our political process . . . [McGovern] remains the wisest, most candid man in the bunch.[64]

Thomas Oliphant reported in *The Boston Globe* that "others may be enjoying a nostalgic mental journey back to 1972 as McGovern campaigns for the Democratic presidential nomination in 1984, but their number does not include the former South Dakota Senator." He reported that McGovern was too busy affecting the politics of 1984, and while it was true that there had been more interest in his campaign in recent days, it was also true that his position in the race was as a "thinking man's" Jesse Jackson.[65]

A blizzard of telephone calls and political rhetoric hit Iowa as Democratic presidential candidates fought for support in the last weekend before the state's precinct caucuses. Meanwhile, a blizzard of another sort played havoc with campaign schedules. Reubin Askew was forced to cancel campaign appearances in the western part of the state because of snow falling at the rate of three inches per hour. John Glenn was forced to cancel three appearances, and Gary Hart missed five scheduled stops. Glenn flew through a heavy snowstorm to Sioux City, where he told a news audience, "I obviously hope to do very well in Iowa." Jerry Vento, Glenn's campaign manager, expected Glenn to finish second with between 15 and 20 percent of the vote.[66]

That weekend, the candidates all tried to make their last-minute appeals to the Iowa public. At a news conference in a Des Moines soup kitchen, Hart called the Reagan budget deficits "this administration's Vietnam," and offered his own plan to reduce them.[67] Mondale used a five-minute radio broadcast to appeal to his backers to attend the Monday night caucuses. "Don't take anything for granted," said Mondale. "You are needed." A native of neighboring Minnesota, Mondale also told Iowans in a taped appeal, "I am your neighbor and friend, I know Iowa."[68] Mondale's effort was getting a big boost from phone banks set up by the AFL-CIO, United Autoworkers, and the National Education Association, all urging their members to support Mondale.[69]

Hart attacked the other candidates, including Mondale, for seeking simply to divide up a shrinking economic pie more fairly. "That is not the option that this country faces. The option is to make the pie grow again."[70]

With all the candidates scrambling for last minute media attention, McGovern knew he needed something to make him stand out from the pack. The answer he came up with was to speak at a place called Trainland U.S.A., a model train exhibit in Colfax. The museum, run by Red and Judy Atwood on their Iowa farm a couple of miles up I-80, boasted twenty model trains, zero gauge, tooting continuously on a mile of track that wound through display cases arrayed like a miniature United States. The trains passed a Statute of Liberty in New York, a coal mine in Kentucky, the San Francisco International Airport, and, in the Rockies, a miniature ski lift so authentic that the chairs carrying the tiny skiers uphill came back down empty. McGovern's instincts paid off, for he attracted a herd of reporters, photographers, and television cameras. They were as captivated by the displays as was McGovern, who acknowledged that mixing politics and trains was the merging of "two nostalgia trips." McGovern said that his own life reflected the hold that railroads still exerted on American life and that it would mean so much to the country to rebuild them. McGovern, from Mitchell, South Dakota, a town named for a railroad president, still had his toy train in his attic.[71]

The former senator said he chose the site to dramatize his plan to re-build American railroads. McGovern said he would cancel the MX Missile and B-1 Bomber and put the money into railroad improvement, which he said "would contribute more to the security and prosperity of the country than moving ahead on these redundant and unnecessary strategic weapon systems."[72]

President Reagan flew to Iowa for a brief visit on the day of the Iowa caucuses in order to steal some of the thunder from the Democrats and fire up the Republican partisans going to their own caucuses that evening. An Iowa poll by the *Des Moines Register* showed that he trailed both Mondale and Glenn in hypothetical general election contests. Mondale led Reagan 53 percent to 39 percent, and Glenn beat Reagan 50 to 39 percent.[73] In his prepared remarks, Reagan sounded themes ridiculing the Democratic hopefuls as big spenders too closely tied to special interest groups. Aping a line from the American Express slogan, "Don't Leave Home Without It," Reagan quipped, "If the big spenders get their way, they'll charge everything on your taxpayer's express card. And believe me, they never leave home without it."[74]

Reagan countered the Democrats' accusation about fairness and said that it should be looked at carefully. "Just below the surface you'll hear an appeal to greed and envy totally inconsistent with the American spirit. I predict, when given the chance, the American people will choose opportunity and economic growth over greed and envy any day of the week," the president said confidently. He charged that his Democratic challengers had a "dinosaur mentality that offers nothing for the future but repeating their failed past." At a speech in Waterloo, he added, "Let them promise the moon, they'll deliver green cheese."[75]

Concerning his slippage in the polls, Reagan responded, "I think it's what you would expect if eight guys have been running around the state for a year kicking my brains out. I would not expect people to have a good opinion of me." Reagan was attempting to undo in Iowa what the Democrats had done to him in more than a year of campaigning. "I am a little curious about some of the things the Democratic Presidential candidates have been saying," Reagan admitted. "But aren't these people who talk so much about fairness for all Americans the same ones who can't see you unless you belong to a special interest group?" he asked. "And don't you get a little nervous when these born-again budget balancers tell us there's only one way to reduce deficits, and it begins with raising your taxes?"[76]

It was Reagan's first political trip outside of Washington since announcing his reelection bid on January 29, and it was choreographed from start to finish in an effort to upstage the eight Democrats and their presidential caucuses. Reagan spoke to more than 7,000 people in Waterloo and 9,000 people in Des Moines, crowds many times larger than what his Democratic campaign rivals could hope to find campaigning in the state.[77]

Try as he could to take the spotlight off the Democratic contenders, Reagan's visit did not detract much from the fact that the day of truth had almost arrived. Mondale, leading in the polls both in Iowa and New Hampshire, predicted that he would do well. It was the conventional wisdom that Senator Glenn was locked in a tight race for second place behind Mondale. Glenn headed off to New England for some campaigning, and Mondale traveled to Illinois. Jackson and Hollings were concentrating on New Hampshire and its February 28 primary. Thus, only Hart, Cranston, McGovern, and Askew remained in Iowa to do some last-minute campaigning.[78]

A poll by the *Des Moines Register* found Democrats likely to go to the caucuses giving Mondale 44 percent of their votes, far more than any other candidate.[79] Sure enough, Mondale came out on top. His sweeping victory in the Iowa caucuses was a triumph of organization, and his support came mainly from middle-aged and older voters, according to a *New York Times*/CBS News poll of caucus participants. The poll also showed that 70 percent of Mondale's supporters came to the caucuses at the request of his organization. Only 43 percent of those who backed other candidates said the same. Mondale's support came from labor, with 62 percent of union members voting for him. But teachers, whose organizations also endorsed him, gave him only 38 percent of their votes. A little over half of all participants over age 65 voted for Mondale, and 45 percent among those between 45 and 64 years old voted for him as well. Among those aged 30 to 44, Mondale received 34 percent of the vote, and only 16 percent of the vote of those aged 18 to 29 years old.[80]

According to the poll, when voters were asked to give as many as two reasons for supporting a candidate, 69 percent of Mondale's backers said he had the "best chance of beating Reagan," and 50 percent cited "experience."[81] Mondale, clearly happy to have the first hurdle behind him, said the vote represented "a great victory, perhaps a spectacular victory" that rested on the same appeals he would use in New Hampshire on February 28.[82] Mondale summed up his victory by saying, "Tonight is the beginning of the end of the Reagan Administration. Let the word go forth from Iowa to the nation: To all Americans who want a safer world, I am on your side."[83]

While everyone expected Mondale to do well in Iowa, virtually no one had predicted the near-collapse of John Glenn's campaign there. His strategy of depending on his personal celebrity as an astronaut rather than on grassroots organization appeared to put him at an insurmountable disadvantage.[84] Glenn was speaking to VFW, American Legion, and service club groups that gave him a good reception but whose members seldom attended a caucus. Mondale, on the other hand, depended on a big, disciplined organization that fielded an estimated 1,000 door-to-door canvassers and an estimated 100 paid staff people.[85]

The same logic that helped Mondale in the caucus helped cripple Glenn's effort. The *New York Times*/CBS News poll indicated widespread rejection of Glenn's theme that he was the Democrat most likely to defeat Reagan.[86]

Senator Glenn said without hesitation that his campaign took a hit in the Iowa caucuses, but that didn't dampen his political spirits. "I'm very up right now, I'm not down in the doldrums," Glenn told reporters after the results from Iowa showed him barely registering. "I'm not going to make any big statements tonight about what happened," he said. "I don't know what happened. I'm not making any excuses. We got whipped tonight in Iowa."[87]

Glenn, who had been seen as the second-strongest Democratic contender, placed fifth among the eight candidates. He congratulated the candidates who placed ahead of him. "Obviously, it is a disappointment . . . [but] to say it is a devastating blow would overdo it, I think," Glenn said. "We took a licking tonight, but we are on to New Hampshire. Naturally I am disappointed."[88] Most analysts agreed that John Glenn's performance had dismantled his claim to be the only one with a chance to stop Mondale's drive for an early lock up of the nomination.[89]

Hart knew that in Iowa, being the first caucus (and one of manageable size, at that), a few hundred votes would be telling. The *Times* observed that he had visited counties that hadn't seen a Democratic candidate since Adlai Stevenson. The *New York Times* described Hart working like "an artisan, hand-crafting votes that the process would magnify."[90]

Hart's hard work and grassroots style paid off. He was in the shower in his room at the Sheraton Wayfarer Inn in Bedford, New Hampshire, when an aide banged at the bathroom door and yelled, "Come out! You're second in Iowa!" The door opened and Hart's damp head poked out. "If I come in second," he exclaimed jubilantly, "I'll be President!"[91] He was 33 points behind Mondale, 6 percent ahead of McGovern in third place, and had supplanted Glenn as the only alternative to Mondale. Perceptions were everything in the nominating process. And the perception after Iowa was that it was becoming a Mondale versus Hart race.[92] But the perception of McGovern also changed after Iowa, as he was now "hailed as the new conscience of his party."[93]

McGovern called his surprising third place finish a "minor miracle." He stated that "a great many Iowa voters . . . voted their convictions and voted their conscience." McGovern, just shy of the required 15 percent, was close to winning Iowa delegates, and could end up with a couple at the state convention in June.[94] Hart's and McGovern's placing in the caucuses is particularly impressive when one takes into account that neither man had impressive war chests or the campaign machinery to defeat Mondale in Iowa.

Just seven months earlier, the *New York Times*/CBS News Poll found no gap between Mondale and Glenn. However, a few days before the caucuses, Glenn's crowds were noticeably shrinking. Meanwhile, buses were unloading from Minnesota with "Fritz Blitz" volunteers. Glenn knew that, given it was Mondale territory, Iowa would be at best a long shot. Nevertheless, he felt he could not sit it out, but he was late to organize and he ran a lackluster campaign. The results, therefore, should not have come as an utter surprise to Glenn.[95]

As in any political contest, it did not take long for the postgame analysis to begin. Iowa's Democratic chairman, David Nagle, accused the national television networks of interfering with his party's precinct caucuses by reporting, before they began, that projections showed Mondale had won them. The caucuses generally convened at 9:00 P.M. EST, but the Democrats weren't supposed to register their preferences until 9:30 P.M. Results from the first two precincts were reported by the News Election Service (NES) at about 9:15 P.M., and CBS News reported at 9:12 P.M. that Mondale would win. NBC projected the Mondale victory at 9:18 P.M., and ABC at 9:46 P.M.[96]

Nagle believed that the television reports had intruded on the process. "I think they've interfered," he alleged. "I think there's a line and I think they crossed it. We haven't even started the process, we haven't even started the game," he said. He called it a "disservice" to all the candidates because Mondale supporters were told in effect that their man had won and there was no more need to participate, while the message to those who backed the losers was "don't bother to go, your guy isn't going to do it."[97] Nagle's complaint was one that would be echoed by political analysts in presidential campaigns for years to come.

The breakdown of the numbers was telling. While Mondale dominated the first voting of the new campaign year by getting 49 percent in the Iowa caucuses, stronger than expected showings lifted Gary Hart and George McGovern from the back of the field to new prominence. Hart received just over 16 percent of the vote, while McGovern received just over 10 percent. Nine percent of the voters were uncommitted, Cranston had 7 percent, and Glenn placed at just over 3 percent. Askew, Jackson, and Hollings received less than 3 percent each.[98]

Those attending the Democratic caucuses were electing delegates to county conventions in April. Those delegates would then select delegates to the May 5 congressional district convention, and the June 9 state convention. At the end of this process, Iowa's national convention delegation would account for only 58 of the 3,933 delegates at the national convention in San Francisco.[99]

The Iowa caucuses were interesting in that, political predictions aside, nothing was a sure bet beforehand. The Mondale camp had been fairly well organized, calling out supporters to turn up and vote specifically for their man.[100] The McGovern campaign, on the other hand, did not have that sort of organization and support. One example of how the process played itself out was told by Josie Floerchinger, a twenty-six-year-old housewife, who was initially a pessimistic supporter of McGovern. "I was trying to figure out who my second choice would be," she said. "Then when I stood up, I was really surprised how many people stood with me." Twenty-nine McGovern supporters stood up with her, to place second to Mondale's forty supporters in the test of strength in Ankeny, Iowa.[101]

After that initial count, supporters of candidates who failed to reach the threshold of 15 percent were free to move to another candidate or uncommitted status. Only Mondale, McGovern, and Hart made the threshold on the initial vote, meaning that, under party rules, only those three could have delegates chosen at the precinct meeting. The presiding officer again called for a division and found that Mondale and McGovern had moved up to 43 and 31 votes, and Hart remained at 22, while the uncommitted rose to 24.[102]

The same spontaneity was evident among McGovern's supporters in other towns. Terry Durand-Gumbille, a twenty-eight-year-old religion teacher, said he went to Des Moines earlier Monday to obtain some literature but did not have time for any organizational effort. Both Hart and McGovern supporters, as well as others at the meeting, covered a wide age range and included blue-collar and white-collar Democrats.[103]

It was estimated that about 85,000 Democrats took part in the caucuses. Mondale received 48 delegates to Hart's 2. Democratic consultant Robert Squier predicted that Iowa had all but knocked Glenn out of the race. Mondale's advisers sought to spread the view that Glenn was on the ropes.[104]

McGovern's third-place finish made many people pontificate on his campaign style, as compared with the other candidates. Irwin Harrison, a poll taker in Boston, said that McGovern had "a message." "He was saying something about himself and about conscience." Glenn, on the other hand, wasn't offering up any particular message so much as he was mud slinging, saying, "Mondale is a tool of the special interests." Hart, for his part, looked forward to a Hart-Mondale race and called it a contest between the party's future and its past. Hart believed that Mondale's support was "very soft" and described Mondale as the candidate of labor and "Democratic bosses," rather than of the average voters.[105] It seemed that McGovern was in the unique position of taking the high ground and not attacking his opponents.

Several political professionals observed that McGovern's strong showing, perhaps the biggest surprise of the Iowa caucuses, now meant that McGovern faced an unexpected choice. Prior to the caucuses, he played the peacemaker, warning the other candidates against dividing the party with their attacks on Mondale. "Now," observed Robert Squier, "McGovern must choose between running for Miss Congeniality and running for the nomination."[106] The former senator, for his part, never suggested that taking the high road and making a serious bid for the White House had to be mutually exclusive propositions.

McGovern, campaigning in Boston the day after the Iowa caucuses, indicated that he would seek campaign contributions needed to make a full-scale effort in New Hampshire and Massachusetts. "When I came into this race in September, everyone was talking about a two man race as though it were entirely between Mondale and Glenn," he said.[107] "Now it's quite clear the rest of us have a crack at it." *The Washington Post* reported that fire was back in George McGovern's belly the morning after the Iowa caucuses. Buoyed by the results, McGovern no longer sounded like a candidate who was in the Democratic presidential race primarily to keep the others from veering to the right.[108]

Partially as a result of Iowa, press opinion was turning around for McGovern. Earlier doubts when he announced his candidacy were being laid to rest by his campaign of conscience. At each debate, as he appeared poised, thoughtful, and bold, McGovern's style was paying off.[109]

The Chicago Tribune reported that the biggest surprise in Iowa "was the strong vote for McGovern, who had almost no organization to cajole supporters to come to the polls. The evidence . . . pointed to McGovern being the beneficiary of a late surge of enthusiasm that led thousands of people to walk into their caucuses unbidden by any political agency."[110]

Even *The New Republic* reversed its position about McGovern. A March editorial asked:

> What has come over McGovern? He used to be a whiner now he's relaxed and seigniorial. Well, why not say it? He's Presidential. While the others prattle vacuously about leadership, he acts like a leader, dispensing calm wisdom about how the campaign should be conducted. His left-wing platform is neither demagogue gobbledygook like Jackson's nor clotted with prosaic details like Gary Hart's. He's even become witty, making amiable jokes about himself as well as the other candidates.[111]

Sandy Grady may have summed the new McGovern up best. Grady wrote in *The Philadelphia Daily News* that McGovern once seemed a tattered, beaten man; now he reminded him of a Hemingway quote: "The world breaks everyone and afterward many are strong at the broken places."[112]

His third-place Iowa finish was indeed a moral victory for the man everyone had reported was washed up. He looked forward to the Massachusetts primary on March 13, where he said "they have the smartest voters in the country."[113] McGovern told his supporters that the Iowa caucus was heavily influenced by professional political "insiders" and massive campaign organizations and felt that it was more a test of campaign logistics than an accurate reading of voter sentiment. He reminded his supporters in a campaign mailing that Mondale and Hart spent over a year working the state of Iowa, and he spent less than four months, relying on a handful of staffers and a small core of committed volunteers.[114] Years later, he praised Judy Wilson for working remarkably hard in Iowa. "The fact that I came in third there, almost second, [she] deserves a lot of the credit."[115]

Mondale, in fact, spent the maximum allowed under federal campaign laws and in comparison, McGovern's spending—a paltry $50,000— amounted to pocket change. Both Mondale and Hart fielded huge staffs, thousands of volunteers, and highly paid advance team operators. McGovern did well in Iowa despite being massively outspent, massively outnumbered in volunteers and staffers, and despite receiving less coverage by mass media.[116] The McGovern campaign was shaking up the assumptions and premature conclusions of the professional pollsters and political pundits. Iowa helped him in many ways by igniting strong, compelling images about his candidacy which were picked up rapidly by the national press and shared with citizens across the country. Before Iowa, many political pundits doubted his campaign could survive. Iowa routed most of the doubters and proved that he was a major force in this presidential race.

McGovern, recalling the terms in which he had acknowledged his longshot status upon entering the race, said his strong finish in Iowa "serves as a reminder that lightning can strike at any time." He also felt his showing said something about what the voters wanted in a campaign. "This proves that ideas are still powerful, that, if we are willing to state our views candidly and address the issues in a substantive way, the voters will respond."[117] Although the pundits said it couldn't be done, that Iowa would be only decided by organizational strength and by money spent, McGovern was at the back of the pack in both respects and he still survived.[118] When all was said and done, McGovern was just barely edged out of second place in the nation's first tally of popular support. With Iowa giving his campaign a boost, McGovern began to look ahead to the big primary contests in Illinois on March 20 and in New York on April 3. However, his greatest need was to do well in the Massachusetts primary, in order to escalate his campaign's momentum and bring in new supporters. (In fact, volunteers were already beginning to set up phone banks in Massachusetts. McGovern's mass media strategy included a major ad in *The Boston Globe* and a series of hard-hitting TV spots costing about $66,000 to reach voters in Massachusetts and New Hampshire. It was estimated that he would need another $32,000 for phoning and mailing.)[119]

Ultimately, McGovern's Iowa results recalled the beginnings of his 1972 campaign, where he vaulted to prominence on the basis of a second-place finish in Iowa. That year, he had an emotional issue, Vietnam, and a solid grassroots organization. This year, McGovern campaigned almost alone and ran only one television commercial, but drew on a strong showing in a debate a week earlier and on a deep well of public affection.[120] If Iowa illustrated anything, it was that nothing in American politics could be predicted with any concrete certainty. McGovern knew this fact going into Iowa, though he could not foresee that within a month, his race to the White House would be over. However, after he did leave the race, McGovern in a good-natured way quipped that he could have taken second place in Iowa—"with a little more money, and a little less walking pneumonia."[121]

CHAPTER SEVEN

Running on a Shoestring: New Hampshire

I would like to think historians will look back and say, if that agenda I was recommending had been followed, it would have been a sound one. I have no doubt that the various speeches I've made around here are going to look pretty good. If they don't I'll be sad that I misread what the times called for.

—George McGovern

Gary Hart's campaign manager, Oliver Henkel, observed that "the power of the press is enormous. The press does not have the power to elect someone, but it does have the power to defeat someone."[1] This is certainly a topic that factored into the 1984 presidential campaign. A constant theme throughout this book has been the phenomenon of the media's treating presidential politics as a horse race, with great coverage being paid to those candidates the media perceives are most likely to have a true shot at the White House, and scant coverage given to those who are considered long shots. The prophecy, of course, is self-fulfilling, for those who are given more coverage gain more name recognition, as well as the "serious contender" label with the voting public, whereas those who are given less coverage have a harder time making a connection with the voters, and almost always end up dropping out early.

In his book, *The Power to Lead*, Pulitzer Prize–winning historian James MacGregor Burns, an adviser to Presidents Kennedy and Johnson, discusses this issue. Burns is particularly troubled by the way various political candidates play into the horse race scenario, manipulating the game so that they come out ahead in the polls, rather than trying to stress the issues they stand for. He noted that television newspersons spent twice as much time commenting on trivial personality quirks and campaign tactics than on issues of substance.[2]

Another interesting and troubling phenomenon is that presidential primaries increasingly have been used not only to choose delegates to the national convention, but also to test the candidates' popularity. Although the voter is usually unaware of the connection between the two decisions, the ultimate effect narrows the field of candidates. The media claims an exclusive relationship with the primaries and virtually dominates them. According to Burns, this "symbiotic bridge between mass media and presidential primaries has further implications."[3] The candidates play the ultimate game of "King of the Rock." In order to reach the public, they must exploit the communications industry without being destroyed in the internal processes. Because they largely bypass party leadership and organization, they are forced to build their own following on a grand scale. As a result, they tend to play down policy questions and build for themselves personas that will interest the networks and newspapers and set them apart from the other candidates. The result, argues Burns, is personality over policy, politics that seeks votes by appealing to short-run, superficial, and narrow needs and hopes.[4] Such was the political climate George McGovern was running in throughout 1983, and in such a field as this, he was indeed playing against a stacked deck.

For months, most of the candidates in the Democratic presidential campaign had been frustrated by the way the media covered the campaign as a two-man race between Mondale and Glenn. In the major newspapers and news magazines, the two men received more coverage than the rest of the candidates combined, and after the three-hour Dartmouth College debate on January 15, the five-minute shout-fest between Mondale and Glenn dominated news reports. Of course, even those involved in the campaigns at the back of the herd recognized that the press was bound to make only one or two candidates the focus of coverage.[5] James Bacchus, the press secretary for Askew, said, "I don't think it's a question of the press making it a two man race improperly. I think the press has done so inevitably. . . . It's an institutional bias. . . . It's not easy to report the nuances of the views of all eight candidates."[6]

The reason the media portrayed Glenn and Mondale as the most newsworthy candidates was money and poll numbers. Since Labor Day, Mondale's ratings in the polls and in financial contributions were double those of Glenn. Glenn's were double those of any of the other candidates.[7] It was felt that either Glenn or Mondale, having the most money and most positive poll results, was most likely to secure the Democratic nomination as a result. Still, had each candidate received equal press coverage—thus leading the public to accurately believe that each candidate had a credible shot of going the distance—there is no telling who the ultimate nominee might have been.

Cranston campaign manager Sergio Bendixen argued, "The press can't make you or break you. If the press can break you, then your candidacy wasn't worth very much. . . . As long as there is an Iowa and New Hampshire in the beginning, there is always a chance for a long shot to succeed."[8]

Iowa and New Hampshire were indeed important to the 1984 campaign. McGovern, who in the months leading up to the first caucus was considered to be the longest of long shots, was suddenly taken a little more seriously after Iowa. Coming in third in the caucus immediately made people rethink their position on McGovern's campaign, for he had invested precious little money there and had started campaigning later than the other candidates. If he performed that well with so little money and campaign time, the question now became, how would he perform in New Hampshire? One strong caucus showing early on could still be taken with a grain of salt, but if McGovern placed second or third in New Hampshire, then all the disadvantages, all the lack of serious news coverage, and all the tongue wagging by political pundits would be erased. Another strong showing might make the chance of replicating his 1972 nomination more possible than even McGovern himself had thought.

One must remember that the road to that Democratic nomination was never a sure thing, as well. On the network news back in 1971, McGovern was barely mentioned at all, and then it was usually in the context of how he was having a tough time.[9] This time, McGovern now had some early momentum on his side, and he realized that, in order to build upon this, he must continue to do well in New Hampshire.

Since New Hampshire initiated its primary in 1952, no one had been selected president without first winning there. But New Hampshire, it can be argued, is unsuited for its impact. With just over 900,000 people, it was the eighth smallest state in 1983. It had a nonwhite population of 1 percent, and only nine other states were more rural. New Hampshire had the lowest unemployment rate in the nation and was the only state, along with Alaska, without either a state income tax or a sales tax. New Hampshire's students achieved the highest scores on the Scholastic Aptitude Test for ten straight years. Clearly, this was not a state to use as a measuring stick for the rest of the country.[10]

McGovern's campaign in New Hampshire started off on a strong note. He was ahead of all the other candidates, except for Mondale and Glenn, in the polls. Voters recognized that he offered the Democratic Party—with a single, bolder platform—its starkest alternative to Reagan.[11] Above all, though, McGovern just seemed to click with the people of the quaint New England state. An example of this occurred one evening when McGovern sat down for dinner at the Millyard Restaurant in Manchester with George Cushman. During World War II, both had been bomber pilots who successfully landed a plane with one engine out, the other on fire, on a one-way strip designed for smaller craft on the Isle of Vis. Now, years later, both men sat on opposite sides of the political spectrum; Cushman was the chairman of the Republican Party in Dunbarton, New Hampshire. Following the dinner, Cushman announced, "I am a Republican, but I would like all those veterans who are Democrats to consider voting for McGovern . . . a man who knows what war is, knows what peace is." McGovern's small-town appeal appeared to play quite well with New Hampshire voters, with Republicans and Democrats alike feeling at ease with him.[12]

On January 14, 1984, the candidates engaged in a three-hour debate moderated by ABC News's Ted Koppel and talk show host Phil Donahue. The debate, aired live on public television and public radio to a national audience, was organized by the House Democratic Caucus and the Rockefeller Center for Social Studies at Dartmouth College. The format was broken down into two segments: the first ninety minutes was a wide-ranging discussion among the candidates, moderated by Koppel. Donahue, in the second ninety minutes, moderated a question-and-answer session with the candidates and the audience.[13] The forum provided many interesting moments, as the candidates had one of their first major opportunities to lash out at each other.

The expected clash between front-runners took place, when Glenn took several swipes at Mondale, charging that he was very vague on the major issues and that he had promised the American people too much. Mondale countered by saying that Glenn was merely supporting Reagan's economic policies. Mondale tried to assert that leadership was the key issue and that he was the only true leader in the field. The two bickered back and forth, which prompted Reubin Askew to quip: "What I'd like to say is that you're both right—you're both right in what you're saying about each other." Meanwhile, Hart once again stressed that he offered "a new generation of leadership" for the party, as contrasted to the "establishment" represented by Mondale and Glenn.[14]

McGovern realized that the televised debates provided him with his best opportunity to "debate the issues and to demonstrate personal qualities of intellect, wit and performance under pressure." These debates provided him with his one long shot at the nomination, and when they came to an end, he realized that his long shot was also being foreclosed.[15]

McGovern found the Dartmouth debate unevenly moderated. To make matters worse, early in the winter he developed "walking pneumonia" that was to plague him for weeks, reaching its worst point at his crucial appearance on *Meet the Press* and during the Dartmouth debate.[16]

Despite feeling lethargic and emotionally empty, McGovern more than held his own on that stage.[17] For example, each time Alan Cranston attempted to make nuclear weapons and the nuclear freeze the focal point of the discussion, McGovern would remind Cranston that he was not the only one who regarded the advent of nuclear war as the most urgent issue.[18]

On the subject of the military budget and defense, McGovern said that he could not imagine anyone there who wasn't for an adequate national defense, and he agreed with Hart, who said, "You don't get it just by spending money." "You don't measure a person's patriotism by how big a military spending binge they want this country to go on," McGovern said. "There is such enormous waste in the way we're now procuring weapons and supplies at the Pentagon, that if the American people were fully aware of it, we'd have a revolt in this country." McGovern said that he would appoint someone like Lee Iacocca the secretary of defense and order him to cut the Defense Department budget by $50–$60 billion by getting rid of fat and boondoggling.[19] At one point, Mondale called Reaganomics the worst mistake in modern American times, and McGovern answered this by saying:

> The problem with Fritz Hollings' freeze on everything right now the way it is, is that for three years this Administration has been gutting the domestic programs—gutting education, gutting the environment, gutting conservation, [applause] gutting the food stamp and the school lunch programs, programs to help the poor, and they've been on a wild military spending binge that's completely out of hand. What we need to do at this point is come out for a flat cut in military spending.[20]

Only McGovern and Jackson were against any increase in the military budget, with McGovern again calling for a cut of between 20 and 25 percent. "If we cut that by 25 percent, that gets us down to $207 billion. That's hardly unilateral disarmament. You can buy a lot with $207 billion," he said.[21]

The candidates also clashed over foreign policy. With regard to the Middle East, Cranston said that he didn't think the United States could have an even-handed policy with nations that resort to violence and terrorism, regard holy war with Israel as a viable option, and refuse to accept Israel's right to exist. On the subject of sending the Marines to Lebanon, Senator Hollings called it a mistake to put the Marines there. There were "too few to fight," he said, and "too many to die." Mondale charged that he felt Reagan didn't even know what he was doing in most places.[22]

McGovern called for normalizing relations with Cuba and pointed out that U.S.-Cuban policy was dead wrong. He felt that the policy of economic boycott and diplomatic isolation maximized Soviet influence in Cuba and minimized that of the United States. Jackson agreed with McGovern, saying that the United States helped Castro's rise to power with its foreign policy. Mondale was not in agreement with formally recognizing Cuba, and Hart called upon the United States to challenge Castro to join America to elevate the standard of living in Central America and fight poverty.[23]

In the second half of the debate, Mondale was questioned about the direction of the Civil Rights Commission. Mondale responded by saying that he would "fire everyone hired" and "hire everyone Reagan fired." Hart chastised Mondale for his answer and said that that was not responsible leadership. Mondale retorted that a number of people that were fired were, in fact, fired in error.[24] On the issue of education, McGovern advocated that the federal government should relieve the states of the burden of welfare and Medicaid costs so that the states could divert that money into education.[25]

At one point, the discussion turned to Reagan's policies toward South Africa. McGovern asserted that the South African government was let off the hook by the Reagan administration, and he compared the U.S. position of not pressing South Africa until the Cubans got out of Angola as treating two problems entirely differently. McGovern called for breaking the "nonsense" about constructive engagement. "This is what happens when your foreign policy is based on what you're against, rather than what you are for. But are we willing [applause] to embrace every scoundrel around the world, including the South Africans, as long as they wave that anti-Communist banner, ignoring the fact that that's the kind of government that produces sympathy for the Communists all over the world?" [applause].[26] McGovern explained that "the problem with what we're doing in foreign policy is to rely excessively on military methods to deal with problems that are essentially economic, diplomatic, political and moral."[27]

When audience members questioned Mondale about how he would balance the federal budget, he responded by saying that he would scale the defense budget back to reality, impose health care cost controls, administer an agricultural budget, and restore revenues progressively. Time after time, he indicated that his administration would restore "fairness" and reduce the Reagan deficits by one-half. He suggested that the reason for the $200 billion deficit was because Glenn voted for Reaganomics.[28] This prompted an attack by Glenn, who said Mondale's promises were the "same vague gobbledygook" that Mondale had been giving throughout the campaign. Glenn alleged that his own campaign was much more "specific" on how various programs would be carried out, and he scolded Mondale for promising "everything to everybody." Mondale then shot back that he listened to Glenn's six-minute speech, and all of it was "baloney." The room erupted into applause.[29]

It seemed that all roads eventually led back to attacking Mondale, the front-runner. When Hart was asked what he could offer the American people, he spoke again of his "new leadership" and "new ideas," but when pressed against the wall, he attacked Mondale, saying that one could not lead if he promised everybody everything. Mondale retorted by saying, "America is about promises."[30] Getting visibly aggravated with the attacks on Mondale, and feeling that the candidates were avoiding seriously discussing the issues at hand, McGovern interjected:

> I'd like to speak to this issue, because as you listen to this discussion here this afternoon, and the criticism we've offered to each other, you get the impression that we're basically responsible for the deficit that faces the country. We've been out of the White House for three years and in all the history of this country we've never had such a big deficit spender as we have in the White House right now. And the reason is not because of Social Security, it's not because of education, it's not because of these social programs most of which have been cut—cut in the last three years. So why are we aiming comments now on cutting programs like that when everybody on this stage knows that the thing that's out of hand on the federal spending side is the military? Even President Reagan's own deputy secretary of defense has said in the last ten days that he could cut this military budget by 20 percent without touching one thing that's essential. Why don't we go after that?[31]

To an extent, McGovern's words fell on deaf ears, and the attacks on Mondale continued. When he was asked how he could promise so much and fulfill those promises, Mondale indicated that he would cut spending by $70 billion in defense, agriculture, and health care costs, and pick up $60 billion in revenue, adding $20 billion in education and science, research and development, industrial exports, restoring compassion to children, the elderly, and legal services. Hart blasted Mondale for his answer and charged that it was unresponsive to the question. Mondale countered that his "new policies" would grow and expand the economy. Glenn again charged that Mondale was being too vague, that Mondale's additional expenditures would be irresponsible, and would cause the United States to lose jobs. He said that Mondale's positions would paint the Democrats as everything the Republicans tried to portray them being: big spenders, weak on defense, and the party that makes promises that cannot be kept. Mondale reminded Glenn that it was Glenn who voted in support of Reaganomics, which all of the candidates seemed to be attacking now. Glenn shot back that 80 percent of the Senate voted in favor of Reagan's economic plan. Back and forth went the two politicians, and once again, McGovern tried to interject with a bit of common sense.[32]

> *McGovern*: I'd like to say something. Can one of the rest of us inject something here? Listening to this argument here, I think it's fine that we air our differences. But all of us are jumping on the front-runner here and I didn't expect to come here today to defend Fritz Mondale, but sometimes front-runners get nominated and I think we [applause] . . . our response . . . but just a minute, Alan, let me just say this, I'm going to support anybody here who's nominated. Everyone will be a hundred miles ahead of Ronald Reagan. I'm the best, but I will support the next best if I'm not . . .

Phil Donahue: Mr. McGovern, your generous observations about your colleagues and especially former Vice President . . . bespeak an insincerity on
your part regarding . . .

McGovern: It's not insincere, Phil, at all. I happen to know that all of these
men around here . . .

Donahue: I'm talking about your commitment to this campaign. I believe you
when you say you admire these men. What America wants to know is how
serious are you? Is this a nostalgic run . . .

McGovern: It's not a nostalgia run. You don't run for the presidency out of
nostalgia. And I've spelled out as clearly over the last few months my differences with the Reagan Administration and with the other candidates as
it's possible to do it. There's no question in my mind that I've got a good
solid program. I have some differences with Fritz . . . let me just finish . . .
what I object to is this tendency that develops in every campaign to clobber
the front-runner whoever it happens to be. Everybody on this platform
knows that Fritz Mondale is a good, decent, intelligent man. He's had a good
record in the Senate. He doesn't need a defense from me.

Donahue: No, but you sound like his second man.

McGovern: I'm not his second man. What I'm trying to get across is that we
have two obligations as candidates for the presidency: one is to analyze the
faults and the weaknesses of the incumbent administration we are trying to
replace. The other is to offer an alternative. Instead of knocking down our
colleagues here, let's talk about our own program. I haven't seen anything
he's proposed that's all that irrelevant. [Applause]

Hollings: The audience has said it better than I could. I was George
McGovern's desk mate and you don't ever accuse him of being insincere, I
can tell you that.

Donahue: He's sincere about his interest in becoming President?

Hollings: Everything. I can tell you that right now. I know him. [Applause][33]

Hollings then lashed out against John Glenn's vote for Reaganomics,
called his "description of Reaganomics" the "biggest charade," and
charged that it was "revenue-hemorrhaging the economy." Cranston interjected at that moment, saying that if McGovern could come to the defense of Mondale, then he was going to defend Glenn's vote, which
Cranston happened to share. Cranston said that they did not, in fact, vote
in favor of Reaganomics, and were against cruel budget cuts, Kemp-Roth,
and the MX Missile.[34]

When asked whether it made any difference who was in the White
House, McGovern's response, reminiscent of the words of Robert F.
Kennedy in 1968, was:

> I think we need a leadership that, instead of appealing to our selfishness and our worst instincts, honors those people who are trying to make this society the kind of a good and decent place it ought to be. In other words, a society of compassion where we care deeply about each other and care about others around the world.[35]

McGovern offered his opinions in the most direct way he could, and he did so without cutting down his opponents. Within a couple of weeks of the debate, McGovern sent out a letter to his supporters, which was written at his room at the Savary Hotel in Des Moines, Iowa. He wanted his supporters to know that he was not so far back as many cynics and skeptics believed, and he told them that *The Boston Globe* predicted that he was going to finish third in the Massachusetts primary. The letter was written on the night of the Iowa caucuses, and McGovern had just returned from meeting with a group of senior citizens, where they talked about their hopes and dreams for America. According to McGovern, the conversation centered around a strong sense that America was in danger of "losing its soul," and the sense that citizens in general were losing their will to care deeply about the suffering and pain of those around them. The ascendancy to power of Ronald Reagan and the New Right had been a "driving force behind this loss of our soul force as a people," wrote McGovern. He charged that Reagan built his presidency on the notion that care, compassion, and fairness were "out of style" with the American people. Reagan believed, wrote McGovern, that most people felt as he felt, that government should "get tough" with the poor, intervene with the politics of small foreign nations, and cut out "government waste" by slashing the Social Security and Medicare benefits of older Americans living on fixed incomes. Instead of giving the country Abraham Lincoln's noble vision of "government of the people, by the people and for the people," Reagan had given them a "government of big businessmen and millionaires" run by special interest leaders and political operatives for the benefit of the wealthy and privileged top 10 percent of the population.[36]

McGovern also deeply believed that America was losing its traditional sense of moral outrage over injustice, unfairness, and intolerable human suffering. He decried the fact that infant death rates in many cities were as high as in many Third World nations. He lamented the fact that the numbers of homeless and unemployed people were growing so rapidly that it was commonplace to see people sleeping on the streets all across America, while Reagan would have the nation believe that this was all "by choice." McGovern charged that in Ronald Reagan's America, hunger was "studied by Commission" and dismissed as not being a real problem. McGovern felt it was entirely inappropriate to criticize people who stay alive by eating at soup kitchens as "free loaders."[37]

McGovern continued to rail against the current president, saying that he saw hypocrisy in Reagan's charge that the public schools were too permissive, while at the same time cutting billions of dollars from scholarships for moderate-income students. Money was being cut from special programs for handicapped children, while it was being added to funds to "manufacture more weapons of death and destruction." He reminded his supporters that, in the past, Reagan said that "the problem in America is government." McGovern charged that no president in that century had been more unfair to the average citizen and more biased toward advancing the interests of his own elite social class. He was now asking America to "come home once again to sanity and common sense," and to put employment, health care, and education before multibillion dollar Pentagon weapon systems. "Nuclear annihilation," for McGovern, was "the real problem facing America," and he noted that the Nuclear Age grew ever more hazardous with each passing day and with every new missile that was added to the stockpile. He told his supporters that he believed his campaign was a critically needed forum to raise the fundamental moral questions of peace and national priorities that he felt were not being addressed seriously. He said that he never "campaigned harder" in his life, and was preparing to launch a hard-hitting series of television and radio spots to get his message before the voters of New Hampshire and the other states.[38]

McGovern was not the only candidate who was lashing out at the current president. On February 21, in Manchester, Mondale, buoyed by his victory in Iowa, delivered his strongest attack on Reagan yet. "The people of New Hampshire won't settle for government by staff, policy by default, management by alibi, and leadership by amnesia," said Mondale. According to Mondale's campaign chairman, James A. Johnson, Mondale's attack represented a new strategy in the candidate's campaign to win the Democratic nomination: to focus on Reagan's leadership qualities and his overreliance on staff.[39] He would also focus attention on Reagan's work hours and his periodic vacations.

Mondale, at a news conference, spoke with unusual bluntness about Reagan. "I'm not sure what's more damning: the failure of this president's leadership, or the success of this president's isolation." He added that the $200 billion federal budget deficits had paralyzed the administration, and there was "no leadership at all on the central domestic question of our time. The only one who doesn't seem to see this problem is the President."[40]

Glenn, meanwhile, entered New Hampshire still licking his wounds from Iowa, hoping to regain some of his lost momentum. His New Hampshire coordinator, Paul Shone, insisted that the Glenn campaign was not dispirited and expected Glenn to "finish a strong second" to Mondale in the upcoming contest. He indicated that his internal polling, as of February 20, showed Glenn would win between 20 and 27 percent of the vote, based on a strategy of reaching out to the independent voters.[41] Still, Glenn's top campaign officials acknowledged that they were facing their toughest challenge to date. The task now was not merely to consolidate Glenn's position as number two in New Hampshire, but also to stave off Gary Hart.[42]

From the start of the campaign, Glenn's campaign was predicated on the notion that he was the only serious challenger to Mondale;[43] he was now unable to present himself as the major alternative to the front-runner. Glenn argued that even those who finished ahead of him in Iowa would present no long-term obstacle. "If anybody's going to be a true alternative, and have a chance at going all the way, I'm the only one with the money, organization in delegate slates," Glenn insisted. "We're the only alternative." Glenn campaign officials indicated that reaching out to non-traditional voters did not work in Iowa, but if Glenn was in trouble, he didn't show it. He was unusually relaxed, greeting voters amid snow flurries and saying that his defeat in Iowa was "not the end of the world." He pledged to press on with his campaign in New Hampshire.[44]

For his part, Senator Gary Hart was enthusiastic about his second-place finish in the Iowa caucuses. "It is a two-person race between myself and Vice President Mondale," he said in a speech at the New Hampshire Vocational Technical College. He observed that most Democrats were "still looking for an alternative" (to Mondale) and predicted that he would be the nominee.[45] Hart had the strongest campaign organization in New Hampshire after Mondale and was managed there by Jeanne Shaheen, who ran Carter's successful campaign there in 1980. Hart's campaign consisted of a large staff, including many volunteers from colleges throughout New England.[46]

In a public opinion poll published on February 17 by *The Boston Globe*, before the Iowa caucuses, Hart placed third among likely voters, with 13 percent, Mondale at 36 percent, and Glenn at 16 percent. In a December poll by the *Globe*, Hart attracted only 8 percent.[47]

The results in Iowa also gave a look to former Senator George McGovern. McGovern's New Hampshire campaign coordinator, Woody Woodland, said that McGovern's third-place finish, 10 percent of the vote, had been "terrific," especially because "we were only organized in something like half of the precincts" and spent only $50,000.[48]

Woodland, a longtime friend and supporter of McGovern's, wanted the campaign to make a vigorous effort there. But McGovern regarded the New Hampshire primary as a very special test and, because Hart had been working there for almost two years, McGovern thought it would be "futile to try to come in there the last minute." Had McGovern entered the race earlier on, he, of course, would have made a serious effort there. He could not see the point in using time, energy, and money when Hart's organization was so carefully built over a long period of time.[49]

McGovern was one of the last candidates to start campaigning in New Hampshire and had one of the smallest organizations, but Woodland asserted that, based on his showing in Iowa, "the uncommitteds will decide he's a viable candidate." An uncertain factor in the primary, according to Woodland, would be the candidacy of Rev. Jesse Jackson, who did not campaign actively in Iowa. Jackson was traveling extensively around southern New Hampshire and was greeted by large, enthusiastic audiences.[50] In New Hampshire, McGovern was campaigning hard, traveling throughout the state. "Win or lose, this will be well worthwhile," McGovern said. "I'm more patient now, and a little bit more philosophical about things," he added. His campaign had an earnest yet "shoestring" operation, according to McGovern, who often traveled alone with one aide, reporters, and a Secret Service entourage. And there is always a chance that, as McGovern's wife Eleanor put it, "[L]ightning will strike" again.[51]

In Concord, at a meeting of the People's Alliance, members of the audience freely displayed their nostalgia, wearing vintage campaign buttons. McGovern told the group that he was the only one of the eight Democratic contenders calling for specific and substantial military spending cuts. "There's so much boondoggling, sweetheart contracts and deals going on that I think 25 percent of every dollar the Pentagon gets is wasted," he said. "What are they pounding over there at the Pentagon that's so precious that they have to hit it with a $400 hammer?" he asked. McGovern was aware that defense workers worry about their jobs when they hear a public figure talk about military cutbacks. But he insisted that they should first hear him out. "I'm talking about investing the savings in other things the country needs which would produce even more jobs." He would reallocate those funds to create jobs rebuilding the country's infrastructure, he told his audiences.[52]

At the New England Human Services Coalition rally, McGovern stressed his continued support for social programs. "The political genius of the Reagan people was to convince the middle class that their taxes went up because of programs for the poor," he said. "The major federal 'welfare' program today is the tax giveaways to the wealthy." McGovern said that "everybody making over $80,000 a year should vote for Reagan. They couldn't do any better, if money is the end-all of life. But those in the middle or lower end are clearly being hurt, painfully hurt, by the cutbacks."[53]

Things seemed to be looking up for McGovern, as he arrived at New England College in Henniker for an afternoon speech and found that the room slated for the talk was too crowded. In moving to another room, students and teachers sat on windowsills and on the floor, and stood in the doorway to hear him. David Dillman, a political science professor, introduced him. "I know many of you worked for him and voted for him in 1972," he said. "I know many of you in '72 were probably six or seven years old." For McGovern, the turnout was "inspiring." When challenged by a student on why the wealthy should be penalized for making money, McGovern said that "the rich shouldn't pay one dime more than their share. But they're getting away with murder under the present tax system."[54]

At the end of the day, McGovern pondered the campaign and said that someday, some historian is going to be going over the whole thing. "I would like to think historians will look back and say, if that agenda I was recommending had been followed, it would have been a sound one. I have no doubt the various speeches I've made around here are going to look pretty good. If they don't I'll be sad that I misread what the times called for," he said.[55]

On February 23, the Federal Election Commission awarded George McGovern $100,000 in matching funds. The action made McGovern the last of the eight candidates to become eligible for them. It also approved $1.2 million more in matching funds for six other Democrats, including $579,347 for Mondale. This raised nearly $12.3 million in total matching funds awarded the Democratic candidates. The McGovern campaign submitted documents on January 18 listing $190,000 in contributions, well above the $100,000 needed to qualify for them.[56]

The campaign was quickly becoming perceived as a three-way contest in the New Hampshire primary. In a debate in Goffstown, New Hampshire, on February 23, Mondale pursued his strategy of distancing himself from his opponents, stressing his experience and saying that the main issue was "presidential leadership." The debate was sponsored by the League of Women Voters. Both Glenn and Hart appealed to what Glenn described as "Yankee independence" and urged voters to reject Mondale as the inevitable nominee.[57]

"The issue in New Hampshire is whether the debate will end here or whether, as in the past, it will begin here," said Hart in his opening statement. The debate was just five days before the first primary of 1984 and in the wake of Mondale's victory in Iowa.[58]

The most dramatic exchange of the ninety-minute program was when Barbara Walters, the *ABC News* interviewer who served as moderator, asked Jackson if he had made anti-Semitic statements, including referring to Jews as "Hymies." Three times Jackson said, "I am not anti-Semitic" as he confronted the issue that was beginning to disrupt his campaign. Pressed on whether he had used the terms "Hymie" and "Hymietown" in reference to New York City, Jackson stopped short of a categorical denial. "I have no recollection of that," he said about remarks attributed to him in a *Washington Post* article.[59]

One of the rare combative moments of the debate came from Walter Mondale after Hart challenged him about the failure of the Carter administration's attempt to rescue the Iranian hostages in 1980. "One of the joys of running for office, not having been there, is that problems always seem more simple on the outside than on the inside," Mondale explained, describing the period of the Iranian hostage crisis as "some of the worst days of my life." Mondale said that, as president, "every once in a while you get in a predicament where there are no good options, and that's when you earn your pay."[60] Mondale's remarks came in response to Hart's assertion that Mondale represented an outdated leadership that ought to be replaced by a new generation represented by him. Hart said that "if we want a representative of this party and its past, we nominate Vice President Mondale." Hart called upon voters to choose him as the voice of "new ideas and new proposals that the people of this country are desperately hungry for and in doing that defeat Ronald Reagan and save this nation."[61]

Glenn offered a call for New Hampshire voters to exert their "independence of thought" and repudiate the idea that the Iowa caucuses set the pattern of the campaign. "This idea that what was cast in Iowa was cast in stone and is irreversible is nonsense," Glenn said. He repeated the theme that the "sensible center" should stop a Mondale candidacy.[62]

Askew, who had not expected to run well, adopted a tone of conciliator. "We're going to leave San Francisco united to beat Ronald Reagan," he vowed.[63] Askew's campaign was now openly appealing to the antiabortion movement. And a few days prior to the New Hampshire primary, parking lots of Roman Catholic voters were leafleted with Askew campaign literature in an effort to turn out the prolife vote.[64]

McGovern's New Hampshire campaign was the focus of a *CBS News* story on Sunday, February 26, titled "George McGovern: The Elixir of Politics." In response to an interview question in which McGovern was asked why he kept coming back even though the conventional wisdom was that he couldn't win, McGovern responded:

> We're very tough on losers in this country. It doesn't make any difference whether it's a politician or a football team or what have you. Some of my more idealistic supporters in 1972 couldn't quite forgive me for losing. And that, incidentally, is one of the reasons why they didn't want me to try it again in some cases. They didn't want to run the risk of being hurt again. My family was opposed to the decision, at least several of them were, and it was very hard for me to come in against their objections at this stage in my life.[65]

So why was it so important for McGovern to enter the race? "Fantasy may be good entertainment on the movie screen; it is not good policy for a great nation," he said. According to Woody Woodland, McGovern's New Hampshire coordinator, McGovern loves politics "and as a public figure, it's his job to discuss issues and he does it very well."[66]

Washington Post columnist David Broder believed, at first, that McGovern's candidacy would be a fiasco. "I thought it was an embarrassment and I thought it would be a terrible embarrassment to him," he said. But it turned out to be quite different. Broder recalled that in New Hampshire at the time of the state convention the previous fall when McGovern was introduced, spontaneously the entire audience got to its feet. Broder believed that the hundreds of people who had come into politics, in part because of George McGovern and what he had done in New Hampshire in 1972, were taking the chance to "tip their hats to their old leader."[67]

McGovern was a seasoned and mature politician and knew from bitter experience that even if you lost an election, you could have an impact on what happens. "If you do it right, if you do it with a certain amount of good humor and yet strong conviction, you'll be heard. You'll influence the tone of the debates, you'll influence the content of the debate."[68]

In New Hampshire, McGovern's staff consisted mainly of five individuals. *CBS News* reported that he lacked campaign funds and had one headquarters in a "store-front office" where the roof would leak whenever it rained. David Culhane reported that the McGovern campaign machine was hardly a "computer age operation" with only two telephone lines and "lick every stamp yourself." With just two days to go before the New Hampshire primary on February 28, Culhane reported that McGovern was still running well back in the pack. McGovern said that "you have to go into a race like this with the odds as heavily stacked as they are against me with a quiet understanding that there is something worse than losing. And maybe one thing that's worse than losing is sitting on the sidelines twiddling your thumbs."[69]

McGovern, however, was not entirely committed to pulling out all the stops and investing an intensive effort in New Hampshire. There were two factors for this, he later explained, the first having to do with his late start in entering the race. Having jumped in so late, McGovern knew that he could not mount more than a "token effort" in New Hampshire and that this would likely not be a terribly effective effort, at that. The other reason for holding back was McGovern's relationship with Gary Hart. Hart, for over a year, had made winning in New Hampshire his top priority. McGovern realized that any inroads his own campaign made would likely have a negative effect on his old friend's chances of winning. Thus, McGovern held back, due to his long association with Hart.[70] His campaign spent a mere $35,000 in New Hampshire, less than any of the other candidates.[71]

Gary Hart achieved an upset victory in the primary and was planning to step up his challenge against wounded front-runner Walter F. Mondale.[72]

Senator Alan Cranston of California announced his withdrawal from the race. "I know the difference between reality and dreams," said Cranston, who finished seventh in New Hampshire after running fourth in Iowa. "I know when to dream and how to count votes."[73] Hollings announced his withdrawal at a press conference on Thursday, March 1, in Washington.[74]

Mondale was setting aside his hope of wrapping up the nomination and acknowledged that his second-place finish showed that voters wanted more time to look over the contenders. He accused Hart of being afraid to run in Southern primaries and caucuses. "I challenge him to compete with me head-to-head," Mondale said.[75] The nine state primaries and caucuses being held on March 13 were being called "Super Tuesday" and included contests in Alabama, Georgia, Florida, and Massachusetts.[76]

As Cranston dropped out of the race, his former competitors were scrambling to hold a place in what Gary Hart was proclaiming "clearly a two-man race" between himself and Mondale.[77]

But Senator John Glenn insisted it was still at least a three-way race that included him. He maintained that Hart's victory merely "opened up" the race by demonstrating that Mondale was vulnerable.[78] Glenn finished a distant third behind Hart and Mondale. After Glenn came Jackson and McGovern virtually tied, for fourth place, followed by Hollings, Cranston, and Askew.

Eighteen delegates to the Democratic National Convention were allocated, with ten going to Hart and eight to Mondale. Hart's advantage of ten percentage points over Mondale was the largest margin of victory reported in a contested Democratic presidential primary in New Hampshire since it was established in 1952. Mondale remarked, "I didn't discriminate against anyone—I ran poorly everywhere." Mondale's campaign chairman, James A. Johnson, said his candidate got only 30 percent of the labor vote despite his labor endorsements. "We will compete everywhere," Johnson told reporters on the Mondale plane. "Gary Hart said he will compete in Massachusetts, one Southern state, Washington, Maine and Vermont. That's five out of twenty-five. Do we intend to give him a pass? No. Are we sending more people to Maine and Vermont? Yes," Johnson said.[79]

On February 29, Hart appeared on the NBC News program *Today*. He vowed to run "second or first in every state from now on." Hart also downplayed his failure to file complete delegate slates in Florida, Illinois, and Pennsylvania. Hart aides said they would try to make up for their failure to file by "adopting" delegate slates from candidates who dropped out. Hart vowed not to lose the nomination for tactical reasons.

Hart's advisers credited his success to his strong performance at the Dartmouth College debate on January 15. Before that debate, Patrick H. Caddell, the former poll taker for President Carter, advised Hart to frame his answers to drive home his "new ideas" theme. Caddell also was credited with playing an important role in talking Hart into returning to Iowa where his organization was practically dormant.[80]

The result was Hart's breakthrough to a second-place finish behind Mondale in the Iowa caucuses on February 20. Successes in both Iowa and New Hampshire rested on the gamble of putting all of the debt-ridden campaigns' money into television time in Iowa and in New Hampshire. Mondale's campaign strategy of going for a quick knockout might have caused them to underestimate Hart's approach of "time and patience," and they made a tactical blunder when they kept Mondale out of New Hampshire for the last three days of the primary campaign. Hart took advantage of the free television time.[81]

Mondale's emphasis on the South was based on the 13 percent of the 3,933 delegates to the Democratic National Convention to be chosen on March 13. Both Glenn and Jackson intended to fight hard for the southern region and to prevent the campaign from becoming a two-man contest.[82] Hart received 37 percent of the New Hampshire vote, compared with Mondale's 28 percent. Glenn came in a distant third with 12 percent, and Jackson and McGovern tied with 5 percent each. Hollings, Cranston, and Askew garnered less than 5 percent of the vote.[83]

Both rain and sleet cut voter turnout by one-third compared with the 1980 race. Many voters came to the polls early to avoid the storm, which coated highways and city streets with slush.[84]

Hart said that he was not prepared to claim the position of front-runner. "But I know one thing, in New Hampshire we buried the label 'dark horse,'" Hart proclaimed.[85]

A *New York Times*/CBS News poll showed that Gary Hart put together his surprising upset with an electorate that was younger, better educated, better off, more liberal, more white, more critical of Reagan, and more politically independent than likely Democratic primary voters elsewhere in America.[86]

With Iowa and New Hampshire behind them, the candidates needed to confront the necessity of mass campaigning in nine states for March 13 contests with electorates likely to total more than 2 million or twenty times the size of the New Hampshire vote.[87]

A nationwide poll taken from February 21 through February 25 found New Hampshire differed economically from the rest of the nation. A *New York Times*/CBS News poll found that nationwide 20 percent said their family financial situation was better than one year ago and 26 percent said it was worse. But in New Hampshire, 30 percent said they were better off and 22 percent worse off.[88] Weather possibly affected the outcome. The former vice president defeated Hart two to one among voters over sixty years of age and ran even with him among conservative and regular Democrats. "The weather was brutal," commented George Bruno, the New Hampshire Democratic Party chairman, and "because of that, maybe those senior citizens just couldn't make it to the polls."[89]

By contrast, the *New York Times*/CBS News surveys showed because of Hart's intense campaigning, the New Hampshire primary attracted twice as many college graduates, nearly twice as many political indepen-dents, and one-third more liberals than the national sample—all catego-ries that gave Hart at least 40 percent of their vote and Mondale 27 percent or less.[90]

A *New York Times* editorial contended that Hart's solid defeat of Mondale turned the campaign into a fight and credited Hart with a shrewd use of limited assets in achieving his goal of becoming Mondale's principal challenger. The editorial credited Hart with garnering half of his total vote from people under thirty. Cranston, Hollings, and Askew were casualties of the New Hampshire primary and folded their campaigns. McGovern vowed to fight on.[91]

Mondale's campaign immediately pulled Robert Beckel, the national campaign manager, and Mike Ford, the national field director, out of the Washington office and sent them to Maine and Vermont for those up-coming contests.[92]

A *New York Times*/CBS News poll confirmed that Hart's "new ideas" approach was working. Over 40 percent of Hart's voters in New Hamp-shire said they picked him because of his "new ideas." Mondale blamed an attitude of overconfidence that "seeped into my campaign."[93] But the *New York Times*/CBS News poll of voters leaving the polling places indi-cated that Hart and Mondale ran even among Democrats with Hart getting 37 percent of their vote to Mondale's 36 percent. Among Indepen-dents, Hart got 42 percent and Mondale only 19 percent, and that provided the 11-percentage-point margin that put Hart in first place. These inde-pendents who made up 38 percent of the New Hampshire primary vot-ers were typical of independents around the country. They were younger, more liberal, and better-educated than most Americans, with family in-comes somewhere between those of typical Republicans and typical Democrats.[94]

A national poll completed three days before the New Hampshire pri-mary found Hart exceptionally hard for most Americans to locate politi-cally. Six registered voters in ten could not say whether Gary Hart was a liberal, a moderate, or a conservative and presented him with what in the ensuing weeks would be either an opportunity or a problem.[95]

Before New Hampshire, the Hart campaign was in debt for more than $400,000 and could barely pull in $100,000 a month. After his New Hampshire victory, Hart raised $400,000 nationally in one week alone.[96]

Mondale admitted that he made some key tactical errors. A crucial mistake, he said, was "basically, I have been campaigning against Mr. Reagan and his policies," and not responding to the charges by Senators Glenn and Hart. He now decided to attack Hart directly in his fight to slow the Colorado senator's momentum and began to give the strongest and most emotional speeches of the campaign. "This is not just a horse race," Mondale told a crowd in Tampa, Florida. "This has become a battle for the soul of the Democratic Party and the future of our country."[97]

Meanwhile, President Reagan's strategists agreed that a prolonged Democratic race meant there could be less time for party unity and attacks on Reagan. "On balance, it's helpful to us that there'll be a spirited primary rather than a coronation," said a senior White House official. No longer could the Republicans focus their attention on a single Democratic opponent. Reagan campaign officials would direct their attacks now against the "liberal philosophy" of the Democrats and not any one candidate.[98]

The Reagan campaign planned to tie Mondale to former President Jimmy Carter and looked forward to linking Hart to former Senator George McGovern, whose presidential campaign Hart managed in 1972. "I know there's a lot of nice liberal nostalgia about McGovern," said a Republican strategist, "but in the country, McGovern has as big a negative rating as he ever had. If anything, McGovern is a bigger liability for Hart than Carter is for Mondale."[99]

The Reagan campaign began planning new polls to assess Hart's perception by the voters. Several Reagan campaign aides were concerned that in the latest Republican campaign poll, in early February, Hart had only a 35 percent name recognition, and they expected it to reach as high as 85 percent by "Super Tuesday." "This means he can be anything to anybody in the next two weeks," said Edward J. Rollins, the Reagan-Bush campaign manager. "My gut instinct tells me Mondale is going to be able to put it back together, but I'm not at all sure Hart won't catch on and go all the way," Rollins said. Earlier in the race, it was the general feeling among Reagan's advisers that Senator John Glenn would be the toughest candidate because of his "celebrity factor" and his reputation as the most conservative of the Democrats.[100]

After Iowa, Reagan's campaign staff decided that Mondale would be the most formidable opponent because of his strong organization and ability to appeal to traditional Democratic constituents. James A. Baker III, the White House chief of staff, believed that nothing prepared a presidential candidate better than the experience of running in a national campaign.[101]

Both Rollins and Lyn Nofziger, a longtime Reagan adviser, were warning that Hart should not be underestimated. They compared Hart with former Governor Jerry Brown of California, who entered the presidential race out of nowhere in 1976 and won several Democratic primaries by making liberals, moderates, and conservatives think he shared their beliefs. Reagan campaign officials were less worried about younger voters who had found Reagan's upbeat vision of economic opportunity and growth of high-technology industries attractive. They had been ready to portray Mondale as a man with ideas rooted in the past, and were somewhat concerned that Hart could preempt the issue with his "new ideas" campaign theme.[102]

For John Glenn, there was a silver lining in the New Hampshire result: It meant that a Mondale victory may not have been inevitable.[103] McGovern was intent to stay in the race at least through Massachusetts. Jesse Jackson, on the other hand, was intent on staying in the race to demonstrate his ability to motivate black voters in the South. But clearly, the post–New Hampshire race was Hart versus Mondale. Now, Mondale had to abandon his attacks on Reagan and direct attention and resources toward his new primary foe.

Gary Hart ignited students and young adults in the tradition of Eugene McCarthy, Robert Kennedy, George McGovern, Jerry Brown, and Jimmy Carter. He stood for some as a welcome change from the old coalitions that Walter Mondale personified. Mondale, on the other hand, received strong support from older, more traditional voters who more surely typified mainstream America.[104]

The morning after the New Hampshire primary, Paul Sullivan awoke in Washington to a 5:30 A.M. telephone call from a frantic Mary McGovern. "My dad is on his way down to Boston," she exclaimed. "He has called a press conference and he is getting out!" George McGovern's tie for fourth place "pulled his legs from under him a little," Sullivan recounted later. And so, he decided to yield to the pressure to get out of the race.[105]

Sullivan jumped out of bed, frantically raced to the airport, and got on a plane to Boston. He arrived at McGovern's hotel before McGovern arrived![106]

"Why not let Massachusetts, the state that stood alone with you in '72, decide?" Mary and Paul pleaded. McGovern finally relented. The press conference that was to be his last speech as a candidate suddenly presented the race with a new twist: McGovern was going to make his last stand in the Massachusetts primary and let the people of the state decide whether he should continue. He vowed to step aside if he did not come in first, or a solid second. Given his position, the national campaign moved into Massachusetts and would pull out all of the stops.[107] With *The Boston Globe* showing McGovern at about 4 percent, Sullivan had less than two weeks to turn it around and keep George McGovern's candidacy alive.[108]

CHAPTER EIGHT

Super Tuesday:
Massachusetts or Bust

Nobody would probably go through this without a feeling that
there's some chance. But even if I had been convinced that there was
no chance to win, I might have done it anyway on the feeling that I
could influence the debate. And I think I have.
                                                —George McGovern

The most important day of the race for the Democratic nomination, Super
Tuesday, was fast approaching, and, with it, came George McGovern's
final chance to light a fire under his campaign and genuinely get himself
into this race. If he did not perform well in Massachusetts, he said, then
he would take the will of the voters to heart and drop his candidacy.[1] What
was it, though, that made Super Tuesday such a make-or-break event? For
the answer to that, one must look back to 1982. That year, the Democratic
Party's Hunt Commission worked to draft the 1984 election calendar rules.
The plan, drafted by staff members of front-runners Walter Mondale and
Edward Kennedy, produced primaries and caucuses in nine states in a de
facto nationwide primary stretching from Massachusetts to Florida to
Washington State. At that time, neither side had any way of knowing
whether the rules they were creating would make or break their candidates. They created another rule designed to aid front-runners. That rule
allowed for the direct election of delegates in each congressional district,
rather than apportioning the delegates to the candidates in proportion to
their showings. Under these rules, it was possible for a candidate to sweep
the delegates in larger states even with a very narrow margin in each congressional district. The rules made the prospect of a dark horse emerging
from the pack very bleak, though not altogether impossible.[2]

Throughout 1983 and the first months of 1984, Walter Mondale's top strategists counseled reporters about how the rules that created Super Tuesday would work to the advantage of the front-runners and make it almost impossible for anyone else to emerge from the pack. They said that after Iowa's caucuses and New Hampshire's primary, the state contests would come so quickly and campaigning would become so costly, that only a well-financed front-runner would be able to stay in the race.[3] It was believed that among Mondale's seven challengers, only John Glenn would be in a position politically and financially to challenge him through the Super Tuesday primaries. Hart, they believed, would be so far in debt by January 1984 that it would be unlikely that he would still be in the race by Super Tuesday. So, although the rules were created to allow Mondale to lock up the nomination by the time of the Illinois primary, he was now struggling to frustrate those rules in order to catch a new front-runner, Gary Hart.[4]

As the Massachusetts primary was quickly approaching, George McGovern was telling his audiences there that the fate of his candidacy was in the hands of the voters. "I have decided that if I'm going to make a real test, this is where it should be," he said to over 250 students at Westfield State College, near Springfield. "It would be correct to say that Massachusetts will be the make-or-break state for my candidacy."[5] McGovern was asking the people of Massachusetts to stand with him. Halting the arms race was his highest priority. There simply would be no real security and no sustained economic recovery as long as America was gearing for a nuclear war. Quite simply, Ronald Reagan's domestic and foreign policies defied the national interest, and the United States was missing an opportunity to lead the way away from nuclear peril toward peaceful coexistence. McGovern called on his friends in Massachusetts to make their voices heard on these issues and not to succumb to the media vision of rubber-stamping a front-runner.[6]

When McGovern was asked by a member of the audience at Westfield State if Hart was moving toward the right, McGovern responded, "Yes, and it has made me a little sad." McGovern observed that he "saw that process begin some years ago when he was running in a conservative state such as Colorado. Being from another conservative state, South Dakota, perhaps I was a little more patient with his effort to move toward centrist positions. But I think it is fair to say that he has been somewhat more fearful of taking strong progressive positions."[7] Despite this, McGovern refused to participate in personal attacks on Hart, regardless of the bitterness expressed by some of his staff, who feared that Hart was benefiting unfairly from his identification with "progressive McGovern issues." McGovern continued to express deep respect and affection for Hart but conceded that there were more similarities between the positions of Mondale and Hart than between Hart's positions and his own.[8]

As the Massachusetts effort continued, McGovern spoke about the "near and dear" relationship with the region, which dated back to 1972, when it gave him his only state victory against Richard Nixon. In 1984, he invited his audiences to gloat about the events of 1972, which set them apart from the rest of the country, and which subjected them to a certain degree of ridicule. "I've been under the impression for quite a while that this is where the most intelligent and better-informed voters in the nation reside," McGovern joked at a speech at Williams College. He drew a laugh when he went on to say he did not know how he would explain this statement in other states after Super Tuesday.[9]

McGovern gave some of his best speeches of the entire campaign in Massachusetts.[10] Time and again, he cried out against Reagan's overblown military budget, which he predicted would lead to the final holocaust at the very worst and to economic disaster at the very best. He railed against Reagan's misadventures in foreign policy, such as those in Lebanon and Central America. Reagan, McGovern said, was paying war contractors with money taken from services that Americans had earned and from industry modernization and job development.[11]

Back in mid-February, Paul Sullivan, a veteran of the 1972 campaign, having run the field organization in California with his wife Karen, was taking the roof off of his home in Hawaii when the telephone rang. Karen answered the phone and called up to Paul through the open rafters, "It's George McGovern!" Sullivan, who worked in the late 1980s for Jimmy Carter as the executive director of the Democratic Party, kept in touch over the years with McGovern, a man for whom he had great respect and admiration.[12]

McGovern asked Sullivan to come aboard the campaign: "Paul, don't think that I'm crazy . . . my chances here are very small." McGovern made it very apparent to Sullivan that it was a really big long shot, and the expectation of winning the nomination was not reasonable, but he still felt compelled to run in order to keep the debate focused in a certain direction. Sullivan responded, "Senator, it is such an honor to do it." Thus it was that Paul Sullivan was named national director of the McGovern campaign, replacing George Cunningham.[13]

According to Sullivan, the campaign was prospering financially compared with just prior to the Iowa caucuses of February 20. Sullivan said that there was about $350,000 in campaign donations, and he planned to invest all of what they had in Massachusetts with radio and television commercials. Fortunately, they had virtually no overhead to contend with, and they operated with an all-volunteer staff.[14]

Sullivan hoped that after the March 13 primaries on Super Tuesday, a strong McGovern showing would lend the Massachusetts primary new importance. McGovern himself indicated that he would need at least $68,000 for a last-minute media blitz and massive get-out-the-vote effort

for election day, and his reports indicated that he could carry Massachusetts.[15]

Sullivan's campaign strategy called for McGovern to not actively campaign in any of the other eight major primaries or caucuses on Super Tuesday where his major rivals for the nomination, Mondale and Hart, needed
to do well.[16]

The McGovern campaign purchased five minutes of advertising time
on all three networks to run a five-minute talk by McGovern to the people
of Massachusetts. The paid commercial ran on the eve of the state's primary, between the local and national news broadcasts. Sullivan estimated
that advertising alone would cost about $35,000, the amount spent for the
entire campaign in New Hampshire. The new money that was pouring
in reflected the delayed effects of McGovern's surprise performance in
Iowa. Although McGovern hadn't been able to ride the Iowa momentum
into any significant showing in New Hampshire, at least he was operating his campaign without debt.[17]

The McGovern campaign lacked the finances to conduct its own polling, not that McGovern cared one bit about what the pollsters were saying. His problem was that too many of the voters that favored him were
standing with other candidates who, they believed, had a realistic chance
in being nominated and defeating Reagan.[18]

On March 5, McGovern sent a message to his supporters that, with the
Massachusetts primary less than nine days away, the race was still wide
open for the five candidates who were participating. McGovern said that
he would prove with the power of the votes that the front-runner had "yet
to emerge." He hoped to prove his theory by celebrating a strong win in
Massachusetts on the 13th, followed by victories in Illinois on March 30
and New York on April 3. Delegates from those states alone totaled 595.[19]

One must remember that, in 1972, McGovern did not shore up the
nomination until the final primaries of the season. In 1983, as he entered
the race, he believed that support for the Democrats in the race was luke-
warm. Perhaps his program, which was different from all the others, could
excite the Democratic electorate and translate into delegate strength.
McGovern, an expert on the delegate selection process, understood that
the caucuses and primaries were primarily electing delegates to the national convention and that the voters were not directly voting for the
nominee. The media, however, was not reporting things as they truly
were. By only reporting on the front-runners, the media was feeding into
the notion that primaries and caucuses were a means to vote directly for
the eventual party nominee. Despite this problem, McGovern continued
to plead with the voters to vote for the candidate who best reflected their
views on the issues, and not to vote based on what they felt the candidate's
actual chances of being nominated would be.

George McGovern was clearly a long shot, but he campaigned on the idea that when one settles for someone who does not represent one's views, one actually throws one's vote away. However, a vote for McGovern, should one agree with his views, would send a sensible, sane message to the Democratic Convention, to the Congress, and to the White House itself. That message would discourage military adventurism and U.S. arms buildup. McGovern urged the people of Massachusetts to vote their conscience, and to make their vote count.[20]

McGovern was acutely aware that from coverage in television and the newspapers, one would think that the media was reporting on the Kentucky Derby, not the Democratic primary. The media, as always, was obsessed with reporting the odds and the favorites. For McGovern, however, the votes being cast were not a two-dollar bet; they were a statement about the country's future. The pundits called McGovern a dark horse, and they reported that he got a late start. They reported that his organization was small and that he lost once before. (Of course, they often forgot to report that he won many primaries and a nomination from his party.) For the media, there was less work in reporting why McGovern couldn't go the distance than there was in reporting the potentially devastating consequences of Reagan's winning a second term.[21]

Moreover, there was no arguing against some of McGovern's main gripes. Even the *New York Times* reported that President Reagan's proposed budget for fiscal year 1985 was dangerously out of order. It showed that, since Reagan took office, the increase in interest payments on the federal debt exceeded all the savings his administration achieved in health, education, welfare, and social service programs. Those cutbacks in domestic spending were at the heart of Reagan's program for economic recovery. He initially said such cutbacks would permit him to balance the budget while increasing military spending and cutting tax rates.[22] McGovern addressed this problem during his campaigning through Massachusetts:

> All the cuts in social services, education, medical aid to the aged and the poor, all the cuts to the hungry and to dependent children, all the cuts in funds available to repair America's bridges, clean its waters, depollute the air . . . all went to pay the extra interest incurred solely by the Reagan Administration for the grotesque military budget![23]

James McGovern (no relation to the senator), the twenty-four-year-old state coordinator for the McGovern campaign, said concerning the people's sense of the candidate, "There's a great deal of admiration. I've felt that grow and grow and grow." And it was, in fact, McGovern, not Mondale or Hart, who received the largest and loudest standing ovation at the Democratic State Committee Dinner that kicked off the final week of campaigning in Massachusetts.[24]

While all the other candidates went south to campaign, only McGovern remained in Massachusetts. He drew scores of people who were eager to touch or speak to him. McGovern moved through large crowds in the closing days of the Massachusetts campaign, stopping for conversations here and there. He appeared elated with the reception he was given. "I always receive a warm reception in Massachusetts," he said en route to campaign at another shopping mall. He wondered, though, whether those good feelings would translate into votes on the 13th.[25]

Others hoped that McGovern's call to cast a vote of "conscience" would succeed. A good showing for McGovern would "force a platform more favorable to McGovern's point of view," said Stephen Maloney, a shipping supervisor in a Connecticut warehouse. "Plus, he might get appointed to a cabinet position." Maloney and his father, Arthur, a fifty-nine-year-old retired firefighter, traveled to Massachusetts to attend McGovern's final rally on a campaign bus sponsored by the Connecticut McGovern campaign. The Connecticut volunteers were among thousands of people who braved the fourteen-degree midday temperature on Monday, March 12, to attend what was to be McGovern's last rally ever.[26]

McGovern, who was not so optimistic that he had his head in the clouds, knew that there was a real probability that Massachusetts was going to be the end of the line. However, he strongly believed that, win or lose, his candidacy had a positive effect on the overall campaign. "No candidate was even talking about Central America when I came in. . . . No candidate was even hinting at the possibility we might reduce military spending," McGovern said in Framingham. Whether he won the party's nomination or not, McGovern knew that, just by raising the issues he cared about, he was making an impact on what the eventual nominee would have to address in his own platform.[27]

Since the primary in New Hampshire, that eventual nominee was looking more and more like it might be Gary Hart. His debt-bedeviled campaign was dramatically altered by his upset victory in New Hampshire's primary. Within hours of his win, his organization took in $100,000 in cash donations, one-third as much as it had raised in the entire month of February, according to his campaign manager, Oliver Henkel. "The results in New Hampshire blew the lid off this campaign, both organizationally and financially," said Henkel.[28]

Hart, who was faced with a lack of money, incomplete delegate slates, and token field organizations, was now scrambling to flush out a skeletal campaign organization in several key states. He was also trying to add more than one hundred delegate candidates from his fallen rival colleagues. Hart had concentrated so heavily on Iowa and New Hampshire that he had mounted only modest efforts in other states, and he was now striving to catch up.[29]

Hart began February with a reported debt of over $500,000, and was counting on the excitement and momentum generated by his surprise victory in New Hampshire to get him some free publicity. Before February 28, Hart had spent only $200,000 in nine states, three-fourths of it in Massachusetts. Mondale, by comparison, spent more than $1 million in those same states, about half of it in Boston.[30] Some thought that Hart's campaign might end soon due to his financial problems, but he announced that, in addition to competing in Massachusetts, he would also compete in Maine and Vermont. "I intend to compete full out in the state of Massachusetts," Hart said at a news conference in Manchester, New Hampshire, where he spent fifty-seven days campaigning in the past year. Still, Hart's debt continued to grow; by March 1, it was nearing $850,000.[31]

Hart had more than financial problems to contend with. In Florida, for example, he had filed for only thirty-four of eighty-four congressional district delegate positions. The conventional wisdom among the Democrats was that Hart had done little organizing and was perceived as "too liberal" for the South. The "McGovern connection" was also believed to be a disadvantage for him.[32] On March 6, Hart was calling upon Southerners to choose him over Mondale to show that Southerners "will not submit to insiders' rule and special interests." Meanwhile, Mondale was in Florida and Georgia pursuing what his advisers described as an urgent effort to break Hart's victory streak. "It's a place where we have to fight like hell," said John Reilly, Mondale's senior campaign adviser, in Orlando. (John Glenn, of course, saw things a little differently, and considered himself to be the only real moderate left in the South. "I think that's important in this area. We have some very clear differences with Mr. Mondale and Mr. Hart," Glenn said. He campaigned in Alabama, a state among the most conservative in the region, as one who has "not gone out courting the liberal wing, which for so long has controlled the Democratic Party.")[33]

The Massachusetts Democratic organization, headed by Governor Michael S. Dukakis, was supporting Mondale. But Jack Weir, Hart's state coordinator, believed that Massachusetts was "a very good state for Gary Hart." Weir was not overly concerned by McGovern's decision to campaign full time in Massachusetts for the next two weeks, bypassing other primaries and caucuses. "McGovern's candidacy was predicated on Mondale as the front-runner. Now there is an alternative," Weir said.[34]

The Maine caucuses, being held on March 3, became a closely watched battleground, since it was the first two-man fight between Hart and Mondale.[35] John Glenn had abandoned his campaign there, and neither Jackson nor McGovern was making a serious effort in the state. The Maine caucuses began the process of selecting the state's twenty-seven delegates

to the convention, and—with only four electoral votes to be won there—
had been considered one of the minor political events on the calendar.
Political pundits were waiting to see whether or not Hart's newfound
momentum and popularity could overcome Mondale's advantage in
money and organization. Although Mondale had the backing of most of
the state's prominent Democratic elected officials, including Governor
Joseph E. Brennan, he also had the only statewide campaign organization.
Hart, on the other hand, relied on the momentum of his New Hampshire
victory, which created a rush of new volunteers in Maine. The Maine caucuses gave Mondale an opportunity to make a quick rebound after his
second-place finish in New Hampshire.[36]

Hart predicted that the campaign would not turn on organization and
telephone banks, but on voter perceptions and issues. "Organization," he
said at a news conference in Alabama, "turns out the vote only if the vote
is there." His strategy at that time called for running in select primary and
caucus states to keep up the momentum, while waiting for a transfusion
of money. Hart boldly predicted that he would finish first or second in
every remaining contest and would then go on to win the nomination.[37]

Hart was describing the Maine caucus as "a David versus Goliath."
Mondale, he charged, had spent "literally hundreds of thousands of dollars" in Maine, and had the support of "constituency groups and special
interests." Barry Hobbins, the Maine Democratic chairman, called the
caucuses "a contest between Mondale's organization and Hart's momentum, Big Mo versus Big O." According to Hart, "we have one thing the
front-runner doesn't have, and that is a vision of this nation's future and
the possibility of winning in November."[38]

On March 6, Hart scored his third victory in a week, winning 70 to 20
percent over Mondale in Vermont's preference vote. The triumph gave
Hart a clean sweep of three New England states: New Hampshire, Maine,
and Vermont, and it positioned him for Super Tuesday.[39] Hart was feeling energized, as he pursued his new generation theme, and he characterized Mondale as part of a leadership generation that was "past its
prime."[40]

Mondale, for his counterattack, went after Hart's character, personality, and life history, making these the themes of his speeches. In Orlando,
Mondale said he was "fighting from behind, trying to catch up" with Hart
in the South. Hart and Glenn's charges that Mondale was making too
many promises to too many different groups was starting to hurt
Mondale, according to his private polls. The former vice president was
thus forced to make some reassessments of his campaign.[41]

Mondale's failure to win in New England, and Hart's momentum, were
attributed by one Mondale adviser as a "mosaic of factors," ranging from
Mondale's natural reserve and caution to his selection of staff members
who largely mirrored his personal conservatism. "No one out there really

knows Mondale, but they think they do. He's been around for years, he's been around the track, and people already defined him," said one Mondale aide. "People have not defined Gary Hart, they're willing to give him one more run around the track."[42] Another Mondale adviser said, "We have allowed other people to define what we were. To say we are working for people should not be seen as a negative, but we allowed the perception to stick. We fed into our own perceived weaknesses." Mondale's caution was perceived as a weakness—a perception that hurt him—but his campaign did nothing to dispel the weakness.[43]

In the Des Moines debate, for example, Hart asked Mondale to name one issue on which he disagreed with labor. Mondale declined to do so, and it took him four days to cite any disagreements. This failure to criticize labor turned into an embarrassment for his campaign. One official close to Lane Kirkland, head of the labor federation, said Mondale's caution was "crazy," and added, "Lane Kirkland himself has a list of things where he and Mondale disagree, just to point out their mutual independence."[44]

Another problem for Mondale was that he could be a bland speaker who failed to ignite crowds. "I'm campaigning on what I believe. I don't know what else to do. What you see is what you get. I believe what I'm saying," Mondale said. For Mondale, Hart's "new ideas" were an anathema to what the Democratic Party stood for. "These days, there's a new idea about what our Democratic Party is, and where it should go," Mondale said in Tampa, Florida. "The new idea is the essence of the battle we're in. The idea is, if you fight for the values that Democrats have always believed in, you're supposed to be on a guilt trip. But if you fight against them, you're supposed to be applauded. If you fight for better schools, you're old. But if you fight for big oil, you're new. If you fight for civil rights, that's a special interest. But if you buckle to the hospital lobby, that's a new idea. I don't accept that."[45] He went on to add, "and I won't cut my values to fit this year's fashions. What I'm doing is to campaign for what I believe. I don't know what else to be for." Both Mondale and Glenn had been advised by their pollsters that "leadership of the future" was the key public concern in the 1984 election, but they both let Hart make "new ideas" the centerpiece of his campaign. Even McGovern, who had the freshest, most original ideas of all the candidates, had somehow let Hart capitalize on this yearning of the voters.[46]

For many people, Mondale's attacks on Hart were harsh, and therefore seemed out of character. But Mondale altered his message to include a full load of anti-Hart material in an effort to put negative writing on the "clean slate" of Hart's public image.[47] When Gary Hart won in Vermont, he received just over 70 percent of the vote to Mondale's 20 percent, and he had touched on a wide range of issues to appeal to the poor, to blacks, and to the young. Mondale knew that he needed to go after these groups as well, and when he was campaigning in Georgia and Alabama, he said, "I come to you today really needing you, and I think you know it." Mondale's losses in New England unsettled his organization, and he was trying to hold on to the support that he was reported to have built. When he traveled to Atlanta, he received the endorsements of the widow and father of the late Rev. Dr. Martin Luther King Jr. This was a crucial weapon in Mondale's fight against the new front-runner.[48]

But was Gary Hart indeed the new front-runner? "There's no question in my mind," said House Speaker Thomas P. O'Neill Jr., a Mondale supporter. "He's going to be hard to overtake. Mondale has got his problems."[49] Governor Mario Cuomo of New York also considered Hart the front-runner going into Super Tuesday, adding that he was less certain than before that Mondale would win the New York primary.[50] And in Florida, three weeks earlier, in mid-February, Gary Hart's campaign consisted of a half-dozen volunteers with neither an office nor a telephone. Mike Abrams, a Miami legislator, who was the campaign state chairman, said that, until recently, "we didn't see much future in Florida." Mondale's campaign had been working Florida for over a year, but Hart's chances were enhanced by the decision of former Governor Reubin Askew to drop his "Favorite Son" candidacy, and many undecided voters became Hart supporters. Hart made his first trip to Florida in nearly a year, because his strategy, until recently, did not call for him to campaign in any southern states where he had little or no support in public opinion polls.[51]

Now that he had shaken things up in the Democratic contest, however, Hart was working to spread his message in the southern states. He was successful in identifying a yearning in the electorate for a new way of doing things, and he constantly stressed his theme of new ideas. It seemed that an entire generation of Americans under forty-five was searching for something new in politics; their generation was shut out of political power, and felt that it was time to elect its own candidate. Although some older Democrats dismissed Hart's theme as an empty phrase, Hart certainly knew how to use it to fire up an audience. "To understand this election, you have to get out of the linear, left-right spectrum. This is not a left-right race," Hart explained. "This is a future-past race. That's what '32 was. That's what '60 was."[52]

In a *New York Times* interview, Hart said that he thought that there was a pent-up desire in America to break out of the old political modes and arrangements.

> I think people thought they got it in '76, and I think some people think they got it in '80, but I think there's still an awful lot of people out there that have been frustrated for a long time by assassinations, by Watergate, by Vietnam, and I think there's been a tremendous desire for somebody to express that latent idealism, that desire for national unity, for a common purpose.

He believed that it had little to do with him, and more to do with that need to identify with a national purpose. "I am not saying I'm the only human being on earth to turn this country around by any means. But I do think a second Ronald Reagan term means a serious decline in so many ways for this country, and perhaps for the world," Hart explained.[53]

On March 11, 1984, the League of Women Voters sponsored their second presidential debate of 1984. It was held at the Fox Theater in Atlanta, Georgia, and was moderated by journalist-commentator John Chancellor.[54]

Chancellor remarked that the field had shrunk from eight to five candidates and observed that Jackson was on the verge of losing his eligibility for campaign matching funds; McGovern was only campaigning in Massachusetts; Glenn had not yet obtained a victory; Mondale's desire for a quick and decisive lead was unfulfilled; and Hart's "new ideas" theme was attacked by his opponents as glamour without substance.[55]

In this debate, McGovern appeared relaxed. He was witty, joking, funny, and addressed his most passionate issues—avoiding nuclear war and U.S.-Soviet relations. Chancellor's first question to McGovern involved McGovern's criticisms of Gary Hart. Chancellor asked him whether Hart's talk of the future was much different from what he was saying in 1972. McGovern answered with a quip about how he had been rethinking 1972 and had probably trained Gary Hart too well. He believed that some legitimate questions had to be asked when the issue was posed as Gary had posed it.[56]

He says the election is a contest between the past and the future. Now, I'm not sure what the past means in those terms. I'm very sensitive about this as Gary knows because I'm an old history teacher. I've always revered the past. But does the past include George Washington and Thomas Jefferson? Does it include Franklin Roosevelt and John Kennedy? Does it include the human rights policy of President Carter? If it does, I'm glad to come here today and claim the past and defend it as a good guide to the future.[57]

For his part, John Glenn discussed the "experience factor," claiming that his business experience combined with his government experience made him the most attractive candidate. Glenn was critical of Reagan's economic policies suggesting that anyone could live on borrowed money for a little while. He advocated about a 6 percent increase in the military budget compared with President Reagan's 17 percent increase and was critical of both Mondale and Hart for cutting defense beyond all reality and especially Mondale for "emasculating" the military. Glenn was also critical of Hart's position on the military, saying that it showed a "fundamental lack of understanding."[58]

Mondale took issue with Hart's new ideas theme and argued that we don't elect momentum and images, that we had "better pick someone who knows what he's doing." Mondale suggested that he was seasoned and experienced and the right man at the right time. Mondale called Reagan's economic policies the "worst deliberate major economic mistake in modern times" and called for about a 4 percent increase in military spending. He agreed that the buildup of arms to scare the Russians would fail and committed to arms control negotiations and annual summits. But Mondale claimed that the Soviets were using their power irresponsibly and dangerously all over the world, and the United States had to be serious in its defense posture. Mondale called for a president who would lead a strong federal government to solve problems essential for the future. He attacked Hart and asked what was so new about entrepreneurship. Mondale claimed that Hart's positions reminded him of the slogan, "Where's the beef?"[59]

Hart claimed, in answer to Chancellor's question about his campaign being more impressionistic than specific, that he objected to how the primaries were set up and told the Hunt Commission back in 1982 "not to do this." He felt that if he had the necessary time to campaign, his ideas would sell well in the South. He agreed with Mondale that Reagan's policies were stealing from our children's future for purposes of greed and in order to satisfy an election year recovery. Where he differed with Mondale, however, was that it required a new generation of leadership in order to restore entrepreneurship. Hart attacked Mondale for being too committed to special interests. He also disagreed with McGovern and Jackson on their proposed decreases in military spending.[60]

Jesse Jackson charged that Mondale's and Hart's proposed increases in the military budget went in the same direction as Reagan's, "just slower." He called for sharing the burden of conventional troops in Japan and Europe by the Japanese and Europeans and advocated a cut of between 20 and 25 percent in defense spending.[61]

McGovern observed that Reagan brought the United States an artificial recovery for some people by spending $200 billion a year more than he took in.[62]

> Now I'm sure some of the viewers listening to the five of us think we're making partisan judgments here today about the president, but his own top economic advisor, Martin Feldstein, the chairman of the Council of Economic Advisors, has said that this $200 billion dollar deficit is a time bomb. It's going to go off after the election. It'll drive interest rates right through the ceiling and that's the end of the recovery. He also said what's causing this enormous deficit: It's a wildly inflationary and extravagant military spending binge that goes way beyond any defense requirement we have. And secondly, it's an inefficient and unjust tax law that's permitting billions of dollars to go through the loopholes to the highest income corporations in the country.[63]

McGovern became almost animated when Chancellor asked the candidates if most of them supported an increase in the military budget and jumped right into the debate. He said that he was for a 25 percent cut in the president's budget and that it could be done without "touching anything that's important to our national defense." He reminded Chancellor that he was a bomber pilot in the Second World War and would not advocate anything that he believed would touch the essential defense of the country. He pointed out, however, that some of the most thoughtful people who have looked at that budget observed that it was loaded with waste and cost overruns and noncompetitive bidding. He said that if we had someone like Lee Iacocca as secretary of defense, to do for the Pentagon what he did for Chrysler Motors, we could have a "good, lean, tough defense force" for less money.[64]

After Mondale, Hart, and Glenn spoke about the need to increase defense spending rather than cut it, McGovern jokingly responded that there was one thing really clear, and that was that there were no new ideas coming from that side of the room. The audience erupted in laughter.[65]

> What we've got is this same old argument, the Russians are coming, the Russians are about to jump on us. You can be very sure that that same argument is being made over there in the Kremlin: The Americans are gaining on us.[66]

McGovern explained that both of the superpowers were literally scaring each other to death, each side arming in the name of defense and piling up more and more weapons of destruction at a time when our societies are deteriorating. He compared his position with that of President Eisenhower who said that if the military spends too much, it actually weakens the country by depriving us of other sources of power—education, housing, transportation, a balanced economy—things that also have to do with our national strength. He observed that Reagan had undertaken this unjustified buildup on the theory that the Russians would be more humble; however, they walked out on the arms negotiations.[67]

McGovern directly challenged Mondale on his position of an increase in military spending:

> Fritz, how [are] you going to stop that with another 4 percent of military spending or another 40 percent? That's not going to change their relation in Poland or Afghanistan or these other areas.[68]

Mondale tried to portray himself as the experienced candidate who supported a strong, sensible defense. McGovern responded:

Every gentleman on this platform knows that if we let fly just 10% of the nuclear weapons we have targeted on the Soviet Union, every single man, woman and child in the Soviet Union would die instantly. Now, what are we going to achieve building any further than that? What is it we're trying to do with a 4% increase or a 6 . . . why not a cut in this enormous escalation that the President has on the drawing board?[69]

When Hart asked McGovern why Glenn was attacking him for all of the cuts he wanted to make and why McGovern was attacking him for making too few cuts, McGovern responded that the reason was that "John Glenn [was] 'further off' [than Hart]." The room erupted in laughter.[70]

McGovern passionately argued that there was a necessity for better communications between Washington and Moscow. He observed that one of the great tragedies of the last three years was that the president of the United States hadn't talked for even sixty seconds to the leader of the Soviet Union. In fact, two of their leaders died during the time President Reagan was in office without even meeting our president. If we had systematic regular talks between the president and his counterpart, McGovern said, it was quite possible that we would have avoided the Korean Jetliner incident. "I think if World War III comes, it'll be because of a communications breakdown." Chancellor asked the seasoned Democrats whether there would be more federal government involvement in people's lives if one of them prevailed in 1984. McGovern responded that there are two types of concentration of power we have to worry about. One is the danger of too much federal concentration and the other is too much corporate concentration of power.[71]

On the federal side, to my surprise, President Reagan has increased the percentage of GNP now being taken up by the federal government. The reason for that is obviously the dramatic increase in military spending. He has cut nutrition, education, the environment and things like that but those cuts are less than the increase in the interest rate on the federal debt since he took office because of this escalating deficit that he's brought on.

On the corporate side, we've had more huge corporate mergers in the last three years than at any other previous time in American history. Enormous oil companies taking over others to the point where I think it's a real call on all of us to see what we can do to strengthen our anti-trust laws.[72]

In their closing comments, Hart predictably called for new leadership while Mondale portrayed himself as the sensible seasoned leader. McGovern said that while Gary Hart and Fritz Mondale both objected to being called the front-runner, he hoped that they would let him be the "peacemaker" and take that label with him back to Boston when he left that evening.[73] McGovern concluded:

Franklin Roosevelt once said that the presidency is preeminently a place of moral leadership. I think that's true, and I think it means the next president is going to have to seek above all else our salvation from nuclear annihilation. But second only to that, we've got to learn in this great country to quit intervening in these Third World revolutions, whether it's El Salvador or Nicaragua or Lebanon or wherever it is. Unfortunately, in the name of fighting Communism, we can embrace virtually every scoundrel around the world who is willing to wave [applause] an anti-Communist banner, and I think the time has come for the United States once again to assert in foreign policy, not so much what we hate and fear, but what this great country is for. And that ought to be the goal of the next president.[74]

For Jim McGovern, the Massachusetts coordinator, one of the stand-out moments of the entire 1984 McGovern campaign was a speech delivered by Senator McGovern titled "Old Values and New Directions." Given to a standing-room crowd in the middle of a blizzard at Faneuil Hall in Boston on March 9, the speech summed up the essence of the public man and his belief in the founding ideals of the Declaration of Independence, the Bill of Rights, and the Judeo-Christian ethic from which those ideals flow.[75]

In Boston's historic Faneuil Hall, McGovern was reminded of the glories and values of the American past and stood on the same hallowed ground on which patriots from Sam Adams to John Kennedy called the nation forward. As one who treasured a sense of history, he saw "the test of leadership turning on our capacity to draw on the wisdom and to learn from the mistakes of the past as the surest guide to the future." He warned America, with an obvious reference to Ronald Reagan, that "a leader who scorns the past is an unsound guide to the future. A man separated from history is like a ship captain without a compass."[76]

McGovern quickly put Hart's new ideas theme to bed, asserting his lifelong-held philosophy that the central issue in the campaign—or in any presidential campaign—"is not between the past and the future; rather it is as always the long and patient struggle between right and wrong, justice and injustice, peace and war. It is not enough to say that we stand on a platform of new ideas. What are the new ideas? Newness does not describe the moral and intellectual worth of an idea." And he pointed out that it is well to be a little modest in claiming authorship for new ideas.[77]

That week in the U.S. Senate a great debate was unfolding over the precious constitutional principle of the separation of church and state. On this, as on all issues of national importance, McGovern was clear and unwavering. He charged that Reagan sought to overturn the U.S. Supreme Court decision against state-sponsored prayer sessions in the public schools. Said McGovern, "Although the President's position is supported in current public opinion polls, I disagree with him on both constitutional and theological grounds. The Constitution is a safer depository of the nation's principles than the latest election-year opinion poll."[78]

"The God of the Bible," said McGovern, "is present at all times: omniscient and omnipresent." In quoting from Matthew, McGovern took an obvious swipe at Ronald Reagan's moral theatrics:

> And when thou prayest, thou shall not be as the hypocrites are: for they love to pray standing . . . in the . . . streets, that they may be seen of men . . . but thou, when thou prayest, enter into thy closet, and when thou hast shut thy door, pray to thy Father which is in secret: and thy Father which seeth in secret shall reward thee openly.[79]

McGovern observed that the Bible does not command us to public prayer. It commands us to "feed the hungry." McGovern continued:

> A president who turns his back on the hungry cannot expect God to heed his prayers.
> If we truly wish to teach our children reverence for our Creator, we should stop the poisoning of his creation by acid rain.
> If we truly believe in communion with God, we must learn to communicate with the creatures of his world—our fellow humans.
> For as the Bible observes: "He that loveth not his brother whom he has seen, how can he love God whom he hath not seen?"[80]

Given the "precarious mutual suicide pact" between the Soviet Union and the United States, McGovern could not understand how the two leaders of the two superpowers had failed to meet during the previous three years. McGovern promised to end that deadly silence the day of his inauguration in order to lay the basis for peace. As true believers in the "right to life," he promised to "turn away from that nuclear abyss that threatens to destroy all of God's children." If we want our prayers to be heard, we must recall that scriptural promise: "Inasmuch as ye have done it unto one of the least of these, ye have done it unto me."[81] McGovern then called upon prayer:

> The spirit of the Lord is upon me, because he hath anointed me to preach the Gospel to the poor: He hath sent me to heal the broken-hearted, to preach deliverance to the captives, and recovering of sight to the blind, to set at liberty them that are bruised.[82]

These were the very concerns that compelled George McGovern to enter the 1984 presidential race. He believed, deep within his soul, that as a nation, America was losing sight of her "finest traditions and noblest dreams."[83]

America, he said, was focused upon what we are against rather than "affirming what we are for and charting a course to make real that vision for our children."[84]

We have the historical richness and the national ideals to lead the world toward a more hopeful and peaceful day. Yet in the grip of materialism and militarism, we have stifled our dreams and dulled our vision. . . .

But I am personally convinced that it makes no sense to stand with leaders who leave our souls untouched and our hearts unmoved.

My decision to seek the presidency was based on my belief that there were issues vital to our future that none of the other candidates were addressing.

And when the choices before us embrace national solvency or national bankruptcy, justice or injustice, life or death—each of us must answer to a moral imperative that we not remain silent.

I am not in this race to run interference for any of my fellow contenders. Neither am I in the race to make these others stumble.

Rather I am discharging a duty, to myself and to my country, to voice my opposition to policies which are taking us astray.

I still would like the chance to lead this nation into a new day, where the ideals of our founding fathers can be finally realized.

And I believe with all my strength that I am prepared as never before to heed the cries of spiritual hunger heard throughout this land, by nourishing what Lincoln called "the better angels of our nature."[85]

For McGovern, national security meant more than merely amassing a nuclear stockpile. He saw the strength of America dependent upon the "vitality of our economy, the quality of our education, the purity of our environment, and the sense of justice and compassion that we bring to each other."[86]

It was clear to George McGovern that national security included "the effectiveness and the fairness of our political system" and the "vision and the credibility of our leaders." Put simply, national security included what Ronald Reagan did not comprehend and his fellow Democrats neglected to address: the health and well-being of our citizenry, and the moral underpinnings of our society.[87]

Again quoting from the Bible, he said, "I have set before you two choices: Life or death. Therefore, choose life that thou and thy seed may live."[88]

In this age when for the first time in human history mankind can destroy itself, that "ancient wisdom takes on new force." With that, George McGovern called upon a prayer for wisdom on Super Tuesday and a rededication of "our lives, our fortunes and our sacred honor."[89]

Super Tuesday, then, was seen as a must-win by all candidates. Hart needed to capitalize on the gains he had made in New England and to establish himself as the unquestionable front-runner. Mondale needed to quash Hart's momentum before he threatened to make Mondale seem totally irrelevant. Mondale, it must be remembered, had his last victory in Iowa on February 20. The other candidates—McGovern, included—needed big wins just to keep their candidacies alive at all. All told, at stake on Super Tuesday were 500 delegates, more than one-fourth of the number needed to secure the nomination at the Democratic National Convention in San Francisco.[90] The South was seen as the major battleground; it was where Hart was the favorite. (Hart, realizing that he had to make up for lost campaigning time in the South, had invested $550,000 on television ads there stressing his new ideas theme. Mondale, in turn, ran a television campaign stressing why he was the best candidate for the southern voters—while also attacking Hart.)[91]

While Mondale and Hart were battling it out to see who the legitimate front-runner was, McGovern was looking ahead to Super Tuesday to see if his candidacy would survive. Less than a week before the Massachusetts primary, *The Boston Globe* ran an editorial, titled "Has Conscience, Should Travel," in which McGovern was called a figure of "already historic dignity and decency" and which took issue with the fact that McGovern would drop out of the race if he did not finish first or second there. *The Boston Globe* called on McGovern to reconsider his pledge to drop out if he did not perform as hoped.[92] The editorial complimented the clarity with which he spoke and the charm of his sparse campaign, which made unique contributions to the political process, adding:

> George McGovern represents stronger values than the current political atmosphere allows. His clarity of vision might seem even more vivid in the New York primary in April, or in California in June. His referee's role might also be needed by then, since Democrats have a habit of becoming more strident as the season wears on.[93]

The *Globe* editorial concluded by stating that McGovern's words deserved to be heard beyond Massachusetts, regardless of the primary results.[94]

In other states throughout the country, the McGovern campaign was kicking into full gear, playing catch-up in order to rectify its late beginning. In Connecticut, for example, the campaign was finding its footing and becoming competitive. There, McGovern had a volunteer state coordinator, as well as coordinators in each of the six congressional districts. What the McGovern campaign lacked in funds, it more than made up for in enthusiasm. The committee held a series of organizational meetings around the state, and its state coordinator participated in multiple debates at various Democratic Town Committees, one of which was televised by the League of Women Voters.[95]

Because of Super Tuesday, the Connecticut primary was suddenly more relevant than had been expected, and it commanded national attention as the only state selecting national convention delegates on March 27.[96] Yet, throughout the Connecticut effort, McGovern had to fight the claim that "he doesn't want to be president" and that he was mostly indulging in nostalgia as he made his way along the campaign trail. But his coordinator, speaking at numerous events, urged the Democrats not to "allow the primary system to become nothing more than a series of public opinion polls." He also said, "A vote for McGovern is a positive vote for a return to common sense and American values."[97]

A survey conducted back in November 1983 by the Institute for Social Inquiry at the University of Connecticut showed that the public at large favored Mondale over Glenn, 32 to 24 percent, while each of the other six challengers was under 6 percent in the poll.[98] Glenn, meanwhile, was believed to have had strong support in Connecticut and had made several fund-raising stops there. State Democratic Party Chairman James M. Fitzgerald indicated that there was a lack of enthusiasm for the choices. "Maybe some guys who are supporting them think they're lighting fires," Fitzgerald said of Mondale and Glenn, "but I haven't seen any big fires for anyone at this point." Fitzgerald believed that people were getting on board campaigns due to the fact that time was running short and they had to go with somebody.[99]

Everett Carll Ladd, a political analyst with the Roper Center for Public Opinion Research at the University of Connecticut, described the American electorate in 1984 using the analogy of an unanchored boat drifting about in the middle of a lake. "If a puff of wind comes up, the boat will move," said Ladd. Ladd's point was that one cannot necessarily describe the precise nature of the wind by watching the boat bob around. The presidential primary in Connecticut scheduled for March 27 would be the twenty-fifth state delegate-selection of the contest.[100]

Most of the leading Democratic figures were supporting either Mondale or Glenn by early September 1983. Nominally heading the Mondale campaign were U.S. Representatives William R. Ratchford and Sam Gejdenson, House Speaker Irving J. Stolberg, Senate Majority Leader Richard F. Schneller, and former U.S. Representative Toby Moffett.[101]

Moffett, who had been defeated in 1982 in his bid to unseat incumbent U.S. Senator Lowell P. Weicker Jr., was active in antinuclear causes, as well as many other liberal arenas. "I think it's early, and you do have a particular problem here in that Jackson's the only person who seems to excite any group," he said. "You don't have any inspirational, charismatic candidates among the front-runners."[102] Just as McGovern had predicted prior to entering the race in September, support for the candidates was soft, and the party leadership was choosing either to remain neutral, or to endorse one of the perceived front-runners. As such, the survey showed that a large bloc of respondents remained undecided. According to the survey, 32 percent of the public—the same percentage as those who supported Mondale—had no choice yet for the Democratic nominee. It was an even larger percent of voters than those who supported Glenn.[103]

Back in late January, the Caucus of Connecticut Democrats, a liberal Democratic organization that had been founded in the late 1960s by supporters of Robert F. Kennedy and Eugene McCarthy, held their nominating convention. Senator Alan Cranston closely aligned his campaign with the national Nuclear Freeze Movement, and the Freeze supporters dominated the delegates, who comprised a loose collection of liberal intellectuals, college professors, and veterans of the Vietnam antiwar movement. Thus, Cranston won 64 percent of the vote to Mondale's 29 percent on the third ballot.[104]

Mary Sullivan, a member of the Democratic National Committee and Cranston's acting Connecticut coordinator, believed the victory would give Cranston's campaign a significant boost.[105] Several Mondale supporters, however, were disgusted. "This whole thing is ridiculous. We all know Mondale's going to be the nominee, and we're all going to unite behind him against Reagan. Voting for Cranston is merely an exercise in political self-gratification," lamented a political science professor at the University of Connecticut, who happened to be a former chairman of a Democratic Town Committee.[106] It is interesting to note that, before Iowa, Gary Hart's campaign in Connecticut was virtually on life support.

The McGovern camp believed that Senator Hart's New Hampshire win boded well for their own candidate, insofar as it demonstrated that anyone could still come from behind. It was felt that McGovern represented the only clear alternative to Reagan's policies and that McGovern was the only candidate offering specific policies, as opposed to vague campaign promises about the better life ahead.

Just prior to the Iowa caucuses, dozens of supporters from the City of Waterbury, Fairfield County, the Naugatuck Valley, and Greater New Haven met to organize McGovern's statewide effort. At that time, between 39 and 47 percent of the Democrats were still undecided. A *Los Angeles Times* poll putting McGovern solidly in third place in mid-January excited his supporters, who sent a busload of volunteers to campaign in Massachusetts.[107] Much of McGovern's financial support in Connecticut came from Fairfield County—from Greenwich, Wilton, and Stamford. By mid-February, about 150 people from Connecticut had donated close to $8,000 to the McGovern campaign. There was a surge of enthusiasm for McGovern, even in Connecticut, after his third-place finish in Iowa.[108]

While Mondale had the endorsements, the money, and the support of the union leaders within Connecticut, the Hart campaign believed that Mondale could be beaten with a well-organized, enthusiastic campaign that focused on his new ideas and his strong chance of defeating Reagan in November. Two weeks prior to the Connecticut primary, the Colorado senator could boast only sixteen state residents who had applied to become delegates for him at the July convention. The day after the Massachusetts primary, that number shot up to 202.[109]

In Connecticut, 612 people had filed to become congressional delegates. Mondale had 238, Hart 202, McGovern had 56, and Jesse Jackson had 50. The McGovern effort in Connecticut was growing steadily.[110]

Like so much of the rest of the country, Connecticut was asleep prior to Hart's upset victory in New Hampshire.[111] U.S. Senator Christopher Dodd held off declaring his support for Hart until March 10, sensing that it was time to climb on the bandwagon.[112]

After the New Hampshire debate, with eight Democrats still running, a longtime Democratic Town chairwoman confided to a friend: "If I could come out publicly for George McGovern, I would; he looks damn good."[113]

Gary Hart won Connecticut's primary handily with 53 percent of the vote to Mondale's 29 percent. Jackson followed a distant third with 12 percent. It is interesting that although only Hart, Mondale, and Jackson still participated, former Governor Reubin Askew led the five candidates who had dropped out of the race in Connecticut in receiving 3 percent of the vote. Askew's votes came primarily and almost exclusively from prolife voters. Askew was followed by George McGovern with just under 2,500 votes followed by Hollings, uncommitted, Glenn, and Cranston.[114]

In Massachusetts, meanwhile, McGovern put on the full-court press to present his message to the voters. He pleaded with 1.4 million Democrats in the state to keep him in the race and to keep his voice alive. McGovern's speeches and television commercials appealed to voters to keep him in the race with their ballots on Super Tuesday. He repeatedly and unabashedly reminded them they "love" him. "If love would decide this primary, I'd win hands down," he told one audience.[115]

Ken Swope dropped everything he was doing and came aboard to produce McGovern's media. He created incredibly powerful television ads titled "El Salvador" and "Don't Throw Away Your Conscience." The "El Salvador" piece showed a close-up of a war-weary little girl, ravaged from the misery caused by the savage death squads. Another ad featured candidate McGovern, appearing quite thrilled, as he mingled about Faneuil Hall in Boston, looking like the Pied Piper, as people swarmed around to meet him, to touch him, to wish him well.[116] In his commercials, McGovern told voters that if the rest of the country had gone along with Massachusetts and the District of Columbia in 1972, many lives would have been saved in both Vietnam and Lebanon. In one ad, the announcer said, "We're the only ones who listened to him. Too bad. Too bad. . . . There would have been no Watergate, no national disgrace. We'd have a freeze by now. Now, he's come back. He's here again. It's up to us—again."[117]

It was almost a miracle how quickly the ads were produced. Swope and Sullivan sat up all night long for three straight nights and created an instant media package. Basically, the theme was very simple: They hit people in their hearts. Since there was insufficient time to run a typical field operation that contacted and identified voters, they sent out McGovern's late hour message directly to the people. They hoped that the love Massachusetts had for McGovern would somehow see him through to an upset victory. And it almost worked.[118]

McGovern spent $90,000 in Iowa and New Hampshire combined, compared with $250,000 on advertising alone in Massachusetts—about double the amount spent by Hart. Mondale canceled television advertising there to concentrate his resources in the South. McGovern's Massachusetts effort was regarded as well organized and highly professional.[119]

Paul Sullivan had been national director for less than a month and found himself in Massachusetts desperately fighting the clock in order to pull off a political miracle. He awoke at 2:00 A.M. from a sound sleep and said to himself, "We've got to do an old-style, old-fashioned McGovern rally." He knew in his heart that the likelihood was that McGovern was not going to pull off a come-from-behind victory. Nevertheless, Sullivan took out his rolodex and immediately began calling all of the 1972 volunteers. "I can't tell you the emotional reaction I received. People left their jobs and came to Boston. We had about 20 of the best advance people arrive in the last 2 or 3 days to set up the rally," Sullivan explained. The one thing that Sullivan didn't do was tell McGovern that it was going to be an outdoor rally. Given the extremely limited time constraints as well as the frigid weather, the whole idea was just too plain risky. Sullivan knew that if it flopped and embarrassed McGovern, his chances of success would be even more remote. The pressure was on. Even several Hart and Mondale staffers, many of whom were former McGovernites, hoped McGovern would pull it off. One call came into McGovern headquarters from Boston Mayor Ray Flynn's staff advising them to cancel the event because it was too cold and would keep people away, thereby embarrassing McGovern. Sullivan felt it was worth the risk, however.[120]

And so it was that on March 12, 1984, McGovern drew several thousand people in sub-zero weather to an outdoor rally at Copley Square in downtown Boston, a rally that was to be McGovern's last. It included a warm introduction by Kathleen Kennedy Townsend, music by folksinger Arlo Guthrie, a marching band, a hot-air balloon, and a variety of other visuals to ensure the needed television coverage.[121] McGovern, stunned at the reception, once more expounded on his ten-point plan, and said, "I need your vote, your voice, and your help." He added his familiar plea, "Look into your hearts, your consciences. The vote you cast is not a bet on a $2 horse race."[122] Then Guthrie sang "Blowin' in the Wind" and "This Land Is Your Land," leading the crowd in a sing-along.[123] The rally was planned to demonstrate his growing momentum, to counter Hart's surge in the polls.[124] However, there was a feeling in the air that this rally was more of a good-bye than anything else.[125] Within the month, Hart had gone from 4 percent to about 50 percent in the Massachusetts polls, while Mondale dropped about 20 points to 24 percent. At the same time, McGovern tripled his standing, but as of March 12, he was still at only 13 percent. The campaign volunteers gave everything they had to this rally. In just a couple of days, the McGovern campaign had garnered about 500 volunteers, many of them college students, working phone banks and distributing literature.[126]

That night in Massachusetts, George McGovern dominated the television news. Shown both on local and national broadcasts was coverage of the Copley Square rally held that day. In between the local and national news was McGovern's five-minute "plea" to the people of Massachusetts to "vote your conscience." And, as if it couldn't get any better, the networks ran a segment on the morning of Super Tuesday titled "The Over the Hill Gang." This story featured coverage of the dozens of 1972 McGovern supporters who left jobs and families to campaign in Massachusetts for their hero.[127]

McGovern focused some criticism on Hart in the final days. He compared the Hart campaign with that of Jimmy Carter in 1976, saying both failed to be specific. "It's less risk to the country when you have a candidate who lets you know where he stands," McGovern said. He had been using historical references in his speeches as a way of criticizing Hart's "past vs. future" theme. He compared his race against Hart as "a contest between a hip tune and an old classical favorite."[128]

Although the McGovern campaign treasury was drained in the Massachusetts primary, McGovern said he had sufficient contributions coming in to wage a low-budget campaign in the March 20 Illinois primary, but he added that he was quite comfortable with being called the party's "conscience" and "elder statesman," titles that he acquired during the campaign. "I expect to be at that platform session in San Francisco, whether I'm the nominee or not," he said.[129]

McGovern, of course, was not the only candidate who had his campaign on the line. Jesse Jackson knew that any hope of capturing the Democratic nomination was slim at best, but he hoped to make a respectable enough showing, regardless. As Super Tuesday drew closer, Jackson stepped up his criticism of Mondale and Hart. He pledged to put a woman on the ticket with him, and noted that they did not. He pledged to cut the military budget, and he challenged the party rules that he believed denied full representation for all voters. Jackson said that on important issues, such as the enforcement of the Voting Rights Act of 1965, nothing separated Mondale and Hart except their rhetoric. "One leans on Humphrey, and the other leans on Kennedy, which is even further back," he said. "Both of them are talking forwards but walking backwards."

When John Glenn criticized Jackson, saying he "has no business experience, no military, science, or research experience," Jackson remarked that "for all the good those assets are doing him, I'm not impressed."[130]

Jackson concentrated his campaign in Alabama, Georgia, and Florida, the first states in the primary season that had large black populations. Jackson desperately needed at least 20 percent of the vote in order to keep his federal matching funds, and both Alabama and Georgia had a voting population composed of at least 20 percent black voters. Jackson asked southern black voters for a show of support, to help send his campaign north with enough credibility to sustain it. He waged an intensive drive to register blacks, who made up more than 20 percent of the registered voters in Georgia and Alabama, and about 16 percent in Florida. Jackson emphasized his association with Martin Luther King (this, despite the fact that Coretta Scott King and several other black leaders endorsed Walter Mondale).[131] Jackson, however, had strong black support in Georgia, and hurt Mondale's efforts there.[132]

John Glenn was feeling a little more positive about his prospects for going the distance, but, realistically, he needed strong victories on Super Tuesday every bit as much as Jackson and McGovern did. In the week before the big contests, he argued that he offered the "last chance for the South" to have a moderate Democratic presidential candidate. He said that, as the only moderate in the race, he best reflected the views of the South. The sixty-two-year-old senator attacked the presumed front-runner, Hart, by going after his views on the military, the economy, and the role of government, saying those views were out of step with moderate and conservative Southerners. He criticized Hart's "imitation" of John F. Kennedy, and questioned Hart's motives in obtaining a naval commission a few years earlier. Glenn, for his part, highlighted his military background in his southern campaign.[133]

Finally, the day of reckoning arrived. Super Tuesday, that "must-win" day for every candidate, had come, ending the speculation of who would survive and who would not. As it had in earlier primaries, the weather made its presence felt. It rained in the South, where Mondale was the big winner, carrying Alabama and Georgia. In the North, Hart carried Massachusetts and Rhode Island, and he won in Florida, as well.[134] According to ABC exit polls, in the three states Hart won, labor was cooler to Mondale, blacks went more for Jackson, and Hart wound up his new coalition consisting of the young, the affluent, women, and Independents.[135]

Voters leaving the polls indicated that Hart's new ideas theme remained a key part of his appeal, and the voter breakdown showed that the more affluent the voter, the more likely he or she was to vote for Hart.[136] (In Massachusetts, for example, Hart received 43 percent support from people living in households with an income of $5,000 to $10,000, while Mondale got 20 percent. Hart won the backing of 46 percent—to Mondale's 19—of those living in homes where the income was between $40,000 and $50,000.)[137] Poorer voters, older voters, and those who placed a high value on "helping the poor" leaned toward Mondale. Helping the poor and protecting social security, in fact, were cited as the most deciding issues in voting for Mondale.[138]

Hart's victories in Florida and Massachusetts, the two largest states to vote thus far, proved that his four victories were not regional flukes.[139] The biggest issue motivating voters in those states was the election of a leader who "would bring needed change," according to an ABC poll.[140] His win of Massachusetts marked the first time a Democratic candidate won both that state and New Hampshire since Lyndon Johnson in 1964. He managed to win with only a small campaign organization and few endorsements from leading Massachusetts politicians.[141] Mondale had been leading Hart in the Massachusetts polls just prior to the primary, but Hart's organization showed a sudden surge of energy when it counted most. The two largest factors in Hart's Massachusetts victory were his stand on controlling the nuclear arms race, and his prospects for defeating Reagan—which 70 percent of those who voted for him credited as their main reason for doing so—in November. Part of what helped Hart was that his image was just vague enough so that he could be many different things to many different people.[142]

Hart was elated with his results, and called Super Tuesday a "watershed for this candidacy," which demonstrated "strength outside of New England. Tonight is a victory not only for this campaign and this candidacy, but tonight is a victory for the people of this country." And it came after an astonishing two-week surge in which Hart rose out of nowhere to score four consecutive victories over the former vice president.[143]

Hart's convincing victories were seen as illustrating Hart's having broad national appeal and the ability to unite the Democratic Party to take on Ronald Reagan in November. "This is a big night for us, especially when you consider that we weren't supposed to win in any of these states a few weeks ago," said Hart's deputy campaign manager, David Landau. Morris Dees, chief fund-raiser for Hart, boasted that, at a meeting of party fat-cats on Super Tuesday, he received pledges totaling $1 million, which indicated that the party establishment was coming around to Gary Hart.[144]

Several political analysts felt that Hart consolidated his strength with his Super Tuesday victories. Although most voters did not know very much about him, they knew a lot about Mondale, and apparently they didn't like it. There was an antiestablishment feeling in the air, and Mondale was very clearly a member of the Democratic establishment.[145]

Yet, in spite of Hart's psychological advantage in winning the big states on Super Tuesday, Mondale continued to maintain a lead in delegates won. "It's not very solid for anyone," Everett Carll Ladd said in a Tuesday evening interview. The shift to Hart made it "evident that an enormous number of people are capable of being moved without an enormous effort." Ladd did not accept the concept of a starkly split voting population along generational lines with young people for Hart and older ones for Mondale.[146]

The mixed bag of results left both the Mondale and the Hart camps agreeing that neither would have it easy from that night until the night of the Democratic National Convention. "This is going to be a long, tough fight," said Oliver Henkel, Hart's campaign manager. Mondale's campaign manager, Robert Beckel, said, "We're back and ready to run. Yes, I think we're out of trouble. We had a rough couple of weeks." Still, Mondale was quite happy to have finally slowed the Hart steamroller.[147]

"I've come back into the race," said a jubilant Mondale. "A month ago, this was a bandwagon. Now it's a crusade.[148] When this race began, it looked like Mondale doing a hundred-yard dash," he told his supporters. "Then it looked like Hart doing a 100-yard-dash. But tonight that's all changed. . . . It's going to be a marathon from now on. . . . A tough fight makes me a better candidate, and it's gonna make you a better President," he said to chants of "Where's the beef?"—a reference to his remark about Hart's new ideas theme lacking substance.[149]

Mondale proclaimed his victories in Alabama and Georgia to be the "turning point of the campaign." He vowed to fight to the end for the Democratic nomination. He told a crowd of supporters, "There are 40 contests yet to come, and we'll be in every one of them. . . . This marathon will be good for our country. . . . Americans will learn a lot about us. . . . We'll be tested under pressure." He also insisted that his Super Tuesday victories had broken Hart's drive for the lead.[150] "Tonight, I came from behind, substantially behind, and I've gained momentum," he said. Mondale believed that the next primaries in the Midwest would give him strength in the Michigan caucuses on March 17 and the Illinois primary on March 20. These would be followed by primaries in Pennsylvania and New York.[151] ABC News found that many people were making up their minds at the last minute and were tending to vote for Mondale. All indications were that the Sunday debate in Atlanta, as well as Mondale's attacks on Hart, had made an impact.[152]

Gary Hart appeared to be broadening his base to include older voters. He was missing one key element, however, of the Democratic coalition: black voters, almost all of whom went to Jackson and Mondale. Hart's failure to attract black voters was evident in his losses in Alabama and

Georgia, where blacks accounted for about one-third of the vote. In Florida and Massachusetts, he split the Jewish vote with Mondale.[153]

However, Mondale failed to attract the young, affluent, better-educated voters, who were desperately needed if he was going to have a real shot at defeating Reagan. Polls of Democratic voters by ABC News showed potentially fatal flaws in Mondale's support. In Florida, for instance, he led Hart only among voters older than sixty, among those with less than a high school diploma, and among those earning less than $10,000 a year.[154]

In Massachusetts, despite strong support from the state Democratic machine, as well as from organized labor, he finished far behind Hart, and just ahead of Senator McGovern. Interestingly, Mondale fared better in Alabama, a state with high unemployment.[155]

Even in Alabama, Mondale trailed Hart among the 34 percent of the electorate that had any higher education. The polling results showed Hart bringing in voters who went for Reagan in 1980, and who would vote for Reagan again, unless Hart was the Democratic nominee. Thus, although Mondale was continuing to gather delegates for the July convention, Hart was the candidate better able to draw Independent and Republican voters into the Democratic Party.[156]

Super Tuesday could also be seen as a victory for Jesse Jackson, who achieved the needed 20 percent of the vote to keep his finances alive. Nevertheless, in Georgia, Jackson ran third in the state, well below his expectations.[157] The *New York Times*/CBS News poll showed Jackson receiving 61 percent of the black vote in Georgia to 30 percent for Mondale.[158] Jackson said that his showing in Georgia positioned him to reclaim his role as the alternative candidate and potential broker if the Hart-Mondale fight went to the convention. In Alabama, Jackson received 50 percent of the black vote to Mondale's 47 percent. Mondale led among older blacks, while Jackson resonated with the younger black voters.[159] At any rate, Jackson vowed to keep his presidential candidacy going, despite his relatively disappointing showings. He insisted that his "Rainbow Coalition [was] here to stay" and would "always remain a conscience in the Democratic Party."[160]

"We shall give people a live option," Jackson said at a news conference. He said that the results showed that "we cannot be taken for granted by the old-line Democratic Party or be written off by the Republican Party."[161]

Mondale continued to hammer away at Hart, attacking his judgment, character, and experience, a strategy that Mondale's aides credited with bringing victories in Alabama and Georgia. Like Jackson, Mondale resonated quite well with the black voters, who responded to his bread-and-butter economic issues and his sharp attacks at the public image of Gary

Hart.[162] Mondale was also aided significantly by the ability of John Glenn to pull 21 percent of the vote in Alabama and 18 percent in Georgia. Glenn's support came from the same sort of Independent voters and pro-Reagan Democrats who formed the core of Hart's support. Dotty Lynch, Hart's poll taker, explained it this way: "My sense is that Glenn's ability to mount an effective campaign and the Mondale attacks probably hurt Gary a lot. If Glenn gets out, I think we'll be able to attract the bulk of the Glenn voters. On Tuesday, Mondale was also saved by the ability to capture enough of the Black vote."[163]

Meanwhile, in Atlanta, John Glenn said that, despite his failure to win a primary in his southern stronghold, the race for the nomination "remains very much alive." He gave no indication that he was about to withdraw as a candidate, and said "I will be returning to Washington tomorrow to map out the future of the campaign." However, a week before the Illinois primary, Tom Joyce, Glenn's Illinois coordinator, was ordered to shut down the remaining operations in the state, as Glenn's campaign was put "in storage." Joyce said "we have no cash left. We've been operating for the last 14 days out of our pockets." Mike McCurry, Glenn's national press secretary, confirmed the orders to close the Chicago office, saying, "Our campaign is broke."[164]

As the dust from the latest primaries began to settle, there was another casualty. Before the votes were counted in Massachusetts, George McGovern appeared headed for a second-place finish. He expressed exuberance and confidence that he would stay in the race at least through the Illinois primary on March 20. "If I had any doubts about it, we're clearing them up today," McGovern said during a dinnertime interview in his hotel suite. "With a first or second here today, we're going to go to Illinois with the surge I've been looking for in this race."[165] His comments came after midafternoon exit polls showed him running a solid second to Gary Hart. McGovern's staff had already scheduled a noontime news conference in Chicago the following day, as well as a meeting with Chicago Mayor Harold Washington.[166] That night, a plane load of McGovern campaigners was flying from Boston to Illinois for a morning airport rally in downstate.[167]

According to state party officials, it appeared that McGovern was being helped by a daylong snowstorm that brought over three inches of snow to all parts of the state. It was believed that the storm kept elderly voters—likely those who would support Mondale—away from the polls. Boston Mayor Raymond L. Flynn, a Mondale supporter, commented that "This weather doesn't help us at all."[168]

Despite a late surge that almost saw him overtake Mondale for second place, however, McGovern didn't quite make it. When the absentee ballots came in and were added to the count, Mondale narrowly edged McGovern out of second place.[169] Coming in third in Massachusetts, McGovern kept his vow to end his candidacy. "I said two weeks ago here in Boston that if I did not place first or second in this important primary race, I would withdraw from the Presidential competition in 1984," McGovern told supporters at a Boston hotel. "And that is what I intend to do."[170]

McGovern said he was willing to "fully accept the verdict of my very special friends, the voters of the state of Massachusetts, who gave us a very strong showing. I think far beyond what anyone expected a short time ago."[171] His announcement came only minutes after George Cunningham said, "If it's only a few points difference, we'll regard that as a win." That was a sentiment shared by many of the McGovern campaign team.[172] "It was such a heartbreaking loss. If we had had one more day . . . [McGovern] would have come in a solid second . . . maybe even first. One or two more days. We were catching them that fast," Sullivan later recounted.[173] McGovern was as good as his vow, though, and he congratulated Gary Hart, whom he called "a brilliant political figure." He added, "His recent surge in the Democratic Presidential race has to be considered one of the most remarkable developments in our recent history."[174] McGovern did hold out the possibility that he might reverse his decision to quit "if the trends changed during the night."[175] He regarded his Massachusetts results as "something of a political miracle." Looking back on it years later, he felt that his 1984 campaign "might have caught on if we'd have had more time [to campaign] and I had not committed myself to drop out at that point."[176] But McGovern did drop out. "I didn't want to do anything that would enable either Hart or Mondale or their supporters to say that I was a spoiler . . . that otherwise their man would have won," he said.[177]

In his brief statement, McGovern also congratulated former Vice President Mondale for "what appears to be an apparent second place showing."[178] In the end, Hart received 39 percent of the vote, Mondale received 25 percent, and McGovern received 21 percent. McGovern's 134,000 votes were only 26,000 shy of overtaking Mondale's second place spot, and remaining in the race.[179] The net result after Super Tuesday in the delegate tally, with 1,967 votes needed to nominate, had Mondale at 333, Hart at 212, Jackson at 37, Glenn at 30, McGovern at 22, and 148 votes still up in the air.[180]

On Wednesday morning, McGovern appeared on ABC's *Good Morning America*. He said that he felt "younger this morning than I did in 1972 when I was defeated by former President Nixon." Gary Hart talked to McGovern, but did not get his endorsement. "He said Vice President Mondale is, in his judgment, a more classic liberal," said Hart of his conversation with McGovern.[181]

McGovern had a long talk at breakfast that morning with Eleanor and Paul Sullivan. He asked Sullivan to take over his political action committee and run it for him. Sullivan responded, "If you'll hang on to your delegates I'll stay with you all the way through to the convention because you don't know what's going to happen, and you don't know what those delegates are going to mean." McGovern agreed. Eleanor turned to Paul and said: "Now, Paul, you're not trying to get him back in the race, are you?" Sullivan smiled at her and said, "No, Eleanor. You think I'd do something like that?" And Eleanor laughed and had a twinkle in her eye.[182]

Super Tuesday, which could have been a make-or-break night for either Mondale or Hart, was seen as a draw. The three other candidates failed to make any breakthrough that would have made them viable contenders. Mondale made good on his only prediction of the year by winning the Democratic primary in Alabama by a large margin. The Alabama and Georgia victories were his first primary wins of the year. Hart and Mondale were now locked in a war of attrition over the next several months, and battled to almost a stalemate in the South. While Hart showed unexpected strength among foreigners, retirees, and the Jewish community, Mondale's union endorsements finally paid off in Alabama. Whereas Hart attracted the young and educated, Mondale attracted the black voters.[183]

As the campaign between Mondale and Hart became more bitter, George McGovern, leaving the stage, warned his fellow Democrats not to press their mutual attacks too hard, for fear of helping the Republicans in November. "Don't do President Reagan's work for him," McGovern warned. "Don't cut each other up." But, with the Mondale campaign predicting a marathon race and discovering a number of Hart's weak points, as well as Mondale's resurgence as a fighting candidate, the McGovern warning appeared to go unheeded.[184]

The 194 delegates in Illinois loomed large, and made up the largest block elected yet in a primary and the first in a major midwestern industrial state. The Illinois primary was to be held in two parts. The first was a popularity contest among the remaining Democratic contenders, which was not binding on the state's delegation to the national convention. The second was an election for 116 delegates committed to a particular candidate, and divided among the state's twenty-two congressional districts. In addition, seventy-eight other delegates would be chosen by the Illinois Democrats in Congress and the state's Democratic Central Committee. Mondale and Glenn were the only candidates with full slates of delegates in each of the districts.[185]

The Mondale campaign's earlier belief that they would have the nomination sewed up by Illinois had a new problem coming to the forefront—

money. Mondale's heavy spending in 1983 and in the early part of 1984 left the campaign with only $6 million to spend before it reached the $20.2 million limit that could be spent on a nomination campaign.[186] The Mondale campaign had believed that no one would be left with sufficient credibility, money, or delegates to overcome the vice president's lead by the time of the Illinois primary. However, the reality was that Mondale's candidacy was on somewhat shaky ground. Playing off Hart's campaign theme of new ideas, Mondale warned that the real fight was between "what's right and what's wrong. If you fight for values that the party has always believed in, you're supposed to be on a guilt trip, but if you fight against them, you're supposed to be applauded."[187]

Hart responded by saying that he was "absolutely committed as a Democrat to the same values and goals" as was Mondale. He alleged that Mondale's charge that he would abandon the party's roots was nonsense "and Fritz knows it." According to Hart, the only substantial difference between Mondale and him was how to accomplish the goals they were both seeking. Hart argued that his program depended on economic growth and that Mondale was more concerned about divvying up "a stagnant economic pie more fairly." Hart believed that the best way to guarantee protection for those less fortunate in society was to put money in the pockets of the wage-earning middle class.[188] His advertising stressed that the election was about the failure of the past and the promise of the future.[189]

In mid-March, House Majority Leader Jim Wright and a dozen other members of Congress, who previously were uncommitted or had supported Senator Alan Cranston, gave Mondale their endorsement. Senator Edward Kennedy further emphasized this neutrality by declining another bid from Mondale for an endorsement.[190]

For Mondale, Hart was consciously deciding to deemphasize what Mondale thought was the human side of public leadership. Mondale believed Hart's record reflected that, and so did his campaign. He viewed his debate with Hart as much more basic than the one he had with John Glenn. Hart's threat to Mondale and old-line Democrats was less an ideological challenge than a threat to the core of the old way of doing business. Hart questioned old assumptions about the role of government and looked at traditional party dogma with a much colder eye. "One of my arguments with . . . [Hart] . . . is that it's not at all clear what he stands for," Mondale said. "He defines himself in negatives, what he's against: the old, the past. Well, who isn't? If the new is good, I'm for it. What really counts here is our values and . . . our objectives. One of the things missing, in my opinion, in Senator Hart's record, is interest in these issues."[191]

George McGovern's quest for the nomination, which began in a sea of ridicule, ended when just over twenty delegates restored him to a respectable position inside the Democratic Party. "It's been one of the very constructive by-products of the campaign," he confessed. "I've found my own standing in the party and in the country dramatically elevated." McGovern was not inclined to endorse any of the remaining candidates, choosing instead to "stand clear and let the voters make the decision."[192] McGovern campaign spokesman Mark Kaminsky said, "One of the most gratifying things has been the turnaround [on] all of the ridicule that was heaped upon him when he announced. Even though they had scorned him, they're now saying that he has been the most class act in the campaign."[193]

Kaminsky recalled how, at precinct caucuses in Iowa, a captain remarked that few of the participants would be for McGovern. But, when they clustered into groups that reflected the candidate they supported, about a third in the room were for McGovern. However, it was in the debates that McGovern attracted the most attention, especially the debate in Des Moines where he pleaded with the voters not to "throw away their conscience."[194]

In other debates, McGovern emerged as a statesman and peacemaker among the hopefuls, and urged them not to attack the front-runner to the point that they would make it difficult for him to defeat Reagan in November.[195] It remained fresh in McGovern's mind how the attacks from fellow Democrats (especially Hubert Humphrey, his main challenger), back in 1972, weakened him for the general election that followed.

"We were just ecstatic at how he performed in the debates," Kaminsky said. "It was so inspiring to watch McGovern outclass the other candidates, and [it was] a tremendous boost to the campaign." It was also McGovern's style that distinguished him as he campaigned through countless towns in Iowa and New Hampshire with his trench coat and Irish hat, absent the trappings of the other candidates.[196]

Throughout most of the campaign, McGovern flew commercially, and declined protection from the Secret Service. McGovern's relaxed pace won him the admiration of many. "Many said in 1972, I was ahead of my time. Well, I'm back," McGovern would say. He also gained respect by his unwavering demands for the withdrawal of American troops from Lebanon. He was seen as a statesman at an hourlong foreign policy meeting that took place in January between himself and Richard Nixon. The McGovern campaign defended the meeting as that same type of gutsy move that made McGovern different from all the others seeking the nomination. However, McGovern's days of campaigning had now come to an end.[197] There were no more votes to seek, no more rallies full of enthusiastic supporters. From this point on, McGovern was no longer going to be on center-stage. With several months to go before the general elections, though, he still had time to make his influence felt.

CHAPTER NINE

The Peacemaker: Emergence of an Elder Statesman

It is not the critic who counts; not the man who points out how the strong man stumbles, or where the doer of deeds could have done them better. The credit belongs to the man who is actually in the arena, whose face is marred by dust and sweat and blood; who strives valiantly; who errs, who comes short again and again, because there is no effort without error and shortcoming; but who does actually strive to do the deeds; who knows great enthusiasms, the great devotions; who spends himself in a worthy cause; who at the best knows in the end the triumph of high achievement, and who at the worst, if he fails, at least fails while daring greatly, so that his place shall never be with those cold and timid souls who neither know victory nor defeat.

—Theodore Roosevelt

To everyone's surprise, Super Tuesday in some ways brought victory to all three of the remaining contenders. Walter Mondale managed to slow Hart's momentum and found that his campaign was still intact and that his dream for the presidency was back on course. Gary Hart, after weeks of surprise and upset victories, could now claim that his "new ideas" message could sell in the conservative South.[1] And Jesse Jackson won enough support to qualify for federal funding.[2] The three men had survived several months of arduous campaigning, witnessed their fellow candidates fall by the wayside, and geared up for the final months of the Democratic contest.

While Mondale, Hart, and Jackson battled it out, Super Tuesday saw the last gasps from John Glenn and George McGovern. McGovern kept his word about leaving the race. While he surely was disappointed that lightning did not strike twice, he did not have much time to dwell on it.

The question of who the Democrats were going to nominate had yet to be answered, and McGovern, who had become something of a peace-keeper in the party during his campaign, still had a role to play. At first he declined to endorse anyone for president, but instead said that he would try to persuade Mondale and Hart not to "turn each other into hamburger." At his first Washington news conference since he withdrew from the race, McGovern said that he would talk to party leaders in an effort to prevent Mondale and Hart from grinding each other up. McGovern believed very strongly that harsh attacks on him during the Democratic primaries in 1972 contributed greatly to his loss to Richard Nixon in the general election. He did not want Mondale or Hart to suffer a similar fate at the hands of Ronald Reagan. "I've come to the conclusion it's better for me not to back any particular candidate, but to do what I can to affect the nominee of this party."[3] If anything, his stateman's touch was needed now more than ever.

Within days of Super Tuesday, the battle between Mondale and Hart grew increasingly acrimonious as they headed into major contests in Michigan and Illinois. At one point, Hart accused Mondale of running negative campaign advertisements against him, yet he quickly apologized when he realized that the ads did not actually exist. Mondale accepted Hart's apology and said, "Occasionally, we get tired in these campaigns. We say things we don't mean, and we ought to have the right to take it back." He added, however, "I do believe there's evidence of a reluctance on the part of the Senator to engage in the merits of the issues I'm raising." Mondale's new approach against Hart was to lure "centrist" and "conservative" Democrats, some of whom supported John Glenn, as well as to create doubts about Hart's experience in foreign policy.[4]

On May 9, Mondale won primaries in Maryland and North Carolina and lost to Hart in Ohio and Indiana.[5] Since May 9, Mondale had suffered big defeats in Oregon, Nebraska, and Idaho, but he nevertheless widened his lead among delegates. According to United Press International, Mondale had 1,643 delegates, Hart had 964, and Jackson had 305. Mondale's campaign chairman, James R. Johnson, was predicting that on June 4, they would have between 1,750 and 1,800 delegates counted for Mondale. Johnson was also predicting that after the last round of primaries in California and New Jersey on June 5, Mondale would have more than the 1,967 delegates needed to assure a first-ballot nomination.[6]

Mondale's campaign was slowly adding to its count by getting delegates from a variety of categories that did not show up in the official count. For example, there were those 568 delegates known as "super delegates." These were elected officials and party leaders who were not pledged to any candidate, but who had reserved seats at the convention. (This category was created by the Hunt Commission, and it was believed that a large bloc of uncommitted delegates could be the deciding factor if

there were a long and undecisive primary season. Mondale's long association with and cultivation of party regulars, coupled with his ability to
play party politics well, put the vast majority of these super delegates
firmly in his corner.)[7]

Meanwhile, McGovern continued to hold fund-raisers in hopes of retiring his campaign debt early. On May 30, Representative Thomas J.
Downey, Carol Haussamen, Stewart Rawlings Mott, Arthur Schlesinger
Jr., Senator Daniel Patrick Moynihan, and Representative Ted Weiss hosted
a cocktail reception at Haussamen's home on Central Park South in New
York City. Among the guests were Shirley MacLaine and former Congress-
woman Bella Abzug.[8]

As the Democratic convention drew nearer, the acrimony between the
Mondale and Hart camps only deepened as the press speculated about
possible running mates. Appearing separately on Sunday news programs
on May 20, Mondale and Hart were drawn into the speculation. Hart said
on a Los Angeles news program that Jesse Jackson had "earned the right
to be considered as a party leader, including Vice President." He said that
he would consider Jackson as a running mate, but that Jackson would
have to modify his views on the Middle East first. Hart noted that the two
disagreed during the campaign on the status of the Palestine Liberation
Organization and on U.S. policy in disputes between Israel and the Arab
states. Ultimately, Hart said that he would not announce his choice of a
running mate until the convention.[9]

Meanwhile, Jackson called speculation about the vice presidency premature. "I would hope that after June 5, we would come together and look
at the broad range of issues, including the long and short lists of Vice Presidential possibilities," he said, although he added "But right now, we are
very much competing in the marketplace to win the nomination."[10]

McGovern, ever mindful of public perception, and wanting to keep the
animosity of the campaign in check, also weighed in with his opinion on
ABC's *This Week with David Brinkley*. He said that there were no "fundamental differences" between Mondale and Hart and that he believed that
Mondale would win the nomination. "I think that if, in fact, this bitterness and acrimony is as deep as some people believe it is, the quickest
way to heal that in the public's mind is actually to put these two men on
the ticket together," he said. "I'd love to see a Mondale-Hart ticket."[11]

Mondale, who appeared on the same May 20 program, said that he
would not exclude anyone as a possible running mate, but he added that
there were "substantial differences" between himself and Hart. He conceded, however, that they were not irreconcilable. When asked about the
possibility of running with Mondale, Hart agreed that it was a possibility, but only if he were the presidential nominee. Asked what he thought
of McGovern's suggestion, Hart said, "Not much."[12]

Jesse Jackson, apparently, shared Hart's opinion. Jackson lashed out at McGovern for suggesting a Democratic ticket consisting of Mondale and Hart, and charged that McGovern had abandoned his role as the "conscience of the party." Jackson stated that "the idea of naming a ticket was not right." He pointed out that both Hart and Mondale proposed an increase in military spending, while both he and McGovern advocated cutbacks. He likened McGovern's "embracing" of a Mondale-Hart ticket to a "dove embracing the hawks."[13]

On June 13, McGovern formally endorsed Mondale for president, and said that placing Hart in the number two spot on the ticket would send a strong message to the country. "I think a Mondale-Hart ticket is the strongest, and that it does gather on one ticket the best vote getters we've got," McGovern said at a news conference. Although he was not pushing Mondale to choose Hart, he reiterated that he felt doing so would be "a logical way to heal wounds quickly."[14] Healing wounds was high on McGovern's agenda, and, in private discussions with top Democrats, he was being looked to as the peacemaker to smooth over raw feelings between Mondale and Hart. McGovern remained friendly with both men and was best positioned to heal the split between them.[15]

At the news conference, McGovern acknowledged that it was not easy to pick Mondale over Hart, whom he referred to as "my special friend and former campaign manager." He noted that while Hart likely would not win enough delegates to gain the nomination, he had won the support and admiration of millions of Americans. McGovern spoke with Hart the previous week about whether Hart might accept a spot on a Mondale ticket, but Hart was not enthusiastic, a posture that candidates at that point in the race usually adopt. However, McGovern believed that it was in Hart's best interest to keep his options open, and to at least consider becoming the vice presidential nominee.[16]

McGovern asked his twenty-three delegates to give their support to Mondale, "the probable nominee of our party," and he called on Democrats to close ranks behind him.[17] "It is imperative that the Democratic nominee be elected next November, because Mr. Reagan does not have the philosophy, realism, or sense of history that can save us from war and economic danger." Although McGovern did not agree with all of Mondale's views, he was convinced that Mondale would reverse the dangerous deterioration of Soviet-American relations and the drift toward war in Central America.[18]

As the weeks wore on, McGovern's 23 delegates—two in Iowa and 21 in Massachusetts—did indeed back Mondale, who, by the time of the Democratic Convention had 1,997 delegates, more than 25 over the number needed to win the nomination on the first ballot. Hart had 1,228, and Jackson had 321. Hart still refused to concede the nomination, and was intent on remaining in the race until the convention.[19] However, Hart assured McGovern that he would be a "good sport" and would not take the party down with his losing presidential nomination.[20]

McGovern appeared at the party's final preconvention platform hearings in June. His major concern was the chilly relations between the United States and the Soviet Union, which he believed should be the Democrats' highest priority in the campaign.[21] Charles Manatt, chairman of the Democratic National Committee, agreed. Manatt, speaking at a news conference, charged that Ronald Reagan's proposed "Star Wars" defense concept of space-based missile defenses represented "a commitment to propel America through a dangerous threshold toward war in space." He believed that "their anticipated deployment would be so provocative that it could risk preemptive attack."[22]

All in all, McGovern saw the Democrats as being more united on issues than they had been since their divisiveness over the Vietnam War. He saw no major issues dividing the party, and believed that the real danger for the Democrats was a convention divided by Hart's newest accusations that some of Mondale's delegates were tainted because of the rules under which they were chosen and the way some primary and caucus campaigns were financed.[23]

After his testimony before the platform panel, McGovern told a reporter that "Gary Hart assured me . . . that he was not going to play a divisive role." McGovern elaborated by stating that "[Hart] said he's going to go to the convention with his delegates, but that he's not going to take a divisive strategy from here on out; there will be no more attacks on Mondale. Mondale gave me the same assurances about Hart."[24] McGovern saw no harm in Hart's pressing for reform of campaign practices if it was done tactfully. "If it gets to the point, though, where it's a bitter head-to-head charge and counter-charge over who's been acting in good faith and who hasn't on things like delegate selection and campaign financing, it's going to be very harmful to us," McGovern said.[25]

Meanwhile, as the general election loomed, it seemed that whether Mondale or Hart won the Democratic nomination was almost a moot point; President Reagan continued to attract more potential voters than either man, according to the Gallup Poll published at the end of May. The poll showed Reagan was the choice of 52 percent of the voters, to Mondale's 43 percent, and the president attracted 50 percent of the voters to Hart's 44 percent. In a Mondale-Hart ticket scenario, the Democrats would still only pick up 46 percent of the vote, to Reagan's 50 percent, and 4 percent of those polled were undecided.[26]

McGovern, though out of the race, was still firmly committed to defeating Ronald Reagan, and in order to lend his support, he kept a full speaking schedule from May until the Democratic Convention in mid-July.[27]

During both May and June, McGovern continued fund-raising. In a letter to his supporters at the end of May, he admitted that the first weeks of the campaign were very hard on him when the national press was making jokes. He was honest enough to tell his supporters that he knew that his run would strike many "as a 'Don Quixote' quest of a man tilting at windmills and longing to recapture the excitement and passion of the 'good old days.'" But McGovern believed that his campaign did make a difference to the nation, to the Democratic Party, and to the tone of the national debate on our future.[28]

In addition, McGovern's committee was making plans to produce a number of nationally televised policy messages to the American people. In those television spots, McGovern planned to speak personally to the voters about why this election was the most critical in history and "why each voter's decision could literally be a life or death decision."[29] Unfortunately, the request that his committee made to the three commercial networks to purchase airtime was declined, because the networks' lawyers considered McGovern no longer a presidential candidate—despite the fact that both the Democratic National Committee and the Federal Election Commission considered McGovern to be a candidate at the time of his request. McGovern was disappointed at the networks' decision, for he felt that this would have been a great way to influence the Democratic Party's platform. Still, McGovern put the money he had raised for the television spots to good use, bringing staff and campaign workers from different parts of the country in to prepare and distribute flyers and issue papers to the convention delegates.[30]

Several operatives of Jesse Jackson and Gary Hart joined forces in June to enhance their campaigns' clout at the Democratic National Convention, and to slow Mondale's drive toward the nomination. The two organizations combined votes in order to attempt to choose state delegation chairmen who, among other things, controlled access to floor passes and telephones at the party's nominating convention in San Francisco. Stoney Cooks, Hart's deputy campaign manager, was the principal link to the Jackson campaign, and he attempted to court the Jackson delegates to put Hart over the top. Jackson strategists, however, were jealously guarding their campaign's independence, and they resisted the heavy courting by the Hart people. With relations remaining tentative, Arnold Pinkey, Jackson's national campaign manager, wanted to leave open the option of operating with Hart's campaign.[31]

Jackson was furious over McGovern's advocacy of a Mondale-Hart ticket, and this led to Jackson's rejection of McGovern's request to attend a fund-raiser in Los Angeles to help McGovern pay off debts from his campaign.[32]

Jackson accused McGovern of being "unprincipled" and "unfair" for not supporting his candidacy. Although Jackson supported McGovern in

1972, he now said that the former senator "chose the two hawks over the dove . . . shifted from conscience to pragmatism. That's not right."[33]

Jackson fired off a letter to McGovern, saying he was "extremely disappointed that your call for party unity comes at a time when the issues you raised with your campaign are still completely unresolved." Jackson believed that the show of unity at the McGovern fund-raiser was too premature, and too forced.[34]

> I believe real party unity can only be founded on party justice. . . . I am deeply disturbed by the lack of progress our party has made in broadening its base. . . . I am deeply disturbed by the failure of Walter Mondale and Gary Hart to take up the issues of peace and justice that you and I have raised in our campaigns.[35]

Jackson's letter also said that, although he tried to discuss the lack of "democracy in the nominating process" with party officials, no action had been taken.[36] Jackson was upset that every effort he made was stonewalled by the party leadership and that "matchmaking" should not take place until the nomination had been decided.[37] By July, however, the convention made it official. Mondale was, indeed, the Democratic Party's nominee.

The 1984 presidential contest had finally found its Democratic contender. But what of McGovern? How had he viewed his campaign? What had he learned? What had others learned from him? Recall that, upon entering the race, McGovern was widely ridiculed for his nostalgia and his foolishness. Yet, by the time he withdrew, the *New York Times*, which had called his campaign "quixotic" at the outset, now said that he left the stage "with a glow of decency, and with the best line of the campaign: Don't throw away your conscience."[38]

If one judges a presidential campaign only in terms of percentages, votes won, and money raised, then it was clear that George McGovern's candidacy was not a success. One major factor that hindered the campaign, besides entering late, was a lack of campaign funds. Kaminsky said that McGovern had spent about $500,000 on the campaign, a paltry amount when compared with what Mondale and Hart spent.[39]

Yet, for McGovern, his 1984 candidacy had been a largely positive experience. Paradoxically, he felt better about himself, his family, the public, and the press in March 1984 than he did in November 1972.[40] Back then, the Vietnam War gave such a grim quality to politics that it took the joy out of the race for McGovern. In fact, the war issue was something of an obsession with him. He went into the 1972 campaign, he said years later, "thinking the fate of the country depended on . . . [my] election." He did not feel the same way in 1984. While he felt just as strongly about the issues—even more so, perhaps—he possessed a more detached, philosophical view than he did when he was fifty years old.[41]

The George McGovern of 1972 was on a mission to change America, and he gave the impression that if he did not prevail in the election, Western civilization itself could be in jeopardy. The George McGovern of 1984, however, was more mature and at peace with himself, although he was even more troubled with Ronald Reagan's policies than he had been with Richard Nixon's.[42] In a moment of self-reflection, McGovern observed that his principles had not changed. "But I think I have a wiser and more thoughtful approach to the country now than I had at any time in my life. I've done a lot more reading, a lot more thinking. . . . Since I've been out from under the pressure of day-to-day discussions, I've been able to probe somewhat more deeply into the problems of the country and also the limitations on what you can do about them. I think I would be a better president now than if I had been elected in 1972," he said.[43]

McGovern described his six-month presidential campaign as beginning and ending with convictions that were in harmony with his ambition.[44] He was content with himself for yielding "briefly to the urge to try again to at least raise the level of the debate," he wrote on January 17, 1988, to Eleanor, as he pondered making yet another presidential run.[45] He was pleased too that he did not have to sacrifice conscience, dignity, or wit. "I think it is fair to say that I did extremely well—with the appreciation of the national press corps, the other candidates and the Democratic Party.[46] It was most gratifying to me," McGovern explained. He later noted that "Presidential ambition can be laudatory," but it also carried "high risks to one's judgment, humor, and emotional health."[47]

McGovern, as well as those who were watching him, felt that his leadership qualities had shown through during the numerous debates that he had engaged in with the other candidates. *The Washington Post* pointed out, for example, that in the first debate in Hanover, New Hampshire, McGovern demonstrated to his fellow contenders that they could "disagree with dignity," and could "emphasize their differences" without losing sight of the fact that they were all still bonded in their desire to topple Reagan.[48] McGovern set ground rules for inflicting damage on one another, and had much to do with the civility of the contest. The *Post* admitted that, at the start of his campaign, it thought McGovern "was an embarrassment and a joke." It now came to the conclusion that it was wrong, and went on to describe McGovern as "a relaxed, amusing and mellow figure who lent good qualities to the campaign, and set a standard of decency and good taste."[49]

It seemed that, until people actually had a chance to hear what McGovern had to say, there was no shortage of preconceived ideas about what a terrible idea it was for him to enter the primaries. The nine debates, however, gave McGovern's "low-budget, issue-oriented campaign" an opportunity. Indeed, those debates, plus the big Democratic Party dinners, where the candidates spoke in succession, "constituted the real substance" of his brief Presidential bid, and they provided him with his best opportunities "to 'debate' the issues and to demonstrate personal qualities of intellect, wit, and performance under pressure."[50]

The brilliant technical campaign that won the nomination in 1972 was missing in 1984. Although his 1972 campaign was begun more than a year in advance, the 1984 effort was hastily put together and lacked a solid foundation. In order to win a nomination, talent, skill, organization, issues and, to a certain degree, luck must all fall into place. The superior message—or messenger—alone cannot win a nomination any more than a great baseball pitcher can win a game without a talented team around him. In an era of highly technical campaigns, McGovern's "special kind of Presidential bid" was not enough to achieve success in the 1984 Democratic primaries.

His was a campaign of genuine volunteers. The candidate shunned a heavily financed professional operation and instead chose to run a campaign fueled by ideas and manned by amateurs.[51] It may well have been one of the last presidential campaigns of that type we will ever see. The true success in McGovern's 1984 run was the candidate himself; he staged a remarkable campaign and turned ridicule at the outset into respect for himself and a serious look at the issues by others.

Although McGovern believed that politics, and the participation in national agenda discussions, was serious business, 1984 saw the former senator let his guard down in public. He was probably the most relaxed candidate on the campaign trail, and, after his run had ended, McGovern even poked a little fun at himself by appearing on NBC's *Saturday Night Live*, the ninety-minute sketch comedy program. After receiving the offer to appear from Dick Ebersol, the program's executive producer, McGovern thought that it would be an interesting thing to do. Other political figures, such as New York Mayor Ed Koch, New York Senator Daniel Patrick Moynihan, and Ralph Nader, had previously appeared on the program, so it was not unheard of.[52]

In addition, *Saturday Night Live* had a great tradition of political satire, ranging from Chevy Chase's portraying a bumbling Gerald Ford, to Eddie Murphy's spoofing the Rev. Jesse Jackson. McGovern quipped that "Anybody who's arrogant enough to run for president shouldn't fear 'Saturday Night Live,'" although he added that he "couldn't find any of my advisors who thought it was a good idea." McGovern felt that the program would be a good way to express his humorous side, in contrast to his very serious political appearances. McGovern also thought that the appearance would show that he was being a good sport about his recent candidacy. He was paid a fee of $5,000, which was his usual lecture fee.[53]

One source of humor in the show was McGovern's campaign debt, which he addressed in his opening monologue. In one sketch, McGovern, playing himself, was an unemployed, deadbeat sponger, living in his sister-in-law's house. In the sketch, his family berated him for embarrassing him, and his sister-in-law exclaimed "How dare you run again!"[54]

McGovern's only suggestion to the writers was that they didn't involve him in any ethnic or racial slurs. "It's just having the guts to do it," he said. "It's a question of having the nerve to expose yourself to spoofs and have the capacity for self-deprecation." Ironically, Richard Nixon would appear that weekend on *60 Minutes*. The difference, though, was that Nixon was making much more money for his television appearance than was McGovern. "George doesn't have as interesting a truth to tell," said *SNL* writer Kevin Kelton. "Nixon has a better agent," retorted McGovern.[55] Ultimately, the whole experience was a nice way for McGovern to let his supporters know that his withdrawal from the race was not the end of the world for him.

When the Democratic National Convention reconvened on Wednesday, July 18, and while George McGovern was not going to take the stage as the nominee of his party, he did take the opportunity to address his fellow Democrats for one final rumination on the campaign and the issues of the day. McGovern's name was placed in nomination by twenty-four-year-old James P. McGovern, the Massachusetts state coordinator, and a close friend of McGovern's.[56] (James McGovern, it might be noted, would later be elected to Congress to represent the Third District of Massachusetts in 1996.)

In his speech, James McGovern summed up McGovern's 1984 campaign as a venture in which the former senator saw his government willing to risk the very survival of the planet in the vain pursuit of military superiority; he witnessed the moral commandment of love for one's neighbor being replaced by a "cynical celebration of materialism and self interest." He explained that George McGovern entered the race understanding that the highest duty of an elected official was to voice dissent from policies that are wrong, regardless of what the political pollsters or pundits may say. He called George McGovern's 1984 platform a commonsense approach for national rebirth. McGovern, he declared, was "guided by conscience" in shaping a brighter future for America.[57] The seconding speech was delivered by Ellen Kurtz, another dedicated and hardworking campaign volunteer. She gave a vivid description of how different our nation's future would be under a McGovern presidency. "Our country's wealth would be wisely spent on the true source of our national strength: education, health care, jobs and the environment, instead of squandered on a bloated military budget," she said. In introducing her "political hero," Kurtz described McGovern as the "conscience of the Democratic Party, the peacemaker, a man with endless compassion, wisdom and integrity—a man who dares to speak the truth, even if it hurts."[58]

George McGovern, in his last address at a Democratic National Convention, referred to the event "as a time of national soul searching . . . a time to define the national purpose." His vision of the country was unchanged from the vision he had had a decade earlier. McGovern wanted America to be a witness to the world for what was "decent and just in human affairs." He believed in an America, borrowing Jefferson's words, that held "a decent respect for the opinions of mankind," an America where people care deeply about each other, as well as the fellow inhabitants of the planet. He envisioned a union that would build prosperity, and peace, from the bottom up, not from the top down. This vision was required not only because it was right, but also because it was the only way that the American economy and American foreign policy could work. Lastly, McGovern said that he envisioned for America a quiet, steady effort to build a nation that matched its performance with its most enduring ideals.[59]

In his address McGovern conceded that the odds against his winning the nomination this time around were against him, but he noted that he felt compelled to run due to his questions over the present course of the Democratic Party and the nation. His candidacy, he said, was his way of joining the national dialogue and steering it in the direction he thought it needed to go. The issues he thought the Democrats needed to address included terminating all military activity in Central America, bringing the Marines home from Lebanon, freezing the nuclear arms race, and assuring farmers a fair price for their wares, while also trying to stamp out hunger.[60] This last point prompted McGovern to reminisce about a moving experience he had had, years before:

> One night in 1968, I was watching a television documentary on hunger in America. In those days, a child who did not have the money went hungry during the school lunch hour. Focusing the camera on a little boy standing at the side of the room watching the other children eat, a reporter asked this youngster what he was thinking. He said, "I'm ashamed." "Why are you ashamed?" inquired the reporter. "Because," said the little boy, "I haven't got any money."
>
> Now, I thought to myself, it is not that little lad who should be ashamed. It is I as a United States Senator who should be ashamed. And that shame led to the creation of the Senate Committee on Nutrition and Human Needs of which I was the Chair. [Applause] And for the next decade, we waged a big victorious battle against hunger and bad diets in America.[61]

From there, McGovern charged that, in the first four years of the Reagan administration, the war on hunger was shortchanged, because money was being diverted for war in the skies. He hoped and prayed, he said, that one day the United States would be able to proclaim that the greatest

nation "is not the one with the most missiles, but the one that best ministers to the health, the education, and the nutrition of its children."[62]

McGovern went on to speak more generally about the goals he had set
for his presidential campaign. His overriding pledge, he said, had been
to say exactly what he thought about the issues. He was being faithful to
his conscience, and he hoped that the nation's voters would do the same.
In addition to his call, he also sounded a conciliatory note among the
Democratic contenders, because, he said, "[I]n a democracy, conciliation
must walk hand-in-hand with conscience." Thus, as his address drew to
a close, McGovern complimented his fellow challengers individually.[63]

He pointed out then that he had once chaired the party's Commission
on Delegate Selection and Party Structure. Its findings were fair and just,
but also controversial and disturbing to some, he acknowledged, and the
attacks were plentiful, especially for asserting that henceforth women and
blacks and Hispanics and young people must be fairly represented in the
presidential selection process. It was that historic action from 1972, he said,
that opened "the way for Geraldine Ferraro to become the Vice President
of the United States."[64]

McGovern acknowledged that his defeat for reelection to the Senate
was caused partly by the accusations of extremist forces who had characterized him as "antifamily." However, it was precisely those values instilled in him by his parents, the love and devotion of his wife, the
inspiration of his children, and the generous opportunities provided to
him by the people of South Dakota—and the larger Democratic family
across the country—that enabled him to come this far in political life.
McGovern thanked the Democratic Party, and America, for giving him,
"a small-town lad from the South Dakota prairies," an opportunity to rise
and be heard. He quoted Oliver Wendell Holmes, who said, "As life is
action and passion, it is required of a man that he should share the passion and action of his time at peril of being judged not to have lived."
Finally, McGovern asked that his name be officially withdrawn from nomination so that the delegates' voice and energy could be given to Walter
Mondale, the next president of the United States.[65]

Of course, history tells us that Walter Mondale was not the next president of the United States. In fact, Mondale lost to Reagan in a landslide
that was reminiscent of McGovern's loss to Nixon in 1972. What went so
wrong? Patrick Caddell felt that the Democrats in 1984 took false hope
from their off-year victories in 1982, during the worst period of the Reagan
recession. In believing in, and working on, their old formulas for nomination, the Democrats nominated Mondale. A consequence of the Democrats' tunnel vision, however, was in nominating a mainstream Democrat
who hadn't even run quite as well as McGovern-Shriver.[66]

Walter Mondale's electoral defeat was the worst in history, and the
Democratic Party would have to wait until 1988 for another chance of

winning the White House. They would have to wait until 1992 for an actual victory.

After the November election, McGovern continued speaking out on the issues that he felt were important, particularly on the nuclear arms race. At a speech delivered at Princeton University to the New Jersey Nuclear War Issues Conference, he said that the nuclear peril ". . . reveals the threats of the Reagan administration's ignorance and attitudes toward the nuclear arms race present—the possible threat of holocaust and the inevitable national impoverishment we already suffer because of spiraling military spending."[67]

Only then, with the election over, did McGovern believe that our country was beginning to face the hard realities of the Reagan deficits. He believed that many who voted for Reagan would feel bitterly betrayed by the shocking flip-flop from his campaign promises to the harsh actions he would now take.[68] Reagan proposals were due to completely eliminate at least fifteen federal programs and to severely slash dozens of others. These were all unwarranted sacrifices, in McGovern's view, and he intended to remain a part of the debate. McGovern regarded the administration as "callous" and "uncaring." His desire was to help the Democrats prepare to regain control of the Senate in 1986, paving the way for the 1988 presidential election.[69]

For McGovern, there was reason for optimism. He believed in the "pendulum phenomenon" in American politics, and saw the swing to the right, which began strongly in 1980, "followed with the practical testing of unworkable extremist policies" finally coming to an end.[70] "I'm not ready to give up on the hope that this country can once again become a greater and a better land if we're faithful to the ideals with which we began," he said.[71]

Through December of 1984, McGovern continued working on retiring his campaign debt, which was now down to about $20,000. As was often the case, his campaign was asked to pay some bills that McGovern's people had expected were being handled by local committees around the country. McGovern proudly boasted that at no time during his quarter-century in politics had he ever left a campaign debt unpaid.[72]

On February 11, 1985, the Federal Election Commission issued a report recommending that McGovern be required to repay more than $25,000 in campaign matching funds.[73] The biggest item, $13,549, involved the publicly funded portion of the $50,000 salary McGovern's 1984 presidential campaign committee paid to him to make up for lost income during his bid for the nomination.[74]

McGovern, who previously had publicly recommended the FEC's abolition, at first intended to fight on the salary issue. He was a bit surprised by the determination, because its general counsel and staff told his campaign earlier that it was acceptable to take the money. McGovern described the report as "miserable, nitpicking."[75]

McGovern was critical of the FEC during his campaign, and he expected to "get it in the ribs" sooner or later. Mary Curtin, treasurer of the Friends of George McGovern, believed that the salary was justified because McGovern made his living on the lecture circuit, and he usually received $5,000 per speech. The six months of lost income would not approach what he would have made had he been active on the lecture circuit. Curtin observed that senators who run for president still receive their Senate salaries. McGovern was especially critical of the FEC for what he regarded as red-tape delays that kept him from receiving federal matching funds until after the Iowa caucuses. At that time, he insisted that he might have come in second in Iowa instead of Gary Hart, if he had had the money in hand.[76]

The FEC audit also said that McGovern's committee should repay $7,457 in "undocumented" expenditures for which receipts could not be found, and $4,099 for expenses in connection with the Democratic National Convention, when McGovern was no longer a qualified candidate. McGovern did not contest those items, but he pointed out that they illustrated his view that the net result of the FEC was to force campaigns to hire auditors instead of relying upon volunteers. He questioned why the six-member commission overruled its own staff.[77]

Although there was no rule or law against paying the candidate a salary, the FEC demanded repayment of $25,104.99 in matching funds for "non-qualified campaign expenses." According to Curtin, there was no precedent for this. She remained the sole employee left in McGovern's campaign. Nothing in the FEC's rules stated that a candidate's salary could not be considered a qualified campaign expense. According to the FEC, the committee paid McGovern a $50,000 salary in three installments: $35,000 on March 9, 1984; $10,000 on May 30, 1984; and $5,000 on June 8, 1984. Although two of the payments were made after McGovern pulled out of the race, the salary was intended solely for the period he was an active candidate. Its current surplus of about $10,000 was not enough to repay the FEC.[78] Because McGovern tried to run a low-budget campaign, staffed almost entirely by volunteers, there were no paid accountants. Every dollar spent to send the twenty-three McGovern delegates to the Democratic National Convention was ruled by the FEC to be unqualified, since, at that time, he was no longer a candidate.[79]

Among McGovern's major financial contributors were actress Shirley MacLaine, actor Shaun Cassidy, radio personality Casey Kasem, actress Shelly Fabares, actor Mike Farrell, actor Charles Grodin, publisher Hugh Hefner, recording artist Don Henley, recording artist and actress Barbra Streisand, Kennedy sister and brother-in-law Jean and Stephen Smith, economist John Kenneth Galbraith, actor Richard Widmark, actress Trish Vandevere Scott, film director Sidney Pollack, actor Jack Lemmon, producer/director Norman Lear, actress Margot Kidder, producer David Meyer Selznick, and stateswoman Pamela Harriman.[80]

In the weeks and months following McGovern's decision to drop out of the campaign, the former senator, along with his many supporters, was given time to reflect upon his campaign effort, the impact he had made, and the lessons that could be learned.[81]

For McGovern, this campaign, more than any other during thirty years of public life, united his family. For him, that alone made it all worthwhile. Paradoxically, it was the one campaign that most of his family opposed at the beginning.[82]

McGovern viewed his seven opponents as the "strongest array of candidates the Democratic Party . . . fielded since 1960," when John F. Kennedy, Lyndon Johnson, Hubert Humphrey, Adlai Stevenson, and Stuart Symington competed. McGovern developed a genuine affection and respect for all his Democratic opponents, and he felt that any one of them would have made a better than average president.[83]

After the race concluded, many people did stop and wonder whether McGovern actually believed that he had a chance to win the Democratic nomination in 1984. The answer to that question was an unequivocal yes. McGovern felt that many Americans were sorry for the decade following the 1972 election and about how they voted. He believed that he could have turned that regret into a successful run for the White House if he had run again in 1976, or if he had come into the competition in 1984 a little earlier.[84] He had had great difficulty being on the sidelines and watching others less experienced and less qualified struggle for the nomination in 1976, 1980, and 1984.[85] Mainly, however, McGovern drew his belief in his candidacy from his own history. Political lightning had struck him in 1972, against all odds and predictions. McGovern had defied the odds once, and he genuinely believed that anything was possible this time around. He tried to present "an honest, straightforward commonsense position," one that he believed would appeal to voters without regard to their ideological stripes.[86]

Despite his late entry into the race and his underfunded and understaffed campaign, McGovern came close to pulling an upset in the Iowa caucuses. An 800-vote shift from Gary Hart to George McGovern could have had him coming out of Iowa on the surge that Hart rode to victory in subsequent tests. Certainly, McGovern considered it quite an accomplishment that he performed so well in Iowa, considering that he was running against multimillion-dollar efforts from the other candidates. McGovern tried to convince the press and the public that his "bargain-rate third-place showing, a handful of votes behind [Hart's] second place, was a minor political miracle."[87]

For McGovern's volunteers, it was difficult to bring to a close an effort of such genuine dedication and caring. They stood together and worked hard to bring his message of courage and common sense to the country. Cathy Powell of McGovern's Washington, D.C., staff, said that her fellow volunteers could be "proud of the difference this campaign made and of what we did accomplish together." Their campaign, which overcame a late start, a skeptical press, and an extremely tight budget, earned them the respect of many political observers.[88]

McGovern had a long record of winning political elections in situations that, on paper, seemed quite improbable. He survived as a Democratic senator in conservative South Dakota longer than almost any other Democrat, a fact of which he was most proud.[89] Historians should not be asking, "Why did George McGovern lose the presidency in 1972, or his Senate seat in 1980?" but, rather, "How did McGovern manage to win all those years as a liberal Democrat in a largely conservative state?"[90]

It must be understood, though, that McGovern had no disrespect or resentment for conservatives. "The longer I live," he once observed, "the more important I think it is that we maintain both a strong liberal tradition and a strong, healthy conservative tradition, provided both stay close to the essentials." In McGovern's view, Ronald Reagan had strayed far from his conservative philosophy and, as a result, America was headed on a perilous course in 1984.[91]

Those who reflect upon McGovern's career tend to be refreshed by the man's faithfulness to his conscience. McGovern was willing to take on two popular presidents against overwhelming odds, because he felt it was the right thing to do.[92] He ran campaigns based on issues, rather than on rhetoric, and refused to play into the horse-race mentality of modern day politics.[93] McGovern's campaign philosophy seemed to sum up a great deal about himself: "If the voters agree with me, that's great, but if they don't, I'm not going to pull back. It never feels good, and I don't think it helps anybody, either. Every time I trimmed or modified in '72, I lost ground."[94]

George McGovern's illustrious career demonstrated that he was driven by a deep sense of compassion for his fellow man. He spoke out, time after time, in anguish against war and want. Robert F. Kennedy once observed that "the future does not belong to those who are content with today, apathetic toward common problems and their fellow man alike, timid and fearful in the face of new ideas and bold projects. Rather it will belong to those who can blend vision, reason and courage in a personal commitment to the ideals and great enterprises of American society."[95]

Back on June 6, 1966, Robert F. Kennedy delivered his now-famous Day of Affirmation Address at the University of Capetown in South Africa, in which he observed that "the enlargement of liberty for individual human beings must be the supreme goal and the abiding practice" of western society.

Few men are willing to brave the disapproval of their fellows, the censure of their colleagues, the wrath of their society. Moral courage is a rarer commodity than bravery in battle or great intelligence. Yet it is the one essential, vital quality for those who seek to change a world which yields most painfully to change . . . I believe that in this generation those with the courage to enter the conflict will find themselves with companions in every corner of the world.

For the fortunate amongst us . . . [there is] the temptation to follow the easy and familiar path of personal ambition and financial success so grandly spread before those who have the privilege of education. But that is not the road history has marked out for us. . . . Like it or not, we live in interesting times. They are times of danger and uncertainty; but they are also the most creative of any time in the history of mankind. And everyone . . . will ultimately be judged—will ultimately judge himself—on the effort he has contributed to building a new world society and the extent to which his ideals and goals have shaped that effort.[96]

Political commentator Bill Moyers advanced an intriguing thesis regarding McGovern's impact on the Democratic contest. He said that a major turning point was McGovern's concluding challenge in *The Des Moines Register* debate, which was "don't throw away your conscience." The wild, sustained applause that greeted this phrase led Mondale to tell McGovern, as they left the stage, "that one really hurt." According to Moyer's thesis, McGovern's phrase was the catalyst people were looking for to answer the invincibility argument that was Mondale's chief asset. Hart must have sensed this too, because he quickly followed the Iowa debate with radio ads that were heard across the state urging Iowans to vote their conscience. Having attacked Mondale directly at the Iowa debate, Hart appeared as the new "conscience alternative," whereas, having warned against destructive attacks on the possible nominee, McGovern was described by some reporters as a "blocking back" for Mondale in search of a Cabinet post.[97] However, these were the opinions of people who viewed George McGovern through skeptical eyes, believing that he was just another politician. This was simply not the case.

As Derek Maurer, endorsing McGovern in *The Daily Iowan*, so eloquently stated:

The 1972 election is not the proper measure of a man whose Washington political career spanned more than 20 years, including four years in the House, two years as special assistant to President Kennedy and director of the Food for Peace program and 18 years in the Senate. . . . In this day when many politicians hedge every bet, lace every statement with escape clauses and employ pollsters as top aides, McGovern would seem to be an anachronism. And what a refreshing anachronism—someone unafraid to espouse the values of charity, of true military restraint and of government's place in the promotion of social betterment. But for all this he does not sacrifice the practical skills of the consummate politician his career proves him to be.[98]

Perhaps Steven Pearlstein, editor of the *Boston Observer*, summed him up best. Pearlstein viewed McGovern as a liberal who brought "a moral perspective to government, not against it." He described McGovern as a "quiet, straight-shooting man with a wonderfully biting sense of humor."[99] Pearlstein's insight into George McGovern continued:

> He reaches for the heart, tugs at the conscience, and appeals to the common sense with programs no more or less radical than Reagan's. He is a seasoned, practical politician unafraid of his ideology or his own ideas. His pitch is to that set of traditional American values on the flip side of the American character: fairness; equality; a commitment to common, as opposed to private, wealth and enterprise.[100]

The final word, of course, should come from George McGovern himself. The former senator once said, "The right to propose new ideas and challenge old ones is the most imperative necessity. It is not simply something we allow, but something a free society demands. It is not just something we can live with; it is something we cannot live without. It is not only consistent with patriotism; it is the highest patriotism."[101] It is ideals like this that guided George McGovern on his long, storied path.

1984 Democratic Primaries and Caucuses

Delegate Total 3,933			
Date	**State**	**System**	**Delegate Votes**
February 20	Iowa	Caucus	58
February 28	New Hampshire	Primary	22
March 4	Maine	Caucus	27
March 6	Vermont	Caucus	17
March 10	Wyoming	Caucus	15
March 13	Massachusetts	Primary	116
	Alabama	Primary	62
	Florida	Primary	143
	Georgia	Primary	84
	Oklahoma	Caucus	53
	Washington	Caucus	70
	Rhode Island	Primary	27
	Democrats Abroad	Mail-In-Primary	5
	Hawaii	Caucus	27
	Nevada	Caucus	20
	American Samoa	Caucus	6
March 14	Delaware	Caucus	18
March 15	Alaska	Caucus	14
March 17	Mississippi	Caucus	43
	Canal Zone	Caucus	5
	South Carolina	Caucus	48

(*continued*)

Delegate Total 3,933

Date	State	System	Delegate Votes
	Arkansas	Caucus	42
	Michigan	Caucus	155
	Kentucky	Caucus	63
	North Dakota (14-28)	Caucus	18
March 18	Puerto Rico	Primary	53
March 20	Illinois	Primary	194
	Minnesota	Caucus	86
March 24	Kansas	Caucus	44
	Virginia (24-26)	Caucus	78
March 25	Montana	Caucus	25
March 27	Connecticut	Primary	60
March 31	Virgin Islands	Caucus	6
April 3	New York	Primary	285
April 7	Wisconsin	Caucus	89
	Louisiana	Caucus	69
April 10	Pennsylvania	Primary	195
April 14	Arizona	Caucus	40
	Guam	Caucus	7
April 16	Utah	Caucus	27
April 18	Missouri	Caucus	86
May 1	District of Columbia	Primary	19
	Tennessee	Primary	76
May 5	Texas	Caucus	200
May 7	Colorado	Caucus	51
May 8	Indiana	Primary	88
	North Carolina	Primary	88
	Maryland	Primary	74
	Ohio	Primary	175
May 15	Nebraska	Primary	30
	Oregon	Primary	50
May 24	Idaho	Caucus	22
June 5	California	Primary	345
	New Jersey	Primary	122
	New Mexico	Primary	28
	South Dakota	Primary	19
	West Virginia	Primary	44

Source: The Washington Post.

The New Realism: A Revival of the Old Common Sense

Presidential Announcement Speech of George McGovern

George Washington University, Washington, DC
11 a.m., Tuesday, September 13, 1983

Through my candidacy I intend to offer the American people a choice—not between party ideologies, not between liberal and conservative or right and left. The choice is whether our civilization can serve the freedom and happiness of every citizen, or whether we will become the ever more helpless servants of a society we have raised up to rule our lives.

We will not be helped to understanding by leadership built on image-making or television commercials; by those who seek power by back-room deals, coalitions of self-interest or a continued effort to adjust their policies to every seeming drift in public sentiment. . . . For my part, I make one pledge above all others—to seek and speak the truth.

I shall seek to call America home to those principles which gave us birth. I have found no better blueprint for healing our troubled land than is found in the Declaration of Independence, the Constitution, and the Bill of Rights.

—Excerpts from George McGovern's 1972
Presidential Announcement

That mission is just as urgent today as it was when nearly thirty-million American voters stood with me in 1972.

—George McGovern's, September 13, 1983

I have decided to seek the Presidency of the United States. I shall make that effort on a platform of realism and common sense. Fantasy may be good entertainment on the movie screen; it is not good policy for a great nation.

The new realism calls for a revival of the old common sense that has guided our greatest leaders since George Washington, who gave this University its proud name.

In the course of the campaign I will set forth what I believe to be commonsense positions on the major issues before the country, but I shall concentrate on these three propositions:

PROPOSITION I: There is no longer any alternative to what President Eisenhower described as "peaceful coexistence" except no existence.

PROPOSITION II: The age of big-power intervention in the internal affairs of small countries is over. It does not work any more.

PROPOSITION III: *American prosperity and power rest on faithfulness to our founding ideals including equal rights and equal opportunities for all Americans.*

As for the first proposition, the system of war as a means of settling international conflict is now obsolete. Both nuclear and conventional weapons have become so costly and so destructive that a peacetime arms race bankrupts the participants and a wartime use of modern weapons destroys the combatants. Modern warfare has erased the distinction between losers and winners: if war comes, all of us lose.

As a combat bomber pilot in the Second World War, I knew the horrors of war firsthand. Many of my young friends, including the navigator on my own crew, died before my eyes.

A decade ago I came to national prominence as a leader in the effort to end the war in Vietnam. After one of the longest and most wide-ranging campaigns in American history, I won the Democratic presidential nomination on a platform to end the war. Although the Vietnam struggle was the transcendent issue of that decade, both the Democratic Party and the nation were painfully divided on the question. In a sense that division led to my defeat by Mr. Nixon in the fall.

But I believed then as I do now that my candidacy helped in ending a conflict that nearly all Americans now realize was a dreadful mistake.

We conducted a campaign of which we can all be proud because it was an honorable campaign of candor, common sense and compassion. The funding of that campaign under the direction of my old friend Henry Kimelman has become a textbook model—not one dollar of deficit—not one hint of dishonesty.

History has already rendered its verdict upon the distortion, deceit, and shameful behavior of our opponents who were driven from office in disgrace a few months after the election.

But, my dear friends, now a decade later the issues before us are far more grave than in 1972. All men, women, and children now face the most awful decision which God has put to them since Creation—the question of whether human life can survive on this planet.

The recent outrageous shooting down of a passenger airliner that had strayed over Soviet territory underscores the folly of the present Cold War tension between Washington and Moscow. The present hair-trigger relationship is too risky. The next blunder might involve the explosion of a nuclear weapon.

Are we to be incinerated in a global war that begins with the folly of a single trigger-happy pilot, or an over-wrought field commander? Will Russians and Americans continue to squander their resources and exhaust their treasuries in manufacturing more and more engines of destruction in the fear that the other side is about to strike?

The President's most substantive reaction to the loss of the Korean airliner has been to renew his call for the MX missile. Is there any thoughtful person who believes that either commercial air travel or America itself will be more secure after we have gone another $100 billion into debt for yet another highly controversial new weapons system?

While the nation must preserve an adequate military deterrence against attack, there is neither security nor victory in either an open-ended arms race or in the actual use of the weapons of deterrence. The only realistic, commonsense course for the United States and the Soviet Union is to relentlessly pursue the discussion and settlement of disputes at the conference table. Better that old men lose their tempers at the conference table than that young men lose their lives on the battle field.

Instead of increasing military spending at a pace of 10 percent annually above the inflation rate as advocated by Mr. Reagan or a 5 to 7 percent increase as advocated by the other Democratic Presidential contenders, we should reduce military spending substantially after ratifying a verifiable arms control agreement with the Soviet Union.

President Eisenhower expressed the hope twenty-seven years ago that "... we will have sense enough to meet at the conference table with the understanding that the era of armaments has ended and the human race must conform its actions to this truth or die."

This is the common sense realism of a man who knew war firsthand—not just the glamourized wars of Hollywood.

I do not advocate unilateral disarmament. But I have no doubt that as President I could work out a realistic agreement with the Russian leaders that would stop the arms race and safely reduce arms spending.

I would not be seeking the Presidency a second time if I did not believe with all my heart and soul that I have the God-given capacity to lead this great nation away from the abyss into the ways that make for peace. I am speaking about hard-headed negotiations with the tough-minded leaders of the Soviet Union. I am speaking about having the informed judgment to end our deepening military involvement in Central America. I am speaking about having the sense of justice and prudence to tell the warring parties of the Middle East that there will be no more American aid and no more American soldiers unless Arabs and Israelis and Palestinians get to the conference table and begin at long last serious negotiations for peace.

As a student of history since childhood and as a seasoned public man who has grappled with political and international issues nearly all of my life, I believe that I am ready now as at no previous time in my life to lead this nation toward justice, honor and peace.

And now for the second proposition: It is no longer possible at acceptable cost for either Washington or Moscow to impose its will against the revolutionary currents of Central America, Afghanistan, Southeast Asia, Poland, Africa and the Middle East.

We Americans love freedom and hate oppression. But we came to greatness not by whimpering what we were *against* but by boldly proclaiming what we were *for*—the liberating, revolutionary ideals of Jefferson and Washington, Jackson and Lincoln, Wilson and Roosevelt.

Yet, we have trembled at and attempted to turn back the revolutionary currents which have convulsed countries from Vietnam and Angola, to Nicaragua and El Salvador. Of course Communists are involved in some of these revolutions. Of course the Russians may support them. But let it never be forgotten that these revolutions, misguided though they sometimes are, are revolts against centuries of oppression and exploitation.

We Americans dislike Communist governments. But we have also learned that with a little-hard-headed common sense and imagination we can live at peace with them and even influence their behavior in a limited way. Yugoslavia is an example of a Communist country that we approached in a practical and effective manner. President Nixon's decision to begin dealing with Communist China is another case in point. Diplomacy and trade are less costly than the shipment of American arms and less precious than American blood.

To be specific, as President, I would cease forthwith the so-called "covert war" against Nicaragua and end all United States military involvement in Central America. Not one drop of American blood would be shed on that soil. And America would not extract one drop of blood from the sons and daughters of Central America.

Certain persons now in power believe that the Russians and Cubans are causing all the trouble in Central America. But remove all Russians and Cubans and Central America would still be caught up in struggle and strife. And which side will we be on? On the side of oppression and shortsighted dictators? Or on the side of desperate peoples trying to find social and economic justice?

To be specific once more, I call for a new day in our relationship with Cuba. Our present policy of boycotting Cuba economically and isolating her diplomatically has been a disastrous failure for more than twenty years. We have done nothing but drive Cuba into the arms of the Soviet Union and into a hated dependence upon that country.

I have endorsed President Reagan's decision to sell American grain to the Soviet Union. I have endorsed former President Nixon's decision to open up the doors of diplomacy and trade to China. But if it makes sense to deal with the two *major* Communist powers, why do we back away in fear from diplomacy and trade with Cuba? Would dealing with Cuba really jeopardize American security?

In addressing the third and final proposition of this campaign, let me assert that there must at long last be an end to unequal treatment of any American and especially of that majority of Americans who are women.

The polling analysts have reported that in 1980 women voters were more opposed to Mr. Reagan's policies than were the men. These same analysts report that the "gender gap" verdict on Mr. Reagan is now widening. Thank God for the women of America! I believe that in 1984 women voters will lead us out of the wilderness of unfairness into that promised land of equality and justice for all Americans.

As for our economic problems, I flatly reject Reaganomics and the Reagan budget priorities. I do not blame Mr. Reagan for all the economic problems that face the country. The economy was in trouble before the present Administration came into power. But I am equally sure that Mr. Reagan's prescription is not the cure for our economic illness. The Reagan supply-side tax plan will cost the government an average of $125 billion annually in lost revenues with very little benefit to the average taxpayer. Nor has the tax cut achieved its announced objective of stimulating savings and investment in job creating enterprises. Savings have declined from 5% of GNP to 3% during the last three years and the tax cut has apparently been used more to finance corporate mergers than to create new jobs.

The Reagan program of military spending is not *really* a program. It is not practical defense. It is a wasteful binge, and it threatens the very vitality of our economy. Until 1965, it cost less than $100 billion to run the entire United States government. Current arms spending has now pushed military outlays alone beyond $200 billion a year. The man who promised a balanced budget has combined an unworkable tax scheme with a foolishly conceived arms spending explosion to produce a $200 billion *annual* federal deficit.

Of the total national debt accumulated since the days of George Washington, 41 percent will have been added by the present Administration. By any test, Mr. Reagan is the most reckless deficit financer in American history. He claims to be a conservative, but these are the facts. He has said in the past that I was too liberal, but if I had said in 1972 that a $200 billion annual deficit was acceptable, I wouldn't even have carried Massachusetts!

We must face the reality that no matter who is President there will be no end to rising deficits and recurring inflation until we end the terrible strain of an open-ended arms race. We must also cancel the unwise tax formula if 1981 and then go on to devise a simplified system of taxation such as the Bradley-Gephardt Fair Tax Bill that will be fair to income receivers of all categories.

Let us recognize, too, that there will be no end to the federal deficit and no increase in our productivity until we educate and train our people for productive work. So let us create a "Second Chance GI Bill of Rights," patterned along the lines of the program after the Second World War but open to all people.

Every American should have the opportunity, through low-cost government guaranteed loans, to have additional education and job training.

Nor will we end federal deficits while twelve million Americans are unemployed and therefore paying no taxes while collecting unemployment compensation or welfare. Each one percent of unemployment costs the national treasury $25 billion in lost revenues and paid out compensation. With ten percent of our people unemployed, the cost to the taxpayers is $250 billion each year. High deficits will not end until high unemployment ends.

So let us develop a carefully designed, businesslike program of public and private works to provide jobs for the balance of this century in rebuilding our railways, roads, water and sewage systems, alternative systems of energy, and the protection of our precious environment. Specifically, with industry and government cooperation let us commit America to building by the year 2000 the finest railway system in the world. Let us undertake an industry-government research effort to find safe and clean methods of utilizing America's vast coal reserves so that we can revitalize our coal industry and strengthen our energy security. Let us undertake a major tree planting and conserving program by our farmers and by a new Civilian Conservation Corps to halt the erosion of life sustaining top-soil. Let us also get the construction industry going again with a concerted effort to bring down interest rates so that the dream of home ownership will once again be a reality. I would recommend the availability of a one-time government-backed mortgage loan below ten percent for any American family.

Believing that the United States government can be a mighty force for human progress, I shall outline additional proposals for strengthening the economy as the campaign progresses. Mr. Reagan seems to believe that government is the enemy of the people. In truth, Democratic government is strength in our hands and hope in our hearts, not a burden on our backs.

American democracy at its best has been undergirded by the spiritual insight of the Hebrew Prophets and the Christian Gospel. Conversely, we have learned again in our time that politics devoid of a moral compass is a destructive enterprise. It is still true that "where there is no vision the people perish."

I believe that the American people want to see the light of this nation shine once again in all its grandeur. Let the light shine on those who long for peace; let the light shine on the despairing unemployed and the discouraged farmer; on the hungry and the homeless; on those who are old and lonely; on the troubled veterans of the Vietnam conflict; let the light shine on the dark recesses of discrimination; and let the light shine on our crime-ridden, drug-infested cities until once again it is safe to walk the streets of America.

And now an exciting and what can be a victorious campaign lies before us. No candidate can predict the public reaction to his appeal. Indeed, as Emerson has written, "None but he knows what he can do, nor does he know until he has tried." I do not know, if I can win this campaign, but I do know that with all my heart and strength I am going to try.

But let me remind you: the success of this campaign lies in *your* hands. Please, those of you at George Washington University and those who watch on television, if you will volunteer send your name, and if you can contribute send your dollars to the McGovern for President campaign. And now let us as Democrats and as Americans join hands around the table of common purpose and then go forward with a strong and active faith.

Address by Senator George McGovern to the Democratic National Convention

WEDNESDAY , JULY 18, 1984

SENATOR McGOVERN: Madam Chairperson, my fellow Democrats, my fellow Americans, I am glad to be in San Francisco tonight—a city with such brilliant political foresight that in the presidential election of 1972 it gave 60 percent of its vote to George McGovern. [Applause]

My supporters didn't win that year, nor did we win this year. But I'm glad we tried. [Applause]

A National Convention is a time of national soul-searching. It is a time to define the national purpose.

The question is not: Are we better off than we were four years ago? The question is: Where will America be four years from now? [Applause]

What is the American future? What kind of America do we want to be? Do we want an America that reserves the most generous benefits and tax breaks for the most powerful, or do we want the America of which Jesse Jackson has spoken that is devoted to justice and dignity for every citizen of this land? [Applause]

Do we want an America that provides guns for dictators and death squads, or do we want the kind of America of which Gary Hart speaks, that recognizes the chief cause of revolution in Central America is not Moscow or Havana but poverty and exploitation? [Applause]

Do we want an America that makes selfishness a public virtue, or do we want a leader like Walter Mondale, who, in Lincoln's phrase, will challenge the better angels of our nature? [Applause]

Do we want an America of confrontation and gunboat diplomacy or do we want an America that strives, as did Jimmy Carter, to uphold the standards of human rights? [Applause]

Do we want an America fearful of revolutionary change in the Third World, or do we want an America which, in John Kennedy's phrase, will make the world safe for diversity?

Do we want an America that treats half of its people as second-class-citizens, or do we want an America that can elevate a Geraldine Ferraro to national greatness? [Applause]

I want an America, as I said a decade ago, that is a witness to the world for what is decent and just in human affairs.

I want an America, in Jefferson's words, with "a decent respect for the opinions of mankind." I want an America where we care deeply about each other and our fellow inhabitants of planet Earth.

I want an America that builds both prosperity and peace from the bottom up, not from the top down. And we must do this not only because it is right, but because it is the only way that the American economy and American foreign policy can work. [Applause]

A selfish, shortsighted, trickle-down economics for the few simply does not work at home, and a foreign policy seeking to project privilege and power for the elite does not work abroad. [Applause]

Reaganism is not only at odds with the Judeo-Christian heritage, it will not work.

I want an America that deeply honors the old values of which Governor Cuomo spoke so eloquently—the values of family, of community, of patriotism, not the patriotism of superficial jingoism, but the quiet, steady effort to build an America that matches its performance with its most enduring ideals. [Applause]

And now may I saw to my fellow Americans: Do not deprive yourselves of the satisfactions of political struggle. Those who don't vote and have given up on politics have no right to complain about public policy. [Applause]

They have surrendered their national birthright—the right to exercise their voice in decisions that affect their lives.

As I. F. Stone has observed recently, "History is not a totally fatalistic drama. People can change it at least a little." I think he said, "It is a citizen's duty—and a journalist's duty—to fight. You never can tell, sometimes you win." [Applause]

Now in 1984 I knew that the odds were against a second McGovern nomination, but there were some questions I wanted to raise about the present course of the Democratic Party and the nation, and a new course I wanted to urge for the future. Those concerns remain, and let me underscore four of them tonight.

Point one: Terminate right now all U.S. military activities in Central America. [Applause] Mr. Reagan believes that all the trouble in Central America is caused by the Russians or the Cubans, but if we had the power here tonight to wave a magic wand and all Cubans and all Russians were to disappear, there would still be revolution in Central America. What we need in Central America is talks for peace, not troops for war.

Point two: Long before any of our marines were killed in Lebanon, some of us urged that they be brought home. Two hundred and sixty-five fine, young marines needlessly died in that ill-conceived attempt to substitute marines for diplomacy. The sacrifice of those marines should have been regarded as a shocking failure of presidential leadership. But instead, Mr. Reagan said, don't worry, it is my responsibility, and then diverted attention from his failure by a Hollywood-style invasion of the little island of Grenada. [Applause]

Four years ago, President Carter lost an election partly because American hostages were still held in Iran. And yet, every one of those hostages came home safe and sound. For his part, Mr. Reagan placed 1,600 marines as hostages in a recklessly exposed position at the Beirut airport, and 265 of them paid with their lives for this thoughtless, ill-advised decision. Never again should any American President send American boys abroad without a clearly defined mission and without the procedural safeguards of the United States Constitution. [Applause]

Point three: We should right now freeze the nuclear arms race and then cut the insane, bankrupting military spending binge of the Reagan Administration. [Applause]

As a bomber pilot in the second World War who saw most of my close friends killed in that conflict, I have always believed in a strong national defense, but I do not believe in wasting and weakening the nation paying for military paranoia. We have enough nuclear weapons right now to kill every inhabitant of this planet no matter what the Russians do.

So, why in God's name, does the President demand that we continue to spend and spend with ever greater deficits for more and more of these engines of death that may bankrupt our treasury and seal the fate of God's creation? [Applause]

Recently, I heard Colonel James Irwin, one of the astronauts who walked on the moon, describe the deep spiritual experience he felt in looking back from the vast reaches of space to our little planet Earth. "I wonder what our Creator thinks as He looks down on His Creatures. He sees a little band here in one corner of the globe digging holes in the ground for missiles to blow up another little band of our fellow creatures who are doing the same thing in another corner of the globe.

He sees people in each camp working hard and giving up needed services to pay for this mutually suicidal arms competition. It does not require the wisdom of God to know that these formulas are wrong morally, and, perhaps more to the point, they will fail practically. [Applause]

Point four: Stop paying farmers not to produce, and instead, assure them a fair price for winning the war against hunger in America and around the world. [Applause]

America has the best and most productive farmers in the world. Their productive abundance should be the glory of their effort, and yet, mistaken economic policies are driving them to bankruptcy. When I consider how hard farmers work and how little they receive, it almost breaks my heart.

So let's elect a Democratic President and a Democratic Congress and get a decent deal for these farmers of the country. [Applause] And then let's use their productive genius as a mighty tool for health and peace. I believe that American food abundance can do more to fill up the swamplands of hunger that breed communism than all the military hardware we have shipped to dictators around the world. [Applause]

I am going to tell you a story tonight, a true story. One night in 1968 I was watching a television documentary on hunger in America. In those days, a child who did not have the money went hungry during the school lunch hour. Focusing the camera on a little boy standing at the side of the room watching the other children eat, a reporter asked this youngster what he was thinking. He said, "I'm ashamed." "Why are you ashamed?" inquired the reporter. "Because, " said the little boy, "I haven't got any money."

Now, I thought to myself, it is not that little lad who should be ashamed. It is I as a United States Senator who should be ashamed. And that shame led to the creation of the Senate Committee on Nutrition and Human Needs of which I was the Chair. [Applause] And for the next decade, we waged a victorious battle against hunger and bad diets in America.

But for the last four years, Mr. Reagan has been shortchanging the war on hunger here on earth so that he can divert money for war in the skies.

I hope and pray that someday we will be able to proclaim that the greatest nation is not the one with the most missiles but the one that best ministers to the health, the education and the nutrition of its children. [Applause]

Now, I launched this recent campaign with one overriding pledge: to say exactly what I think about the Nation's problems. And I called on each American to be faithful to his or her own conscience. But I also thought it important to promote a conciliatory spirit among the Democratic contenders and within this party because in a democracy, conciliation must walk hand in hand with conscience.

And now is the time for all Democrats of conscience to unite behind a leadership dedicated to justice and to the ways that make for peace. [Applause]

These are the concerns that have kept me involved in the political struggle. They are the values that led me into the Democratic Party.

I believe this party is the party that breaks new ground, and, if I may be permitted a personal word on that matter: More than a decade ago, I chaired this party's Commission on Delegate Selection and Party Structure. Our findings were fair and just, but they were also controversial and disturbing to some of our fellow Democrats. We were attacked especially for asserting that henceforth women and Blacks and Hispanics and young people must be fairly represented in the presidential selection process. [Applause] But we were right and this party was right—and that historic action of 1972 helped mightily in opening the way for Geraldine Ferraro to become the Vice President of the United States. [Applause]

I am proud tonight of the sentiments that led my supporters to place my name in nomination. I'm proud too of the splendid Americans who have worked so hard for the nomination of Jesse Jackson and Gary Hart. Jesse Jackson has warmed our hearts and stirred our souls as only he can do. [Applause]

Gary Hart did me the honor of serving as my campaign manager a decade ago and now he has become an eloquent and powerful national voice calling us to the frontiers of the future. [Applause]

I salute also my fellow candidates of 1984, Reubin Askew, one of the greatest governors of one of the greatest states, Florida. [Applause]

Alan Cranston, who has achieved a high place in history by dedicating his campaign to the salvation of our civilization from nuclear annihilation. [Applause]

John Glenn, who has demonstrated both in space and on earth that he has the right stuff. [Applause]

Fritz Hollings, my seatmate for many years in the United States Senate, whom we all love not only for his courage and his conviction, but because he never forgets both the laughter and the tears of our human condition. [Applause]

It has been one of the blessed times of my life that I was permitted to seek high office in the presence of such men.

In 1980 I was defeated for reelection to the Senate partly by the accusations of extremist forces who characterized me as anti-family. And yet it is precisely because of the values instilled in me by my mother and father, the love and devotion for 40 years of dear Eleanor, the inspiration of my children and the generous opportunities provided me first by the people of South Dakota, and then by the larger Democratic family, that enabled me to come this far in political life.

I thank the Democratic Party and I thank America for giving me—a small-town lad from the South Dakota prairies—an opportunity to rise and to be heard in this magnificent national forum.

Thank you, my fellow Americans, for giving me the opportunity, more than once, to respond to these words of Oliver Wendell Holmes a century ago: "As life is action and passion, it is required of a man that he should share the passion and action of his time at peril of being judged not to have lived."

And now I ask that my name be withdrawn from nomination so that you can join with me in giving your energy and your voice to the election of a good, decent and strong man as President of the United States— Walter Mondale. [Applause]

Godspeed to all of you, my fellow Americans.

[Standing ovation]

GOVERNOR COLLINS: And now in order to recognize for the nomination of Reverent Jesse Jackson, the Chair recognizes Mayor Marion Barry, the Mayor of the District of Columbia.

Notes

PREFACE

1. Theodore H. White, *The Making of the President 1960*, (Atheneum Publishers, New York 1961), 338–341.
2. "Enthusiastic Crowd Hails McGovern's Appearance," *Waterbury American*, September 15, 1972.
3. Ibid.
4. Ibid.
5. Ibid.
6. Ibid.
7. Lloyd Shearer, "Senator George McGovern: First at the Starting Gate in the Presidential Race," *Parade*, August 1, 1971.
8. Robert Sam Anson, *McGovern* (Holt, Rinehart & Winston, New York, San Francisco, Chicago 1971), 164–165.

INTRODUCTION

1. "An Interview with George McGovern," *Playboy*, August 1971.
2. Patricia J. Donovan interviews, January 20, 2002 and February 6, 2002.
3. "An Interview with George McGovern," *Playboy*, August 1971.
4. Theodore H. White, *The Making of the President 1972*, (Atheneum Publishers, New York 1973), 118–119.
5. Ibid.
6. Jack W. Germond, *Fat Man in a Middle Seat*, (Random House, New York 1999), 99–104; Theodore H. White, *The Making of the President 1972*, (Atheneum Publishers, New York 1973), 40–41, 118–122; and Jules Witcover, *MARATHON: The Pursuit of the Presidency 1972–1976*, (The Viking Press, New York 1977), 174.
7. Jack W. Germond, *Fat Man in a Middle Seat*, (Random House, New York 1999), 103.
8. "How Radical Is McGovern?" *Newsweek*, June 19, 1972.

9. Lawrence F. O'Brien, *No Final Victories*, (Barone & Company, Washington, D.C. 1974) , 313–322.

10. Theodore H. White, *The Making of the President 1972*, (Atheneum Publishers, New York 1973), 226–227; and Lawrence F. O'Brien, *No Final Victories*, (Barone & Company, Washington D.C. 1974), 313–322.

11. Theodore H. White, *The Making of the President 1972*, (Atheneum Publishers, New York 1973), 221–228.

12. Patricia J. Donovan interviews, January 20, 2002 and February 6, 2002.

13. George V. Cunningham interviews, January 29, 2002 and February 19, 2002.

14. Patricia J. Donovan interviews, January 20, 2002 and February 6, 2002.

15. Letter to the author from Arthur M. Schlesinger Jr. dated July 28, 2000.

16. Miles Benson, "McGovern Resurrects His Dream," *Sunday Star-Ledger*, October 30, 1983.

17. Ibid.

18. Jack W. Germond, *Fat Man in a Middle Seat*, (Random House, New York 1999), 99; and John S. Monagan, *A Pleasant Institution*, (University Press of America, Lanham, Md. 2002), 372.

19. Jules Witcover, *MARATHON: The Pursuit of the Presidency 1972–1976*, (The Viking Press, New York 1977), 174; and John S. Monagan, *A Pleasant Institution*, (University Press of America, Lanham, Md. 2002), 372.

20. T.R. Reid, "Fighting the Loser Image," *Washington Post National Weekly Edition*, March 5, 1984.

21. Ibid.

22. Jack W. Germond, *Fat Man in a Middle Seat*, (Random House, New York 1999), 99.

23. William Greider, "The McGovern Factor," *Rolling Stone*, November 10, 1983.

24. "How Radical Is McGovern?" *Newsweek*, June 19, 1972; and " 'I Have Earned the Nomination,' " an interview by Richard Meryman, *LIFE*, July 7, 1972.

25. *Playboy*, August 1971.

26. "George McGovern: The Elixir of Politics," *CBS News*, February 26, 1984.

27. Lloyd Shearer, "Senator George McGovern: First at the Starting Gate in the Presidential Race," *Parade*, August 1, 1971.

28. Theodore H. White, *The Making of the President 1972*, (Atheneum Publishers, New York 1973), 41–42, 132–136; *GRASSROOTS: The Autobiography of George McGovern*, (Random House, New York 1977) 184–187; *The Keynoter*, Winter 1982, Volume 82, Number 4; and Richard Meryman, "The Infighting Was 'Ferocious,'" *LIFE*, July 21, 1972.

29. "How Radical Is McGovern?" *Newsweek*, June 19, 1972.

30. Paul Hendrickson, "George McGovern & The Coldest Plunge," *Washington Post*, September 28, 1983.

31. James M. Perry, "Teacher McGovern Considers Politics Another Classroom," *Wall Street Journal*, October 19, 1983.

32. George V. Cunningham interviews, January 29, 2002 and February 19, 2002.

33. George McGovern interview, February 13, 2002.

34. Lawrence F. O'Brien, *No Final Victories*, (Barone & Company, Washington, D.C. 1974), 333.

35. "How Radical Is McGovern?" *Newsweek*, June 19, 1972.

36. Theodore H. White, *The Making of the President 1972*, (Atheneum Publishers, New York 1973), 218, 359; and "How Radical Is McGovern?" *Newsweek*, June 19, 1972.

37. George McGovern interview, February 13, 2002.

38. *The Keynoter*, Winter 1982, Volume 82, Number 4.

39. Ibid.

40. Ibid.

41. Patricia J. Donovan interviews, January 20, 2002 and February 6, 2002.

42. George V. Cunningham interviews, January 29, 2002 and February 19, 2002.

43. Ibid.

44. Miles Benson, "McGovern Resurrects His Dream," *Sunday Star-Ledger*, October 30, 1983.

45. Ibid.

46. "How Radical Is McGovern?" *Newsweek*, June 19, 1972.

47. Ibid.

48. *The Keynoter*, Winter 1982, Volume 82, Number 4.

49. Paul Hendrickson, "George McGovern & the Coldest Plunge," *Washington Post*, September 28, 1983.

50. Jack W. Germond, *Fat Man in a Middle Seat*, (Random House, New York 1999), 103.

51. Paul Hendrickson, "George McGovern & the Coldest Plunge," *Washington Post*, September 28, 1983.

52. Lawrence F. O'Brien, *No Final Victories*, (Barone & Company, Washington, D.C. 1974), 319–320.

53. Lawrence F. O'Brien, *No Final Victories*, (Barone & Company, Washington, D.C. 1974), 333.

54. Brochure titled *The Clearest Choice of the Century*, published by the Finance Committee to Re-Elect the President, 1972.

55. Lawrence F. O'Brien, *No Final Victories*, (Barone & Company, Washington, D.C. 1974), 313–319.

56. Lawrence F. O'Brien, *No Final Victories*, (Barone & Company, Washington, D.C. 1974), 323–324.

57. Theodore H. White, *The Making of the President 1972*, (Atheneum Publishers, New York 1973), 226–229 ; and Lawrence F. O'Brien, *No Final Victories*, (Barone & Company, Washington, D.C. 1974), 319–321.

58. Lawrence F. O'Brien, *No Final Victories*, (Barone & Company, Washington, D.C. 1974), 324; and John S. Monagan, *A Pleasant Institution*, (University Press of America, Lanham, Md. 2002), 371–372.

59. Theodore H. White, *The Making of the President 1972*, (Atheneum Publishers, New York 1973), 226–229, 284; "How Radical Is McGovern?" *Newsweek*, June 19, 1972; and Lawrence F. O'Brien, *No Final Victories*, (Barone & Company, Washington, D.C. 1974), 324–326, 328–329.

60. Theodore H. White, *The Making of the President 1972*, (Atheneum Publish-

ers, New York 1973), 226–229, 284; opinion of author; and Lawrence F. O'Brien, *No Final Victories*, (Barone & Company, Washington, D.C. 1974), 295, 312, 320–321, 328–329.

61. "Can McGovern Put It All Together?" *Newsweek,* June 19,1972; and Lawrence F. O'Brien, *No Final Victories,* (Barone & Company, Washington, D.C. 1974), 320.

62. *The Keynoter,* Winter 1982, Volume 82, Number 4; and Richard Meryman, "The Infighting Was 'Ferocious,' " *LIFE,* July 21, 1972.

63. Ibid.

64. Theodore H. White, *The Making of the President 1972,* (Atheneum Publishers, New York 1973), 120; *GRASSROOTS: The Autobiography of George McGovern,* (Random House, New York 1977), 30–49; and Robert Sam Anson, *McGovern: A Biography,* (Holt, Rinehart & Winston, New York, San Francisco, Chicago 1971), 49–63.

65. *The Tumbleweed,* Dakota Wesleyan University, 1952.

66. *GRASSROOTS: The Autobiography of George McGovern,* (Random House, New York 1977), 51–71.

67. T.R. Reid, "Fighting the Loser Image," *Washington Post National Weekly Edition,* March 5, 1984.

68. *GRASSROOTS: The Autobiography of George McGovern,* (Random House, New York 1977), 79–97, 104–112.

69. *The Keynoter,* Winter 1982, Volume 82, Number 4; and David Kranz, "McGovern and LBJ," *Sioux Falls Argus-Leader,* February 17, 2002.

70. David Kranz, "McGovern and LBJ," *Sioux Falls Argus-Leader,* February 17, 2002.

71. Lawrence F. O'Brien, *No Final Victories,* (Barone & Company, Washington, D.C. 1974), 190.

72. Ibid., 250.

73. Ibid., 288–289.

74. *GRASSROOTS: The Autobiography of George McGovern,* (Random House, New York 1977), 108–127; Theodore H. White, *The Making of the President 1972,* (Atheneum Publishers, New York 1973), 40; and Robert Sam Anson, *McGovern,* (Holt, Rinehart & Winston, New York, San Francisco 1971), 193–210.

75. T.R. Reid, "Fighting the Loser Image," *Washington Post National Weekly Edition,* March 5, 1984.

76. *Playboy,* August 1971.

77. Lawrence F. O'Brien, *No Final Victories,* (Barone & Company, Washington, D.C. 1974), 262, 265; and Theodore H. White, *The Making of the President 1968,* (Atheneum Publishers, New York 1969), 396.

78. Lawrence F. O'Brien, *No Final Victories,* (Barone & Company, Washington, D.C. 1974), 289–291.

79. Theodore H. White, *The Making of the President 1972,* (Atheneum Publishers, New York 1973), 41.

80. Lawrence F. O'Brien, *No Final Victories,* (Barone & Company, Washington, D.C. 1974), 289–291.

81. Lawrence F. O'Brien, *No Final Victories,* (Barone & Company, Washington, D.C. 1974), 291–292.

82. Ibid., 292.

83. Ibid., 294.

84. Ibid., 295–297, 306, 319, 328–329.

85. Ibid., 295–296.

86. *The Keynoter*, Winter 1982, Volume 82, Number 4.

87. Lawrence F. O'Brien, *No Final Victories*, (Barone & Company, Washington, D.C. 1974), 306.

88. Ibid., 309–312.

89. Ibid., 312.

90. Ibid., 308.

91. Theodore H. White, *The Making of the President 1972*, (Atheneum Publishers, New York 1973), 175; and Richard Meryman, "The Infighting Was 'Ferocious,'" *LIFE*, July 21, 1972.

92. Lawrence F. O'Brien, *No Final Victories*, (Barone & Company, Washington, D.C. 1974), 307–308, 313–316, 319.

93. Ibid., 295, 315, 319, 323–324. For further discussion and insider views of the problems plaguing the McGovern campaign, read Gordon W. Weil, *The Long Shot*, (W. W. Norton Company, New York 1973); and Richard Dougherty, *Goodbye, Mr. Christian*, (Doubleday & Company, Garden City, New York 1973).

94. Lawrence F. O'Brien, *No Final Victories*, (Barone & Company, Washington, D.C.1974), 326–328.

95. Opinion of the author.

96. "How Radical Is McGovern?" *Newsweek*, June 19, 1972; John S. Monagan, *A Pleasant Institution*, (University Press of America, Lanham, Md. 2002), 371–373; and Lawrence F. O'Brien, No Final Victories, (Barone & Company, Washington D.C.) 1974, 312, 328.

97. "Can McGovern Put It All Together?" *Newsweek,* June 19, 1972; Jack W. Germond, *Fat Man in a Middle Seat*, (Random House, New York 1999), 99; and John S. Monagan, *A Pleasant Institution*, (University Press of America, Lanham, Md. 2002) 371–372.

98. "How Radical Is McGovern?" *Newsweek*, June 19, 1972; and Theodore H. White, *The Making of the President 1972*, (Atheneum Publishers, New York 1973), 40.

99. "How Radical Is McGovern?" *Newsweek*, June 19, 1972.

100. "Can McGovern Put It All Together?" *Newsweek*, June 19, 1972.

101. Thomas P. "Tip" O'Neill with William Novak, *Man of the House*, (Random House, New York 1987) 298.

102. George V. Cunningham interviews, January 29, 2002 and February 19, 2002.

103. David Kranz, "McGovern and LBJ," *Sioux Falls Argus-Leader*, February 17, 2002.

104. George V. Cunningham interviews, January 29, 2002 and Febuary 19, 2002; and John S. Monagan, *A Pleasant Institution*, (University Press of America, Lanham, Md. 2002), 371–372.

105. "How Radical Is McGovern?" *Newsweek*, June 19, 1972.

106. Ibid.

107. "Can McGovern Put It All Together?" *Newsweek,* June 19, 1972; and John

S. Monagan, *A Pleasant Institution*, (University Press of America, Lanham, Md. 2002), 371–372.

108. Gary Warren Hart, *Right from the Start*, (Quadrangle/The New York Times Book Co., New York 1973) 323–330; and Lawrence F. O'Brien, *No Final Victories*, (Barone & Company, Washington, D.C. 1974), 326.

109. *The Keynoter*, Winter 1982, Volume 82, Number 4.

110. "Can McGovern Put It All Together?" *Newsweek*, June 19, 1972.

111. Lawrence F. O'Brien, *No Final Victories*, (Barone & Company, Washington, D.C. 1974), 320.

112. Jules Witcover, *MARATHON: The Pursuit of the Presidency 1972–1976*, (The Viking Press, New York 1977), 179.

113. Ibid.; Lawrence F. O'Brien, *No Final Victories*, (Barone & Company, Washington, D.C. 1974), 333; and Jack W. Germond, *Fat Man in a Middle Seat*, (Random House, New York 1999), 104.

114. Gary Warren Hart, *Right from the Start*, (Quadrangle/The New York Times Book Co., New York 1973), 323–330; and Lawrence F. O'Brien, *No Final Victories*, (Barone & Company, Washington, D.C. 1974), 326.

115. T.R. Reid, "Fighting the Loser Image," *Washington Post National Weekly Edition*, March 5, 1984.

116. Ibid.

117. Ibid.

118. Phil Gailey, "For McGovern, the Second Time Around Is Good," *New York Times*, November 3, 1984.

119. George McGovern, "McGovern's Campaign Not Quixotic," *Waterbury American*, October 7, 1983.

120. Ibid.

121. *The Keynoter*, Winter 1982, Volume 82, Number 4.

122. George McGovern, "McGovern's Campaign Not Quixotic," *Waterbury American*, October 7, 1983.

123. *GRASSROOTS: The Autobiography of George McGovern*, (The Viking Press, New York 1977), 257.

124. Jules Witcover, *MARATHON: The Pursuit of the Presidency 1972–1976*, (The Viking Press, New York 1977), 178–181.

125. Ibid., 174

126. Ibid., 175–176.

127. Ibid., 178.

128. Ibid., 179–180.

129. Ibid., 181.

130. Phil Gailey, "For McGovern, the Second Time Around Is Good," *New York Times*, November 3, 1983.

131. A letter by George McGovern to a constituent, March 29, 1963.

132. Richard Meryman, " 'I Have Earned The Nomination,' " *LIFE*, July 7, 1972, p. 33.

133. Lloyd Shearer, "Senator George McGovern: First at the Starting Gate in the Presidential Race," *Parade*, August 1, 1971.

134. Patricia J. Donovan interviews January 20, 2002 and February 6, 2002, quoting "Friend of Farmers," *New York Times*, March 31, 1961.

CHAPTER 1

1. "Conservatives Plan $700,000 Drive to Oust 5 Democrats from Senate," *New York Times*, August 17, 1979.

2. George McGovern interview, February 13, 2002.

3. "Conservatives Plan $700,000 Drive to Oust 5 Democrats from Senate," *New York Times*, August 17, 1979.

4. Ibid.

5. Ibid.

6. *Daily Republic*, February 12, 1980.

7. "McGovern Reacts to Charges Leveled in Ads," *Daily Republic*, February 14, 1980.

8. Ibid.

9. Ibid.

10. *Daily Republic*, February 12, 1980.

11. "McGovern Reacts to Charges Leveled in Ads," *Daily Republic*, February 14, 1980.

12. Ibid.

13. Ibid.

14. Vince Stricherz, "Byrd Supports McGovern Bid," *Daily Republic*, February 14, 1980.

15. Ibid.

16. Ibid.

17. Ibid.

18. Ibid.

19. Ibid.

20. Vince Stricherz, "McGovern Announces Re-Election Bid In Mitchell," *Daily Republic*, February 14, 1980.

21. Ibid.

22. Ibid.

23. Ibid.

24. Ibid.

25. Ibid.

26. Ibid.

27. Bernard Weinraub, "Million-Dollar Drive Aims to Oust 5 Liberals," *New York Times*, March 24, 1980.

28. Ibid.

29. Ibid.

30. Ibid.

31. Ibid.

32. Ibid.

33. Ibid.

34. Ibid.

35. Ibid.

36. Leslie Bennetts, "Conservative and Anti-Abortion Groups Press Attack against McGovern," *New York Times*, June 2, 1980.

37. Ibid.

38. Ibid.

39. Ibid.

40. Ibid.

41. Ibid.

42. George V. Cunningham interviews, January 29, 2002 and February 19, 2002.

43. Leslie Bennetts, "Conservative and Anti-Abortion Groups Press Attack against McGovern," *New York Times*, June 2, 1980.

44. Ibid.

45. George McGovern, "The Unfinished Agenda of 1980: Survival," *Congressional Record*, Vol. 126, No. 123, August 4, 1980.

46. Ibid.

47. Ibid.

48. Ibid.

49. Ibid.

50. "Doomed McGovern?" *Wall Street Journal*, August 15, 1980.

51. Steven V. Roberts, "McGovern in New Battle for Survival," *New York Times*, September 15, 1980.

52. Wayne King, "McGovern, Long a Target, Finds Rewards in Taking the Offensive," *New York Times*, October 20, 1980.

53. George V. Cunningham interviews, January 29, 2002 and February 19, 2002.

54. Steven V. Roberts, "McGovern in New Battle for Survival," *New York Times*, September 15, 1980.

55. Ibid.

56. Ibid.

57. Ibid.

58. George McGovern interview, February 13, 2002; and Steven V. Roberts, "McGovern in New Battle for Survival," *New York Times*, September 15, 1980.

59. James M. Perry, "Anti-Family Charge and a Popular Foe Endanger McGovern," *Wall Street Journal*, September 23, 1980.

60. "The Senate: Arguing on the Issues," *Time*, October 6, 1980.

61. James M. Perry, "Anti-Family Charge and a Popular Foe Endanger McGovern," *Wall Street Journal*, September 23, 1980.

62. Ibid.

63. Ibid.

64. Lucia Mouat, "South Dakota—Will McGovern Liberalism Be Plowed Under?" *Christian Science Monitor*, September 30, 1980.

65. James M. Perry, "Anti-Family Charge and a Popular Foe Endanger McGovern," *Wall Street Journal*, September 23, 1980.

66. Anthony Lewis, "Backlash in South Dakota?" *New York Times*, October 13, 1980.

67. Lucia Mouat, "South Dakota—Will McGovern Liberalism Be Plowed Under?" *Christian Science Monitor*, September 30, 1980.

68. Anthony Lewis, "Backlash in South Dakota?" *New York Times*, October 13, 1980.

69. Lucia Mouat, "South Dakota—Will McGovern Liberalism Be Plowed Under?" *Christian Science Monitor*, September 30, 1980.

70. "The Senate: Arguing on the Issues," *Time*, October 6, 1980.

71. Ibid.

72. Ibid.

73. Anthony Lewis, "Backlash in South Dakota?" *New York Times*, October 13, 1980.

74. Ibid.

75. Charles Raasch, "Test of a Liberal Handshake. South Dakota," *New Republic*, October 25, 1980.

76. George V. Cunningham interviews, January 29, 2002 and February 19, 2002.

77. Wayne King, "McGovern, Long a Target, Finds Rewards in Taking the Offensive," *New York Times*, October 20, 1980.

78. Michael Barone and Grant Ujifusa, *The Almanac of American Politics 1982*, (Barone & Company, Washington, D.C. 1981), 1016–1022.

79. Charles Raasch, "Test of a Liberal Handshake. South Dakota," *New Republic*, October 25, 1980.

80. Ibid.

81. Anthony Lewis, "Backlash in South Dakota?" *New York Times*, October 13, 1980.

82. T.R. Reid, "Exorcising the Ghost of 1972," *Washington Post*, January 14, 1984.

83. Paul Hendrickson, "George McGovern & the Coldest Plunge," *Washington Post*, September 28, 1983.

84. Ibid.

85. Ibid.; and George McGovern interview, February 13, 2002.

86. Paul Hendrickson, "George McGovern & the Coldest Plunge," *Washington Post*, September 28, 1983.

87. Patricia J. Donovan interviews, January 20, 2002 and February 6, 2002.

88. George V. Cunningham interviews, January 29, 2002 and February 19, 2002.

89. Senator Edward M. Kennedy, "The Commonsense of George McGovern," *Congressional Record*, Volume 126, No. 170, Part II, December 4, 1980. Senator Edward M. Kennedy also delivered a speech on the floor of the U.S. Senate titled "The Greatness of George McGovern." See *Congressional Record*, December 10, 1980.

90. Paul Hendrickson, "George McGovern & the Coldest Plunge," *Washington Post*, September 28, 1983.

91. Fred Barnes, "McGovern Working to Promote 'Common Sense' in Politics," *Sun*, [n.d.] 1981.

92. George McGovern, "The New Right and The Old Paranoia," *Playboy*, January 1981; and Senator Edward M. Kennedy, "The Commonsense of George McGovern," *Congressional Record*, Volume 126, No. 170, Part II, December 4, 1980.

93. Ibid.

94. Ibid.

95. Ibid.

96. Ibid.

97. Ibid.

98. Ibid.

99. Ibid.

100. Ibid.

101. Ibid.

102. Letter from George McGovern in early 1981 to former supporters making them "Honorary Charter Members" of Americans for Common Sense.

103. Brochure for Americans for Common Sense.

104. Letter from George McGovern in early 1981 to former supporters making them "Honorary Charter Members" of Americans for Common Sense.

105. Brochure for Americans for Common Sense.

106. Ibid.

107. Fred Barnes, "McGovern Working to Promote 'Common Sense' in Politics," *Sun*, [n.d.] 1981.

108. Ibid.

109. Ibid.

110. Brochure titled *Public Questions about Americans for Common Sense*, published by Americans for Common Sense.

111. Ibid.

112. Memorandum from George McGovern, Chairman, Americans for Common Sense, to ACS members regarding current ACS actitivies, May 1981.

113. Ibid.

114. "The Election of 1980 and the Future of Soviet-American Relations," a lecture given by George McGovern at the Dr. Karl Renner Institut, Vienna, Austria, on June 29, 1981.

115. Ibid.

116. Ibid.

117. Ibid.

118. Ibid.

119. Ibid.

120. Letter from George McGovern to Americans for Common Sense members regarding the "Common Sense Radio Project," June 1981.

121. Americans for Common Sense newsletter, undated.

122. *RightWatch* 1, no. 1 (August 1981), published by Americans for Common Sense.

123. Letter from George McGovern, Chairman, Americans for Common Sense, to ACS members, August 1981.

124. George McGovern interview, February 13, 2002.

125. Letter from George McGovern, Chairman of the American for Common Sense, to ACS members regarding the "National Campaign on Defense Policy," Fall 1981.

126. Americans for Common Sense *National Campaign on Defense Policy* brochure regarding excessive military spending and an escalated arms race.

127. "American Foreign Policy: Two Idealisms," a lecture given by George McGovern at Northwestern University, March 30, 1981.

128. Ibid.

129. Ibid.

130. Paul Clancy, "McGovern Blends Old and New for Warm George Mason Crowd," *Washington Star*, March 4, 1981.

131. Tom Callahan, "McGovern Criticizes Reagan's Political Agenda," *Fairfield Mirror*, March 11, 1982.

132. John Steinbreder, "McGovern Calls Liberals to Arms," *Fairfield Citizen-News*, March 5, 1982.

133. Ibid.

134. Lecture by George McGovern, "Reagan and the Liberal Alternative," March 2, 1982, Fairfield University, sponsored by the Fairfield University Young Democrats; and George McGovern, "Policies Democrats Should Pursue," *New York Times*, April 3, 1982.

135. Ibid.

136. Ibid.

137. John Steinbreder, "McGovern Calls Liberals to Arms," *Fairfield Citizen-News*, March 5, 1982.

138. Ibid.

139. Ibid.

140. Ibid.

141. Ibid.

142. An interview with George McGovern, undated, sent to Americans for Common Sense members after the 1982 elections.

CHAPTER 2

1. Diane Gross, "Primaries," *George*, April 2000.

2. Rosanah James Benett, "George McGovern: What Makes Him Run?" *American Politics*, January 1984.

3. Ibid.

4. A letter to Eleanor McGovern from George McGovern, January 17, 1988.

5. George Cunningham interviews, January 29, 2002 and February 19, 2002.

6. Rosanah James Benett, "George McGovern: What Makes Him Run?" *American Politics*, January 1984.

7. Lecture by George McGovern, "Reagan and the Liberal Alternative," March 2, 1982, Fairfield University, sponsored by the Fairfield University Young Democrats.

8. Discussion of Senator McGovern with the author, March 3, 1982; and a letter to the author from George McGovern, August 24, 1982.

9. A letter to the author from George McGovern, April 7, 1983.

10. *New York Daily News*, October 6, 1982.

11. A letter to the author from George McGovern, April 7, 1983.

12. Associated Press, "McGovern Weighs Bid for Presidency," July 18, 1983, reporting on a *Los Angeles Times* interview with George McGovern.

13. Ibid.

14. Ibid.; and an interview with George McGovern by the author, February 13, 2002.

15. Associated Press, "McGovern Weighs Bid for Presidency," July 18, 1983, reporting on a *Los Angeles Times* interview with George McGovern.

16. Ibid.

17. Ibid.

18. Ibid.

19. Ibid.

20. Ibid.

21. "A McGovern Run?" *Washington Post*, September 9, 1983.

22. Ibid.

23. Ibid.

24. From poll taker Patrick Caddell's privately circulated paper, "The State of American Politics," October 1983, urging a Democratic candidacy of fresh blood and new ideas.

25. George McGovern, "McGovern's Campaign Not Quixotic," *Waterbury American*, October 7, 1983.

26. George, McGovern, "I'm Glad I Tried," *Washington Post*, March 18, 1984.

27. George McGovern, "McGovern's Campaign Not Quixotic," *Waterbury American*, October 7, 1983.

28. Ibid.

29. Ibid.

30. Ibid.

31. Paul Hendrickson, "George McGovern & the Coldest Plunge," *Washington Post*, September 28, 1983.

32. Ibid.

33. Ibid.

34. A letter to Eleanor McGovern from George McGovern, January 17, 1988.

35. Paul Hendrickson, "George McGovern & the Coldest Plunge," *Washington Post*, September 28, 1983.

36. Ibid.

37. *Meet the Press*, A Public Affairs Presentation of NBC News. Guest: George McGovern, Sunday, November 13, 1983. Volume 83—Panel: Bill Monroe, NBC News; Marianne Means, Hearst Newspapers; Charles McDowell, *Richmond Times-Dispatch*; William Greider, *Rolling Stone;* and Moderator, Marvin Kalb, NBC News.

38. Paul Hendrickson, "George McGovern & the Coldest Plunge," *Washington Post*, September 28, 1983.

39. Rosanah James Benett, "George McGovern: What Makes Him Run?" *American Politics,* January 1984.

40. Ibid.

41. Associated Press, "McGovern to Enter Presidential Race," September 13, 1983.

42. "McGovern Banks on Left," *USA Today*, September 13, 1983.

43. Phil Gailey, "For McGovern, the Second Time Around is Good." *New York TImes*, November 3, 1983; and miscellaneous newspaper reports, September 14, 1983.

44. Announcement to the press, statement of Senator George McGovern, September 13, 1983.

45. Ibid.

46. Ibid.

47. Ibid.

48. Ibid.

49. Phil Gailey, "Restless McGovern Renews Quest for Presidency," *New York Times*, September 14, 1983.

50. Ibid.; and "The New Realism: A Revival of the Old Common Sense," Presi-

dential Announcement Speech of George McGovern, George Washington University, September 13, 1983.

51. Phil Gailey, "Restless McGovern Renews Quest for Presidency," *New York Times*, September 14, 1983.

52. Ibid.

53. Ibid.

54. Ibid.; and "The New Realism: A Revival of the Old Common Sense," Presidential Announcement Speech of George McGovern, George Washington University, September 13, 1983.

55. Ibid.

56. Ibid.

57. Phil Gailey, "Restless McGovern Renews Quest for Presidency," *New York Times*, September 14, 1983.

58. Ibid.

59. "McGovern Banks on Left," *USA Today*, September 13, 1983.

60. Associated Press, "McGovern to Enter Presidential Race," September 13, 1983.

61. Phil Gailey, "Restless McGovern Renews Quest for Presidency," *New York Times*, September 14, 1983.

62. Ibid.

63. Associated Press, "McGovern to Enter Presidential Race," September 13, 1983.

64. Ibid.

65. Rosanah James Benett, "George McGovern: What Makes Him Run?" *American Politics*, January 1984.

66. Ibid.

67. Paul Hendrickson, "George McGovern & the Coldest Plunge," *Washington Post*, September 28, 1983.

68. Ibid.

69. Rosanah James Benett, "George McGovern: What Makes Him Run?" *American Politics*, January 1984.

CHAPTER 3

1. "Candidate George McStassen," *The Chicago Tribune*, September 14, 1983.

2. "Not George, Again," *Waterbury American*, September 14, 1983.

3. For examples of how George McGovern was portrayed in editorial cartoons during the 1984 presidential campaign, see the fourteen cartoons reprinted in this book.

4. Alexander Cockburn and James Ridgeway, "McGovern: Remember What a Real Liberal Looks Like?" *The Village Voice*, September 27, 1983.

5. Ibid.

6. T.R. Reid, "Fighting the Loser Image," *Washington Post National Weekly Edition*, March 5, 1984.

7. Ibid.

8. James Reston, "What Makes Them Run?," *New York Times* [n.d.].

9. R. Emmett Tyrell Jr., "Democratic Celebrities Seek Office." [syndicated column, n.d.]

10. *New Republic*, October 3, 1983.

11. "McGovern Picks Up McGovern's Standard," Letter to the Editor, *New York Times*, October 16, 1983, from Professors Richard Parker, Lewis Sargentich, and Duncan Kennedy, and four additional members of the Harvard Law School Faculty.

12. George Gallup, *Los Angeles Times*, October 9, 1983.

13. *Atlanta Journal*, October 10, 1983.

14. *Sioux Falls Argus-Leader*, October 12, 1983.

15. "Don't Laugh," endorsement in *Philadelphia Daily News* [n.d.].

16. Rosanah James Benett, "George McGovern: What Makes Him Run?" *American Politics*, January 1984.

17. "Progressive Voice," endorsement in *Daily Iowan*, February 17, 1984.

18. *Meet the Press*, A Public Affairs Presentation of NBC News. Guest: George McGovern, Sunday, November 13, 1983. Volume 83—Panel: Bill Monroe, NBC News; Marianne Means, Hearst Newspapers; Charles McDowell, *Richmond Times-Dispatch*; William Greider, *Rolling Stone*; and Moderator, Marvin Kalb, NBC News.

19. *Des Moines Register*, October 5, 1983.

20. Campaign literature authorized by the McGovern for President Committee.

21. Bill Peterson, "McGovern Uses Long-Shot Status to Speak Freely," *Washington Post*, November 28, 1983.

22. David Nyhan, *Boston Globe*, November 27, 1983.

23. William Greider, "The McGovern Factor," *Rolling Stone*, November 10, 1983.

24. Ibid.

25. Ibid.; and George McGovern interview, August 23, 2000.

26. William Greider, "The McGovern Factor," *Rolling Stone*, November 10, 1983.

27. Steven Pearlstein, "Don't Blame Me . . . Endorsing George McGovern, a Democrat Who Remembers What Liberalism Is About," *Boston Observer* 3, no. 2 (February 1984).

28. Ibid.

29. Ibid.

30. Stephen Stark, "The Outsider Is Beginning to Look Good," *Stamford Advocate*, February 1984.

CHAPTER 4

1. T.R. Reid, "Exorcising the Ghost of 1972," *Washington Post*, January 14, 1984.

2. Bill Peterson, "McGovern Is Not a Democratic Harold Stassen," *Washington Post*, December 12, 1983.

3. George V. Cunningham interviews, January 29, 2002 and February 19, 2002.

4. Ibid.

5. Bill Peterson, "McGovern Is Not a Democratic Harold Stassen," *Washington Post*, December 12, 1983.

6. Ibid.

7. George V. Cunningham interviews, January 29, 2002 and February 19, 2002.

8. George McGovern interview, February 13, 2002.

9. Bill Peterson, "McGovern Is Not a Democratic Harold Stassen," *Washington Post*, December 12, 1983.

10. Ibid.

11. George McGovern, "McGovern's Campaign Not Quixotic," *Waterbury American*, October 7, 1983.

12. Bill Peterson, "McGovern Is Not a Democratic Harold Stassen," *Washington Post*, December 12, 1983.

13. Phil Gailey, "For McGovern, the Second Time Around Is Good," *New York Times*, November 3, 1983.

14. Ibid.

15. Ibid.

16. Fay S. Joyce, "McGovern Seeks Effect on Party Policy Debate," *New York Times*, December 29, 1983.

17. Ibid.

18. Ibid.

19. Ibid.

20. *Sioux Falls Argus-Leader*, November 22, 1983.

21. Ibid.

22. Fay S. Joyce, "McGovern Seeks Effect on Party Policy Debate," *New York Times*, December 29, 1983.

23. Ibid.

24. William Keyserling, "It's Wrong for the Media to Write Off the Other Candidates," *Washington Post*, January 9, 1984.

25. Ibid.

26. Ibid.

27. Ibid.

28. Ibid.

29. Ibid.

30. Ibid.

31. Ibid.

32. Ibid.

33. Ibid.

34. Ibid.

35. T.R. Reid, "Exorcising the Ghost of 1972," *Washington Post*, January 14, 1984.

36. Ibid.

37. Associated Press, "Democrats Rap Reagan, and Each Other," October 7, 1983.

38. "Presidential Candidates' Forum on Arms Control," published by the Massachusetts Citizens Coalition for Arms Control.

39. Robert Pear, "7 Presidential Contenders Debate Arms Control," *New York Times*, October 14, 1983.

40. Presidential Debate on Nuclear Arms, cosponsored by the Massachusetts Citizens Coalition for Arms Control and Harvard University's Institute of Policy, October 13, 1983, Cambridge, Massachusetts.

41. Ibid.

42. Ibid.

43. George Gallup, "McGovern Affects Mondale's Lead," George Gallup, *Los Angeles Times Syndicate*, October 9, 1983.

44. Ibid.

45. Frank Lynn, "Cuomo and Moynihan Back Mondale," *New York Times*, October 14, 1983.

46. Howell Raines, "Mondale Had Good '83; Now the Real Test Begins," *New York Times*, December 12, 1983.

47. "From McGovern Headquarters," news about the campaign authorized by the McGovern for President Committee, December 12, 1983, quoting David Nyhan in the *Boston Globe*.

48. "From McGovern Headquarters," news about the campaign authorized by the McGovern for President Committee, December 12, 1983.

49. Ibid.

50. "From McGovern Headquarters," news about the campaign authorized by the McGovern for President Committee, December 12, 1983.

51. Donald M. Rothberg, "Democrats Open Money Drive," Associated Press, December 6, 1983.

52. "Upcoming Events," news about the campaign authorized by the McGovern for President Committee, December 12, 1983.

53. Associated Press. [n.d.]

54. *New York Times*, December 7, 1983.

55. *Time*, December 19, 1983.

56. "On The Campaign Trail," news about the campaign authorized by the McGovern for President Committee, December, 1983.

57. Ibid.

58. Ibid.

59. Ibid.

60. "Media Notes . . ." news about the campaign authorized by the McGovern for President Committee, January 16, 1984, quoting John Patrick Hunter, *Capitol Times*, December 15, 1983.

61. "Media Notes . . ." news about the campaign authorized by the McGovern for President Committee, January 16, 1984, quoting Curtis Wilkie, "McGovern Bid Unusual for Candor, Liberalism," *Boston Globe*, December 18, 1983.

62. "Media Notes . . ." news about the campaign authorized by the McGovern for President Committee, January 16, 1984, quoting Tom Wicker, "The Right Stuff," *New York Times*, December 26, 1983.

63. Ibid.

64. "Media Notes . . ." news about the campaign authorized by the McGovern for President Committee, January 16, 1984, quoting Ellen Goodman, "Did I Say That?" *Washington Post*, December 31, 1983.

65. William Schneider, *Los Angeles Times*, "About Those Polls: Be Wary of Them," *The* (Tacoma) *News Tribune*, December 27, 1983.

66. Ibid.

67. "From McGovern Headquarters," news about the campaign authorized by the McGovern for President Commitee, January 16, 1984.

68. "Upcoming Events," news about the campaign authorized by the McGovern for President Committee, January 16, 1984; and Christopher Lydon, "Campaigning with an Old Pro: Revisionism and the Social Gospel," *Boston Observer* 3, no. 2 (February 1984).

69. Ibid.

70. "Upcoming Events," news about the campaign authorized by the McGovern for President Committee, January 16, 1984.

71. Ibid.

72. George McGovern, "McGovern's View of Yale Debate," *Newsday*, February 22, 1984.

73. Ibid.

74. Ibid.

75. Ibid.

76. George McGovern, "McGovern's View of Yale Debate," *Newsday*, February 22, 1984.

77. Ibid.

78. George F. Will, "McGovern's Politics Quixotic," *Waterbury American*, February 1, 1984.

79. Ibid.

80. George McGovern, "McGovern Calls Will's Column Unfair," *Waterbury American*, February 15, 1984.

81. George Gallup, "McGovern Affects Mondale's Lead," *Los Angeles Times Syndicate*, October 9, 1983.

82. *New York Times/"CBS News Poll,"* December 1983.

83. "From McGovern Headquarters," news about the campaign authorized by the McGovern for President Committee, January 16, 1984, quoting a *Los Angeles Times* poll, December 1983.

84. T.R. Reid, "McGovern: Fighting the Loser Image," *Washington Post National Weekly Edition*, March 5, 1984; and Rowland Evans and Robert Novak, "McGovern Hurts Glenn," *Washington Post* [n.d.] 1983.

85. Associated Press, "Democrats Nice to Each Other, Harsh Toward Reagan," February 1, 1984.

86. James Reston, "On the Morning After," *New York Times*, March 14, 1984.

87. Associated Press, "McGovern Seeks Cuts in Defense," September 1983.

88. John Hyde, "McGovern Rips Democrats Who Support Invasion," *Des Moines Register*, November 16, 1983.

89. Ibid.

90. Ibid.

91. Ibid.

92. Ibid.

93. *Meet the Press*, A Public Affairs Presentation of NBC News. Guest: George McGovern, Sunday, November 13, 1983. Volume 83—Panel: Bill Monroe, NBC News; Marianne Means, Hearst Newspapers; Charles McDowell, *Richmond Times-Dispatch*; William Greider, *Rolling Stone*; and Moderator, Marvin Kalb, NBC News.

94. Associated Press, "Five Democratic Candidates Criticize Reagan for Air Strikes," December 5, 1983.

95. Ibid.

96. *New Republic*, December 12, 1983.

97. George Gallup, "Mondale, Glenn Even with Reagan," January 22, 1984.

98. *New York Times*, January 22, 1984.

99. Memo to state coordinators from Brian Best, director of political outreach, McGovern for President Committee, February 9, 1984.

100. Ibid.

101. Ibid.

102. Ibid.

103. Ibid.

104. Memo to state coordinators from Jeff Biggers, national field director, McGovern for President Committee, January 16, 1984.

105. Undated letter to campaign supporters from George McGovern, February 1984.

106. "From McGovern Headquarters," news about the campaign authorized by the McGovern for President Committee, January 16, 1984.

107. Associated Press, "Mondale Top Fund-Raiser in 1983," February 1, 1984.

108. Ibid.

109. Ibid.

110. George V. Cunningham interviews, January 29, 2002 and February 19, 2002.

111. Undated letter to campaign supporters from George McGovern, February 1984.

112. "From McGovern Headquarters," news about the campaign authorized by the McGovern for President Committee, January 16, 1984.

CHAPTER 5

1. Campaign position paper titled "Campaign '84," authorized by the McGovern for President Committee.

2. Ibid.

3. George McGovern, *War Against Want*, (Walker & Company, New York 1964),120–128.

4. Fay S. Joyce, "An Interview with Former South Dakota Senator George McGovern," *New York Times*, December 29, 1983.

5. Letter written by George McGovern, February 1984, regarding the unilateral weapons freeze, authorized by the McGovern for President Committee.

6. *Meet the Press*, A Public Affairs Presentation of NBC News. Guest: George McGovern, Sunday, November 13, 1983. Volume 83—Panel: Bill Monroe, NBC News; Marianne Means, Hearst Newspapers; Charles McDowell, *Richmond Times-Dispatch*; William Greider, *Rolling Stone*; and Moderator, Marvin Kalb, NBC News.

7. Ibid.

8. Ibid.

9. Fay S. Joyce, "An Interview with Former South Dakota Senator George McGovern," *New York Times*, December 29, 1983.

10. Campaign position paper titled "Euromissiles," authorized by the McGovern for President Committee.

11. *Meet the Press*, A Public Affairs Presentation of NBC News. Guest: George

McGovern, Sunday, November 13, 1983. Volume 83—Panel: Bill Monroe, NBC News; Marianne Means, Hearst Newspapers; Charles McDowell, *Richmond Times-Dispatch*; William Greider, *Rolling Stone*; and Moderator, Marvin Kalb, NBC News.

12. Ibid.

13. Fay S. Joyce, "An Interview with Former South Dakota Senator George McGovern," *New York Times*, December 29, 1983.

14. Ibid.

15. The League of Women Voters' Debate, Atlanta, Georgia, March 11, 1984.

16. Bill Peterson, "McGovern Faults Defense Stands of Mondale, Glenn," *Washington Post*, November 17, 1983.

17. Alexander Cockburn and James Ridgeway, "McGovern: Remember What a Real Liberal Looks Like?" *Village Voice*, September 27, 1983.

18. Campaign position paper titled "Military Budget," authorized by the McGovern forPresident Committee, January 1984.

19. Campaign position paper titled "Federal Deficits," authorized by McGovern for President Committee, January 1984.

20. Campaign position paper titled "Military Budget," authorized by the McGovern for President Committee, January 1984.

21. Ibid.

22. Ibid.

23. *Meet the Press*, A Public Affairs Presentation of NBC News. Guest: George McGovern, Sunday, November 13, 1983. Volume 83—Panel: Bill Monroe, NBC News; Marianne Means, Hearst Newspapers; Charles McDowell, *Richmond Times-Dispatch*; William Greider, *Rolling Stone*; and Moderator, Marvin Kalb, NBC News.

24. Campaign position paper titled "Military Budget," authorized by the McGovern for President Committee, January 1984.

25. Campaign position paper titled "Federal Deficits," authorized by the McGovern for President Committee, January 1984.

26. *Boston Globe*, December 13, 1983.

27. Campaign position paper titled "The Lessons of History," authorized by the McGovern for President Committee.

28. Ibid.

29. Bill Peterson, "McGovern Faults Defense Stands of Mondale, Glenn," *Washington Post*, November 17, 1983.

30. Fay S. Joyce, "An Interview with Former South Dakota Senator George McGovern," *New York Times*, December 29, 1983; and campaign position paper titled "America Held Hostage," authorized by the McGovern for President Committee.

31. Campaign position paper titled "The Lessons of History," authorized by McGovern for President Committee.

32. Ibid.

33. A letter by George McGovern, February 1984, regarding U.S. policy toward Latin America and the Caribbean basin authorized by the McGovern for President Committee.

34. Ibid.

35. Campaign position paper titled "The Path to Peace in Central America," authorized by the McGovern for President Committee, February 1984.

36. A letter by George McGovern to U.S. Representative Bruce Morrison in opposition to the recommendations of the Kissinger Commission, dated February 22, 1984.

37. Campaign position paper titled "The Path to Peace in Central America," authorized by the McGovern for President Committee, February 1984. Senator McGovern's maiden speech in the U.S. Senate, delivered in March of 1963, was titled "Our Castro Obsession versus the Alliance for Progress." The thrust of that speech was that the United States had greatly exaggerated Castro's real significance in the hemisphere. McGovern felt it was a mistake for the Eisenhower administration to break relations with Cuba and set up the invasion that President Kennedy attempted to carry out.

38. Ibid.

39. Fay S. Joyce, "An Interview with Former South Dakota Senator George McGovern," *New York Times*, December 29, 1983.

40. Ibid.

41. *Meet the Press*, A Public Affairs Presentation of NBC News. Guest: George McGovern, Sunday, November 13, 1983. Volume 83—Panel: Bill Monroe, NBC News; Marianne Means, Hearst Newspapers; Charles McDowell, *Richmond Times-Dispatch*; William Greider, *Rolling Stone*; and Moderator, Marvin Kalb, NBC News.

42. Ibid.

43. Campaign position paper titled "The Path to Peace in Central America," authorized by the McGovern for President Committee, February 1984.

44. Address by Senator George McGovern to the Democratic National Convention, July 18, 1984. Also, interview with George McGovern by the author on February 13, 2002.

45. Ibid.

46. "America Held Hostage," a statement by George McGovern dated January 7, 1984, authorized by the McGovern for President Committee.

47. Campaign position paper titled "Federal Deficits," authorized by the McGovern for President Committee, January 1984.

48. Campaign position paper titled "First Time Home Buyer's Mortgage Assistance," prepared by the McGovern for President Committee, for internal use only, January 1984.

49. Ibid.

50. Fay S. Joyce, "An Interview with Former South Dakota Senator George McGovern," *New York Times*, December 29, 1983.

51. Campaign position paper titled "Federal Deficits," authorized by the McGovern for President Committee, January 1984.

52. Campaign position paper titled "Tax Reform," authorized by the McGovern for President Committee, February 1984.

53. Ibid.

54. Ibid.

55. Campaign position paper entitled "Federal Deficits," authorized by the McGovern for President Committee, January 1984.

56. Fay S. Joyce, "An Interview with Former South Dakota Senator George McGovern," *New York Times*, December 29, 1983.

57. Ibid.

58. Campaign position paper titled "Tax Reform," authorized by the McGovern for President Committee, February 1984.

59. Campaign position paper titled "Education," authorized by the McGovern for President Committee, January 1984.

60. Ibid.

61. Ibid.

62. Fay S. Joyce, "An Interview with Former South Dakota Senator George McGovern," *New York Times*, December 29, 1983.

63. George McGovern, *War Against Want*, (Walker & Company, New York 1964); George McGovern, *Agricultural Thought in the Twentieth Century*, (The Bobbs-Merrill Company, Inc., Indianapolis, New York 1967); and campaign position paper titled "The McGovern Farm Program," authorized by the McGovern for President Committee, December 1983.

64. Campaign position paper titled "The McGovern Farm Program," authorized by the McGovern for President Committee, December 1983.

65. Ibid.

66. Ibid.

67. Ibid.

68. Alexander Cockburn and James Ridgeway, "McGovern: Remember What a Real Liberal Looks Like?" *Village Voice*, September 27, 1983.

69. Campaign position paper titled "Issues of Individual Conscience: Free Choice and Reproductive Rights," authorized by the McGovern for President Committee, January 1984.

70. David J. Lynch, "Getting Political with George McGovern," *Family Weekly*, February 5, 1984.

71. Campaign position paper titled "Issues of Individual Conscience: School Prayer," authorized by the McGovern for President Committee, January 1984.

72. Campaign position paper titled "Issues of Individual Conscience: Gay and Lesbian Rights," authorized by the McGovern for President Committee, January 1984.

73. Campaign position paper titled "U.S. Trade," authorized by the McGovern for President Committee, January, 1984.

74. Ibid.

75. Ibid.

76. Ibid.

77. A letter by George McGovern, February 1984, regarding the unilateral weapons freeze, authorized by the McGovern for President Committee.

78. Campaign position paper titled "Can a Friend of Israel Be a Critic?" authorized by the McGovern for President Committee.

79. Ibid.

80. Fay S. Joyce, "An Interview with Former South Dakota Senator George McGovern," *New York Times*, December 29, 1983.

81. Ibid.

82. Alexander Cockburn and James Ridgeway, "McGovern: Remember What a Real Liberal Looks Like?" *Village Voice*, September 27, 1983.

83. Campaign position paper titled "The Realities of Lebanon," authorized the McGovern for President Committee.

84. Fay S. Joyce, "An Interview with Former South Dakota Senator George McGovern," *New York Times*, December 29, 1983.

85. Campaign position paper titled "Environment and Energy Policy," authorized by the McGovern for President Committee.

86. Ibid.

87. Ibid.

88. Ibid.

89. Ibid.

CHAPTER 6

1. Remarks by Senator George McGovern, Jefferson-Jackson Day Dinner, October 8, 1983, Des Moines, Iowa.

2. Ibid.

3. Jack Germond and Jules Witcover, "A Long Shot, but Worth Cheers," *Baltimore Evening Sun*, October 20, 1983.

4. George McGovern, "I'm Glad I Tried," *Washington Post*, March 18, 1984.

5. Jack Germond and Jules Witcover, "A Long Shot, but Worth Cheers," *Baltimore Evening Sun*, October 20, 1983.

6. Hedrick Smith, "Iowa Democrats Say Only Mondale's Margin of Victory Is in Doubt," *New York Times*, November 25, 1983.

7. Bill Peterson, "McGovern Is Not a Democratic Harold Stassen," *Washington Post National Weekly Edition*, December 12, 1983.

8. "Political Report on Iowa," a campaign memorandum by George V. Cunningham, February 10, 1984.

9. Hedrick Smith, "Iowa Democrats Say Only Mondale's Margin of Victory is in Doubt," *New York Times*, November 25, 1983.

10. James M. Perry, "Teacher McGovern Considers Politics Another Classroom," *Wall Street Journal*, October 19, 1983.

11. Ibid.

12. Ibid.

13. Ibid.

14. Ibid.

15. Ibid.

16. Bill Peterson, "McGovern Faults Defense Stands of Mondale, Glenn," *Washington Post*, November 17, 1983.

17. Ibid.

18. Ibid.

19. Ibid.

20. Ibid.

21. Bill Peterson, "McGovern Is Not a Democratic Harold Stassen," *Washington Post National Weekly Edition*, December 12, 1983.

22. Ibid.

23. Ibid.

24. Fay S. Joyce, "McGovern Is Relaxed on Wearying Campaign," *New York Times*, January 15, 1984.

25. Associated Press, "Six Democratic Aspirants Argue over Car-Worker Issues," January 22, 1984.

26. William Robbins, "Specific Views on Farm Aid Sought from Six Democrats," *New York Times*, January 21, 1984.

27. Ibid.

28. William Robbins, "McGovern and Hart Gain Ground with Farmers," *New York Times*, January 23, 1984.

29. Associated Press, "Six Democratic Aspirants Argue over Car-Worker Issues," January 22, 1984.

30. William Robbins, "McGovern and Hart Gain Ground with Farmers," *New York Times*, January 23, 1984.

31. William Robbins, "Farmers at Forum Respond Warmly to McGovern," *New York Times*, January 22, 1984.

32. William Robbins, "McGovern and Hart Gain Ground with Farmers," *New York Times*, January 23, 1984.

33. Ibid.

34. Ibid.

35. Ibid.

36. Ibid.

37. Associated Press, "Six Democratic Aspirants Argue over Car-Worker Issues," January 22, 1984.

38. Ibid.

39. *New York Times*/CBS News Poll, January 25, 1984.

40. Associated Press, "Democratic Rivals Spar over Taxes," February 10, 1984.

41. Ibid.

42. "Shelling of Drug Positions 'The Most Incredible Kind of Nonsense' McGovern Says," press release authorized by the McGovern for President Committee, February 10, 1984.

43. Ibid.

44. Associated Press, "7 Democratic Aspirants Gang Up on Mondale in Iowa," February 12, 1984.

45. Ibid.

46. Ibid.

47. Ibid.

48. "Democrats' Debate in Iowa," *New York Times*, February 13, 1984.

49. Associated Press, "7 Democratic Aspirants Gang Up on Mondale in Iowa," February 12, 1984.

50. "Democrats' Debate in Iowa," *New York Times*, February 13, 1984.

51. Memorandum to State Coordinators from Brian Best, political affairs officer, McGovern for President, February 15, 1984.

52. Gerald M. Boyd, "McGovern Aims Drive at Undecided Iowans," *New York Times*, February 17, 1984.

53. Ibid.

54. Ibid.

55. Ibid.

56. Ibid.

57. George McGovern, "I'm Glad I Tried," *Washington Post*, March 18, 1984.

58. Gerald M. Boyd, "McGovern Aims Drive at Undecided Iowans," *New York Times*, February 17, 1984.

59. Memorandum to State Coordinators from Brian Best, political affairs officer, McGovern for President, February 15, 1984.

60. A statement by Dr. Helen Caldicott, president emeritus, Physicians for Social Responsibility.

61. David S. Broder, "McGovern Walking Tall," *Washington Post*, February 15, 1984.

62. "George McGovern: The Elixir of Politics," *CBS News*, February 26, 1984.

63. "The Sage," editorial in *Philadelphia Daily News*, February 17, 1984.

64. Ibid.

65. Thomas Oliphant, "McGovern Knows What He's Doing in '84," *Boston Globe*, February 18, 1984.

66. "Political Rhetoric Resounds Over Iowa," Associated Press, February 19, 1984.

67. Ibid.

68. Ibid.

69. Ibid.

70. Ibid.

71. Jack Rosenthal, "George McGovern's Toy Train," *New York Times*, February 24, 1984.

72. Associated Press, "Political Rhetoric Resounds over Iowa," February 19, 1984.

73. Steven R. Weisman, "Reagan's Attacks on Democrats Draws Rousing Cheers in Iowa," *New York Times*, February 21, 1984; and Associated Press, "Mondale Favored in Iowa Contests, Reagan Stumping," February 20, 1984.

74. Associated Press, "Mondale Favored in Iowa Contests, Reagan Stumping," February 20, 1984.

75. Associated Press, "Reagan Attacks Democrats before Large Iowa Crowds," February 21, 1984.

76. Steven R. Weisman, "Reagan's Attacks on Democrats Draw Rousing Cheers in Iowa," *New York Times*, February 21, 1984.

77. Associated Press, "Reagan Attacks Democrats before Large Iowa Crowds," February 21, 1984.

78. Associated Press, "Mondale Favored in Iowa Contests, Reagan Stumping," February 20, 1984.

79. Ibid.

80. Adam Clymer, "Poll Shows Victory Due to Solid Organization," *New York Times*, February 21, 1984.

81. Ibid.

82. Howell Raines, "Mondale Wins Handily in Iowa; Close Race for 2nd as Glenn Trails," *New York Times*, February 21, 1984.

83. Associated Press, "Iowa Win Lifts Mondale," February 2, 1984.

84. Howell Raines, "Mondale Wins Handily in Iowa; Close Race for 2nd as Glenn Trails," *New York Times*, February 21, 1984.

85. Associated Press, "Iowa Win Lifts Mondale," February 2, 1984.

86. Howell Raines, "Mondale Wins Handily in Iowa; Close Race for 2nd as Glenn Trails," *New York Times*, February 21, 1984.

87. Associated Press, "'Spirits Up,' Glenn Says after Loss," February 21, 1984.

88. Ibid.

89. Howell Raines, "Mondale Works to Bolster Lead as Others Adjust to New Lineup," *New York Times*, February 22, 1984.

90. "The Glenn Gap and the Fritz Blitz," editorial, *New York Times*, February 22, 1984.

91. Peter Goldman and Tony Fuller, *The Quest for the Presidency 1984*, (Bantam Books, New York 1985), 103.

92. Ibid.

93. "From McGovern Headquarters," news about the campaign authorized by the McGovern for President Committee, undated, quoting Kathy Sawyer, *Washington Post*.

94. Associated Press, "Iowa Win Lifts Mondale," February 21, 1984.

95. "The Glenn Gap and the Fritz Blitz," editorial, *New York Times*, February 22, 1984.

96. Associated Press, "TV Interference Cited," February 21, 1984.

97. Ibid.

98. Howell Raines, "Mondale Works to Bolster Lead as Others Adjusts to New Lineup," *New York Times*, February 22, 1984.

99. Howell Raines, "Mondale Wins Handily in Iowa; Close Race for 2nd as Glenn Trails," *New York Times*, February 21, 1984; and Frank Lynn, "Amity and Democracy Blend at Iowa Meeting," *New York Times*, February 22, 1984.

100. Howell Raines, "Mondale Wins Handily in Iowa; Close Race for 2nd as Glenn Trails," *New York Times*, February 21, 1984.

101. Ibid.; and Frank Lynn, "Amity and Democracy Blend at Iowa Meeting," *New York Times*, February 22, 1984.

102. Ibid.

103. Ibid.

104. Howell Raines, "Mondale Works to Bolster Lead as Others Adjusts to New Lineup," *New York Times*, February 22, 1984.

105. Ibid.

106. Ibid.

107. Ibid.

108. George Lardner Jr., *Washington Post*, February 22, 1984.

109. Robert J. Guttman, *PPI Report*, February 20, 1984.

110. "From McGovern Headquarters," news about the campaign authorized by the McGovern for President Committee, undated, quoting Jon Margolis and Steve Neal, *Chicago Tribune*, February 21, 1984.

111. *New Republic*, March 5, 1984.

112. "From McGovern Headquarters," news about the campaign authorized by the McGovern for President Committee, undated, quoting Sandy Grady, *Philadelphia Daily News*, February 17, 1984.

113. David Nyhan, *Boston Globe*, February 22, 1984.

114. "Urgent Message" to supporters, George McGovern, authorized by the McGovern for President Committee, February 20, 1984.

115. George McGovern interview, February 13, 2002.

116. David Nyhan, *Boston Globe*, February 22, 1984; and "Urgent Message" to supporters, George McGovern, authorized by the McGovern for President Committee, February 20, 1984.

117. "From McGovern Headquarters," news about the campaign authorized by the McGovern for President Committee, undated.

118. Ibid.

119. "Urgent Message" to supporters, George McGovern, authorized by the McGovern for President Committee, February 20, 1984.

120. Howell Raines, "Mondale Wins Handily in Iowa; Close Race for 2nd as Glenn Trails," *New York Times*, February 21, 1984.

121. George McGovern, "I'm Glad I Tried," *Washington Post*, March 18, 1984.

CHAPTER 7

1. Martin Shram, "It's True: The Top 2 Democrats Are Getting the Most Coverage," *Washington Post National Weekly Edition*, January 30, 1984.

2. James MacGregor Burns, "Is the Primary System a Mistake?" *Family Weekly*, February 26, 1984, quoting James MacGregor Burns, *The Power to Lead: the Crisis of the American Presidency*, (Simon & Schuster, New York 1984).

3. Ibid.

4. Ibid.

5. Martin Shram, "It's True: The Top 2 Democrats Are Getting the Most Coverage," *Washington Post National Weekly Edition*, January 30, 1984.

6. Ibid.

7. Ibid.

8. Ibid.

9. Ibid.

10. Fox Butterfield, "Despite Its Anomalies, New Hampshire Is a Key Candidate Proving Ground," *New York Times*, February 21, 1984.

11. David Nyhan, *Boston Globe*, November 27, 1983.

12. "From McGovern Headquarters," news about the campaign authorized by the McGovern for President Committee, undated.

13. George McGovern, "I'm Glad I Tried," *Washington Post*, March 18, 1984.

14. Associated Press, "Not Much Excitement, But Debate Had Moments," January 16, 1984.

15. George McGovern, "I'm Glad I Tried," *Washington Post*, March 18, 1984.

16. Ibid.

17. Ibid.

18. Democratic Debate, Dartmouth College, Hanover, New Hampshire, January 14, 1984.

19. Ibid.

20. Ibid.

21. Ibid.

22. Ibid.

23. Ibid.

24. Ibid.

25. Ibid.

26. Ibid.

27. Ibid.

28. Ibid.

29. Ibid.

30. Ibid.

31. Ibid.

32. Ibid.

33. Ibid.

34. Ibid.

35. Ibid.

36. A letter to supporters, George McGovern, the Savary Hotel, Des Moines, Iowa, early February 1984.

37. Ibid.

38. Ibid.

39. Bernard Weinraub, "Mondale Accuses President of 'Leadership by Amnesia,'" *New York Times*, February 22, 1984.

40. Ibid.

41. Fox Butterfield, "Hart, after Iowa, Sees A 2-Man Race," *New York Times*, February 22, 1984.

42. David Shribman, "Glenn Says His Enthusiasm Is Undampened," *New York Times*, February 22, 1984.

43. Ibid.

44. Ibid.

45. Fox Butterfield, "Hart, after Iowa, Sees A 2-Man Race," *New York Times*, February 22, 1984.

46. Ibid.

47. Ibid.

48. Ibid.

49. George McGovern interview, February 13, 2002; and Paul Sullivan interview, February 1, 2003.

50. Fox Butterfield, "Hart, after Iowa, Sees A 2-Man Race *New York Times*, February 22, 1984.

51. Thom Duffy, "McGovern Running on a Shoestring," *New Haven Register*, January 29, 1984.

52. Ibid.

53. Ibid.

54. Ibid.

55. Ibid.

56. "Election Panel Grants $100,000 to McGovern," *New York Times*, February 24, 1984.

57. Howell Raines, "Democrats Vie for Position in Calm, Mannerly Debate," *New York Times*, February 24, 1984.

58. Ibid.

59. Ibid.

60. Ibid.

61. Ibid.

62. Ibid.

63. Ibid.

64. David Shribman, "Glenn Criticizes Mondale Again on Pipeline Issue," *New York Times*, February 17, 1984.

65. "George McGovern: The Elixir of Politics," *CBS News*, February 26, 1984.

66. Ibid.

67. Ibid.

68. Ibid.

69. Ibid.

70. A letter from George McGovern to the author, December 23, 2001; and Paul Sullivan interview, February 1, 2003.

71. Ronald Smothers, "McGovern Banking on Massachusetts," *New York Times*, March 4, 1984.

72. Howell Raines, "Hart Steps Up Campaign Effort; Cranston Quits Democratic Race," *New York Times*, March 1, 1984.

73. Associated Press, "Hart's Victory Ousts Cranston," February 29, 1984.

74. Howell Raines, "Hart Steps Up Campaign Effort; Cranston Quits Democratic Race," *New York Times*, March 1, 1984.

75. Ibid.

76. Associated Press, "Hart's Victory Ousts Cranston," February 29, 1984.

77. Howell Raines, "Hart Steps Up Campaign Effort; Cranston Quits Democratic Race," *New York Times*, March 1, 1984.

78. Ibid.

79. Ibid.

80. Ibid.

81. Ibid.

82. Ibid.

83. Michael Barone and Grant Ujifusa, *The Almanac of American Politics 1986*, (National Journal, Inc., Washington, D.C. 1985), 822.

84. Thom Duffy, "Hart Challenges Dark Horse Image," *New Haven Register*, February 29, 1984.

85. Ibid.

86. Hedrick Smith, "Polls Outline Bases of Hart's Victory," *New York Times*, March 1, 1984.

87. Ibid.

88. Ibid.

89. Ibid.

90. Ibid.

91. "As Goes New Hampshire," editorial, *New York Times*, March 1, 1984.

92. Howell Raines, "Hart Victory Shakes Up Some, Shakes Out Others," *New York Times*, March 4, 1984.

93. Ibid.

94. Adam Clymer, "The Independent Vote That Made All the Difference," *New York Times*, March 4, 1984.

95. Ibid.

96. Frank Lombardi, "Hart of the City," *New York Daily News*, March 14, 1984.

97. Bernard Weinraub, "How Mondale Faltered," *New York Times*, March 8, 1984.

98. Steven R. Weisman, "The White House Ponders New Hampshire's Message," *New York Times*, March 4, 1984.

99. Ibid.

100. Ibid.

101. Ibid.

102. Ibid.

103. Howell Raines, "Hart Steps Up Campaign Effort; Cranston Quits Democratic Race," *New York Times*, March 1, 1984.

104. "New Frontier or Familiar Fringe?" editorial, *New York Times*, March 4, 1984.

105. Paul Sullivan interview, August 30, 2002.

106. Ibid.

107. Ibid.

108. Ibid.

CHAPTER 8

1. Associated Press, "'Super Tuesday' Victory Is a Must for Mondale," March 13, 1984.

2. "1984 Proves Rules for Front-Runners Don't Always Work," *Washington Post* article published in the *Hartford Courant*, March 14, 1984.

3. Ibid.

4. Ibid.

5. Ronald Smothers, "McGovern Banking on Massachusetts," *New York Times*, March 4, 1984.

6. McGovern for President Massachusetts Campaign brochure titled *The Issue Is the Military Budget and What It's Doing to Our Country.*

7. Ronald Smothers, "McGovern Banking on Massachusetts," *New York Times*, March 4, 1984.

8. Ibid.

9. Ibid.

10. "Bay State Results Keep McGovern in Race," *Knight-Ridder Newspapers*, March 14, 1984.

11. McGovern for President Massachusetts Campaign brochure titled *The Issue Is the Military Budget and What It's Doing to Our Country.*

12. Paul Sullivan interview, August 30, 2002.

13. Ibid.

14. Ronald Smothers, "McGovern Banking on Massachusetts," *New York Times*, March 4, 1984; and Paul Sullivan interview, February 1, 2003.

15. "Urgent Message" to supporters, George McGovern, authorized by the McGovern for President Committee, March 5, 1984.

16. Ronald Smothers, "McGovern Banking on Massachusetts" *New York Times*, March 4, 1984; and Paul Sullivan interview, February 1, 2003.

17. Ibid.

18. Ken Swope interview, August 27, 2002.

19. "Urgent Message" to supporters, George McGovern, authorized by the McGovern for President Committee, March 5, 1984.

20. McGovern for President Massachusetts Campaign brochure titled *The Issue Is the Military Budget and What It's Doing to Our Country.*

21. McGovern for President Massachusetts campaign flyer titled "It's Not a Horse Race."

22. McGovern for President Massachusetts Campaign brochure titled *The Issue Is the Military Budget and What It's Doing to Our Country.*

23. Ibid.

24. *Philadelphia Inquirer*, March 1984.

25. Ibid.

26. Ibid.; and Stephen Maloney interview, September 5, 2002.

27. *Philadelphia Inquirer*, March 1984.

28. Hedrick Smith, "Hart Strategists Say Money and Backers Are Coming In," *New York Times*, March 14, 1984.

29. Ibid.

30. Ibid.

31. Frank Lynn, "Hart Seeking to Exploit Gain in New Hampshire," *New York Times*, March 1, 1984.

32. Ibid.

33. Ibid.

34. Ibid.

35. Phil Gailey, "Caucuses in Maine Test 2 Candidates," *New York Times*, March 4, 1984.

36. Ibid.

37. Ibid.

38. Ibid.

39. Frank Lynn, "Hart Scores Again In Vermont Vote," *New York Times*, March 7, 1984.

40. Howell Raines, "Candidates Battle Hard in 3 Southern Primaries," *New York Times*, March 7, 1984.

41. Howell Raines, "Contest Is Now One of Personality and Message," *New York Times*, March 8, 1984.

42. Ibid.

43. Ibid.

44. Ibid.

45. Ibid.

46. Ibid.

47. Ibid.

48. John Herbers, "Hart and Mondale Striving to Find How to Win South," *New York Times*, March 8, 1984.

49. "O'Neill Depicts Hart as Clear Front-Runner," *New York Times*, March 8, 1984.

50. Ibid.

51. William E. Schmidt, "Hart, Once Weak in Florida, Is Now Seen as One of Top Challengers," *New York Times*, March 8, 1984.

52. Anthony Lewis, "Why Gary Hart?" *New York Times*, March 8, 1984.

53. Ibid.
54. The League of Women Voters' Debate, Atlanta, Georgia, March 11, 1984.
55. Ibid.
56. Ibid.
57. Ibid.
58. Ibid.
59. Ibid.
60. Ibid.
61. Ibid.
62. Ibid.
63. Ibid.
64. Ibid.
65. Ibid.
66. Ibid.
67. Ibid.
68. Ibid.
69. Ibid.
70. Ibid.
71. Ibid.
72. Ibid.
73. Ibid.
74. Ibid.
75. Letter to the author from Congressman James P. McGovern, June 4, 2002.
76. "Old Values and New Directions," remarks by Senator George McGovern, Faneuil Hall, Boston, Massachusetts, March 9, 1984.
77. Ibid.
78. Ibid.
79. Ibid.
80. Ibid.
81. Ibid.
82. Ibid.
83. Ibid.
84. Ibid.
85. Ibid.
86. Ibid.
87. Ibid.
88. Ibid.
89. Ibid.
90. David Lightman, "Super Tuesday: Make or Break Time," *Hartford Courant*, March 13, 1984.
91. Associated Press, "'Super Tuesday' Victory Is a Must for Mondale," March 13 1984.
92. "Has Conscience, Should Travel," editorial, *Boston Globe*, March 8, 1984.
93. Ibid.
94. Ibid.
95. Recollections of the author; Jason F. Isaacson, "Mondale and Glenn Way Out in Front in Connecticut Race," *Litchfield County Times,* December 9, 1983; and

"McGovern Backers Will Meet Thursday," *Waterbury American*, January 13, 1984. In Connecticut, Richard M. Marano was state coordinator; the six district co-ordinators were Jack Zanini, Richard Stroller, Lawrence Hunter, Miles Penny-backer, Prof. Vincent Carrafiello, and Mary Jane Michaels. Other active volunteers were Angie Marano, Mark Sadlowski, and Stephen Maloney.

96. "Life after Super Tuesday," editorial, *Hartford Courant*, March 15, 1984.

97. Tamara Lyttle, "Agents Tout 3 as Reagan-Beaters," *New Haven Register*, February 29, 1984.

98. Jason F. Isaacson, "Mondale and Glenn Way Out in Front in Connecticut Race," *Litchfield County Times*, December 9, 1983.

99. Ibid.; and "Candidate Backers Seek Support in March 27 Democratic Voting,"*Cheshire Herald*, March 1, 1984.

100. Bill Stall, "Hart Sails On; Mondale Buys Time," *Hartford Courant*, March 14, 1984.

101. Jason F. Isaacson, "Mondale and Glenn Way Out in Front in Connecticut Race," *Litchfield County Times*, December 9, 1983; and "Candidate Backers Seek Support in March 27 Democratic Voting," *Cheshire Herald*, March 1, 1984.

102. Ibid.

103. Ibid.

104. Jackey Gold, "Cranston Wins State Caucus," *New Haven Register*, January 29, 1984.

105. Ibid.

106. Associated Press, "State Caucus of Democrats for Cranston," January 29, 1984.

107. "McGovern Bus," *New Haven Register*, March 9, 1984; and Jack Goldberg, "For McGovern Forces, It May Be Uphill All the Way," *Waterbury Republican*, January 20, 1984.

108. McGovern for President Contributor Disk for Connecticut, February 17, 1984.

109. Nancy M. Tracy, "Would-Be Delegates in Connecticut Rush to Embrace Hart," *Hartford Courant*, March 14, 1984.

110. Ibid.

111. Associated Press, "State Primary Drawing Increased Interest," March 12, 1984.

112. Charles F.J. Morse, "In Connecticut, It Will Be a Scramble,"*Hartford Courant*, March 15, 1984.

113. Discussion of the author with Laraine Smith, Cheshire, Connecticut, Democratic Town Committee chairwoman, February 1984.

114. Associated Press, "Askew Led Dropouts in Vote in Connecticut," *New York Times*, March 29, 1984.

115. "Bay State Results Keep McGovern in Race," Knight-Ridder Newspapers, March 14, 1984.

116. Letter to the author from Congressman James P. McGovern, June 4, 2002; and Ken Swope interview, August 27, 2002.

117. "Bay State Results Keep McGovern in Race," Knight-Ridder Newspapers, March 14, 1984.

118. Paul Sullivan interview, August 30, 2002.

119. "Bay State Results Keep McGovern in Race," Knight-Ridder Newspapers, March 14, 1984.

120. Paul Sullivan interview, August 30, 2002.

121. "Bay State Results Keep McGovern in Race," Knight-Ridder Newspapers, March 14, 1984; and Paul Sullivan interview, August 30, 2002.

122. Paul Sullivan interview, August 30, 2002; and Fox Butterfield, "Hart Wins in Massachusetts; McGovern Fails to Place 2nd," *New York Times*, March 14, 1984.

123. Ibid.

124. "Bay State Results Keep McGovern in Race," Knight-Ridder Newspapers, March 14, 1984.

125. Paul Sullivan interview, August 30, 2002.

126. "Bay State Results Keep McGovern in Race," Knight-Ridder Newspapers, March 14, 1984.

127. Paul Sullivan interview, August 30, 2002.

128. "Bay State Results Keep McGovern in Race," Knight-Ridder Newspapers, March 14, 1984.

129. Ibid.

130. Fay S. Joyce, "Jackson Attacks 2 Front-Runners," *New York Times*, March 7, 1984.

131. "South Gives Jax His Best Chance," Combined Dispatches, *New York Daily News*, March 14, 1984.

132. Howell Raines, "Hart Takes Massachusetts, Florida and Rhode Island; Mondale Is Strong in South," *New York Times*, March 14, 1984.

133. Frank Lynn, "Glenn Refuses to Concede Races; Aides Say He Must Have Victory," *New York Times*, March 14, 1984.

134. Howell Raines, "Hart Takes Massachusetts, Florida and Rhode Island; Mondale Is Strong in South," *New York Times*, March 14, 1984.

135. United Press International, "Hart Captures 3 States While Mondale Wins 2," March 14, 1984.

136. Howell Raines, "Hart Takes Massachusetts, Florida and Rhode Island; Mondale Is Strong in South," *New York Times*, March 14, 1984.

137. David Lightman, "Hart Takes 2 Big Prizes," *Hartford Courant*, March 14, 1984.

138. Howell Raines, "Hart Takes Massachusetts, Florida and Rhode Island; Mondale Is Strong in South," *New York Times*, March 14, 1984.

139. United Press International, "Hart Captures 3 States While Mondale Wins 2," March 14, 1984.

140. Lars-Erik Nelson, "His Voters Are Just The Ticket," *New York Daily News*, March 14, 1984.

141. Fox Butterfield, "Hart Wins in Massachusetts, McGovern Fails to Place 2nd," *New York Times*, March 14, 1984.

142. Hedrick Smith, "How Mondale's Flagging Campaign Was Revived," *New York Times*, March 15, 1984.

143. Deborah Orin and Niles Lathem, "Super Tuesday Dems Make It a Race Again," *New York Post*, March 14, 1984.

144. Harrison Rainie, "Call Him Senator Appealing," *New York Daily News*, March 14, 1984.

145. Bill Stall, "Hart Sails On; Mondale Buys Time," *Hartford Courant*, March 14, 1984.

146. Ibid.

147. Associated Press, "Hart, Mondale Running 1–2 After Super Tuesday" March 14, 1984.

148. Deborah Orin and Niles Lathem, "Super Tuesday Dems Make It a Race Again," *New York Post*, March 14, 1984.

149. Ibid.; and Frank Jackman, "Tough-It-Out Fritz Won't Beef," *New York Daily News*, March 14, 1984.

150. Frank Jackman, "Tough-It-Out Fritz Won't Beef," *New York Daily News*, March 14, 1984.

151. Howell Raines, "Hart Takes Massachusetts, Florida and Rhode Island; Mondale Is Strong in South," *New York Times*, March 14, 1984.

152. Deborah Orin and Niles Lathem, "Dems Turn Their Labors to Industrial States," *New York Post*, March 14, 1984.

153. "Mondale Victorious in Dixie," *New York Post*, March 14, 1984.

154. Lars-Erik Nelson, "His Voters Are Just the Ticket," *New York Daily News*, March 14, 1984.

155. Ibid.

156. Ibid.

157. Ronald Smothers, "Bid by Jackson Is Cited In Black's Big Turnout," *New York Times*, March 15, 1984.

158. Howell Raines, "Hart Takes Massachusetts, Florida and Rhode Island; Mondale Is Strong in South," *New York Times*, March 14, 1984.

159. Ronald Smothers, "Bid by Jackson Is Cited In Black's Big Turnout," *New York Times*, March 15, 1984.

160. Doug Feiden, "Heavy Black Jackson Vote Not Enough," *New York Post*, March 14, 1984.

161. United Press International, "Hart Captures 3 States While Mondale Wins 2," March 14, 1984.

162. Howell Raines, "Contest Is Now One of Personality and Message" *New York Times*, March 8, 1984; Hedrick Smith, "How Mondale's Flagging Campaign Was Revived," *New York Times*, March 15, 1984; and Deborah Orin and Niles Lathem, "Dems Turn Their Labors to Industrial States," *New York Post*, March 14, 1984.

163. Hedrick Smith, "How Mondale's Flagging Campaign Was Revived," *New York Times*, March 15, 1984.

164. "McGovern Bows Out of the Race," *Newark Star-Ledger*, March 14, 1984.

165. "Bay State Results Keep McGovern in Race," Knight-Ridder Newspapers, March 14, 1984; and Paul Sullivan interview, February 1, 2003.

166. "Bay State Results Keep McGovern in Race," Knight-Ridder Newspapers, March 14, 1984.

167. Paul Sullivan interview, August 30, 2002.

168. "Bay State Results Keep McGovern in Race," Knight-Ridder Newspapers, March 14, 1984.

169. George McGovern interview, February 13, 2002; and "McGovern Tosses in the Towel," *New York Post*, March 14, 1984.

170. "McGovern Tosses in the Towel," *New York Post*, March 14, 1984.

171. Ibid.

172. "McGovern Bows Out of the Race," Star-Ledger Wire Services, March 14, 1984.

173. Paul Sullivan interview, August 30, 2002.

174. "McGovern Bows Out of the Race," Star-Ledger Wire Services, March 14, 1984.

175. Ibid.

176. George McGovern interview, February 13, 2002.

177. Ibid.

178. "McGovern Bows Out of the Race," Star-Ledger Wire Services, March 14, 1984.

179. Michael Barone and Grant Ujifusa, *The Almanac of American Politics 1986*, (National Journal, Inc., Washington, D.C. 1985), 615.

180. "The Democrats: A Delegate Update," *New York Times*, March 15, 1984.

181. Associated Press, March 14, 1984.

182. Paul Sullivan interview, August 30, 2002.

183. "Mondale Victorious in Dixie," *New York Post*, March 14, 1984.

184. Hedrick Smith, "How Mondale's Flagging Campaign Was Revived," *New York Times*, March 15, 1984.

185. Andrew H. Malcolm, "Illinois to Test Leaders Tuesday for Big Stakes," *New York Times*, March 15, 1984.

186. Howell Raines, "Mondale Is Facing Financial Squeeze in Nomination Bid," *New York Times*, March 15, 1984.

187. David S. Broder, Dan Balz, George Lardner, Jr., Milton Coleman, Paul Taylor, and Martin Schram, "Super Tuesday: A Fight for the Democratic Party's Soul?" *Washington Post National Weekly Edition*, March 19, 1984.

188. Ibid.

189. Ibid.

190. Ibid.

191. Ibid.

192. Gerald M. Boyd, "McGovern Gratified with Respect Won as He Leaves Race," *New York Times*, March 15, 1984.

193. Ibid.

194. Ibid.

195. Ibid.

196. Ibid.

197. Ibid.

CHAPTER 9

1. "The Democrats—And the Democrats," editorial, *New York Times*, March 15, 1984.

2. Ronald Smothers, "Bid by Jackson Is Cited in Blacks' Big Turnout," *New York Times*, March 15, 1984.

3. United Press International, "McGovern Won't Back Anyone for Nomination," *New York Times*, March 16, 1984.

4. Bernard Weinraub, "Mondale-Hart Exchanges Grow Sharper," *New York Times*, March 16, 1984.

5. Dan Balz, "Mondale's 'Body-by-Body' Search for Delegates," *Washington Post National Weekly Edition*, June 11, 1984.

6. Ibid.

7. Ibid.

8. Recollection of the author.

9. Associated Press, "Hart Says He'd Consider Jackson; McGovern Prefers Mondale, Hart," May 21, 1984.

10. Ibid.

11. Ibid.

12. Ibid.

13. Ronald Smothers, "Jackson Attacks McGovern Plea for Mondale-Hart 'Unity' Ticket," *New York Times*, May 31, 1984.

14. Associated Press, "McGovern Swings to Mondale Camp," June 14, 1984.

15. Paul Sullivan interview, February 1, 2003.

16. Associated Press, "McGovern Swings to Mondale Camp," June 14, 1984.

17. Associated Press, "Mondale-Hart Ticket Favored by McGovern," June 14, 1984.

18. Associated Press, "McGovern Swings to Mondale Camp," June 14, 1984.

19. Associated Press, "Mondale-Hart Ticket Favored by McGovern," June 14, 1984.

20. Don McLeod, "McGovern Pleads for United Convention," *Washington Times*, June 13, 1984.

21. Ibid.

22. Ibid.

23. Ibid.

24. Ibid.

25. Ibid.

26. Campaign Notes, "Gallup Reports Reagan Leads Mondale and Hart," *New York Times*, May 31, 1984.

27. Letter from George McGovern to his supporters in May 1984.

28. Ibid.

29. Letter from George McGovern to his supporters dated April 27, 1984, authorized by Friends of George McGovern Committee.

30. Letter from George McGovern to his supporters dated June 1984, authorized by Friends of George McGovern Committee.

31. Milton Coleman, "Hart and Jackson Supporters Team Up to Derail Mondale," *Washington Post National Weekly Edition*, June 11, 1984.

32. Ibid.

33. Ibid.

34. Ibid.

35. Ibid.

36. Ibid.

37. Ibid.

38. "The Democrats—and the Democrats," editorial, *New York Times*, March 15, 1984.

39. Gerald M. Boyd, "McGovern Gratified with Respect Won as He Leaves Race," *New York Times*, March 15, 1984.

40. George McGovern, "I'm Glad I Tried," *Washington Post*, March 18, 1984.

41. Bill Peterson, "McGovern Is Not a Democratic Harold Stassen," *Washington Post National Weekly Edition*, December 12, 1983. See also Phil Gailey, "Restless McGovern Renews Quest for Presidency," *New York Times*, September 14, 1983.

42. Bill Peterson, "McGovern Is Not a Democratic Harold Stassen," *Washington Post National Weekly Edition*, December 12, 1983; Phil Gailey, "Restless McGovern Renews Quest for Presidency," *New York Times*, September 14, 1983; Miles Benson, "McGovern Resurrects His Dream," *Newark Sunday Star-Ledger*, October 30, 1983; "An Interview with George McGovern," *Playboy*, August 1971; "McGovern in Ithaca Speech, Says He's 'Wiser' Candidate," *New York Times*, September 30, 1983; and Phil Gailey, "For McGovern, the Second Time Around Is Good," *New York Times*, November 3, 1983.

43. Miles Benson, "McGovern Resurrects His Dream," *Newark Sunday Star-Ledger*, October 30, 1983.

44. George McGovern, "I'm Glad I Tried," *Washington Post*, March 18, 1984.

45. Letter from George McGovern to Eleanor McGovern dated January 17, 1988.

46. Ibid.

47. George McGovern, "I'm Glad I Tried," *Washington Post*, March 18, 1984.

48. "Mr. McGovern's Success," editorial, *Washington Post*, April 2, 1984.

49. Ibid.

50. George McGovern, "I'm Glad I Tried," *Washington Post*, March 18, 1984.

51. Letter from George McGovern to author dated April 10, 1984; and Paul Sullivan interview, February 1, 2003.

52. "McGovern to Do 'Saturday Night,' " *New York Times*, April 13, 1984.

53. Fred Rothenberg, " 'Saturday Night' Makes Liberal Use of George McGovern as Guest Host," *Newark Star-Ledger*, April 13, 1984.

54. Ibid.

55. Ibid.

56. Nominating Speech for Senator George McGovern by James P. McGovern, Democratic National Convention, July 18, 1984.

57. Ibid.

58. Seconding Speech for Senator George McGovern by Ellen Kurtz, Democratic National Convention, July 18, 1984.

59. Address by Senator George McGovern to the Democratic National Convention, July 18, 1984.

60. Ibid.

61. Ibid.

62. Ibid.

63. Ibid.

64. Ibid.

65. Ibid.

66. Peter Goldman and Tony Fuller, *The Quest for the Presidency 1984*, (Bantam Books, New York 1985), 371.

67. Letter by George McGovern to supporters, December 12, 1984.

68. Ibid.

69. Ibid.

70. Ibid.

71. Lecture by George McGovern, "Reagan and the Liberal Alternative," March 2, 1982, Fairfield University, sponsored by the Fairfield University Young Democrats.

72. Letter by George McGovern to supporters, December 12, 1984.

73. "McGovern's Campaign Told to Repay Some U.S. Funds," *New York Times*, February 13, 1985.

74. "FEC Says McGovern Must Repay $25,000," *Washington Post*, February 12, 1985.

75. Ibid.

76. Ibid.

77. Ibid.; and letter to supporters, George McGovern, April 1985.

78. Associated Press, "FEC demands refund on McGovern 'salary,'" February 12, 1985. On November 25, 2002, the Federal Election Commission agreed to let candidates pay themselves salaries using campaign donations, aiming to encourage people who otherwise couldn't afford to give up their jobs to run.

79. "FEC Says McGovern Must Repay $25,000," *Washington Post*, February 12, 1985; and letter to supporters, George McGovern, April 1985.

80. Friends of George McGovern, Federal Election Commission, Selected List of Receipts and Expenditures (G), March 7, 1985.

81. George McGovern, "I'm Glad I Tried," *Washington Post*, March 18, 1984.

82. Ibid.

83. Ibid.

84. Ibid.

85. Letter from George McGovern to Eleanor McGovern, January 17, 1988.

86. George McGovern interview, February 13, 2002.

87. George McGovern, "I'm Glad I Tried," *Washington Post*, March 18, 1984; and George McGovern letter to author, April 10, 1984.

88. Cathy Powell letter to the author, April 6, 1984; and George McGovern letter to the author, April 10, 1984.

89. T.R. Reid, "Exorcising the Ghost of 1972," *Washington Post,* January 14, 1984; and lecture by George McGovern, "Reagan and the Liberal Alternative," March 2, 1982, Fairfield University, sponsored by the Fairfield University Young Democrats.

90. Lecture by George McGovern, "Reagan and the Liberal Alternative," March 2, 1982, Fairfield University, sponsored by the Fairfield University Young Democrats.

91. Ibid.

92. George McGovern, "I'm Glad I Tried," *Washington Post*, March 18,1984; and George McGovern letter to author, April 10, 1984.

93. George McGovern, "I'm Glad I Tried," *Washington Post*, March 18, 1984.

94. T.R. Reid, "Exorcising the Ghost of 1972," *Washington Post*, January 14, 1984.

95. Speech to students, Senator Robert F. Kennedy, October 22, 1966, University of California, Berkeley.

96. Day of Affirmation Address, Senator Robert F. Kennedy, June 6, 1966, University of Capetown, Capetown, South Africa.

97. George McGovern, "I'm Glad I Tried," *Washington Post*, March 18, 1984.

98. Derek Maurer, "Progressive Voice," editorial, *Daily Iowan*, February 17, 1984.

99. Steven Pearlstein, ed., "Don't Blame Me . . . Endorsing George McGovern, a Democrat Who Remembers What Liberalism Is About," *Boston Observer* 3, no. 2 (February 1984).

100. Ibid.

101. *George McGovern: The Kind of Man He Is*, McGovern for Senate Committee, 1968.

Selected Bibliography

ARCHIVAL SOURCES

Senator George McGovern Collection, Layne Library, Dakota Wesleyan University, Mitchell, South Dakota.
George S. McGovern Papers, Princeton University, Princeton, New Jersey.

ARTICLES ABOUT THE 1972 PRESIDENTIAL CAMPAIGN

"Can McGovern Put It All Together?" *Newsweek*, June 19, 1972.
"Front and Center for George McGovern." *Time*, May 8, 1972.
"George McGovern: Can He Unite His Party?" *U.S. News & World Report*, July 24, 1972.
"How McGovern Brought It Off." *Newsweek*, July 24, 1972.
"How Radical Is McGovern?" *Newsweek*, June 19, 1972.
"Introducing . . . the McGovern Machine." *Time*, July 24, 1972.
"Is It an Era—or Only and Hour?" *Newsweek*, July 24, 1972.
Meryman, Richard. "The Infighting Was 'Ferocious.'" *LIFE*, July 21, 1972.
"St. George Prepares to Face the Dragon." *Time*, July 24, 1972.
"What McGovern Would Do as President." *U.S. News & World Report*, July 24, 1972.

BOOKS ABOUT GEORGE McGOVERN

Ambrose, Stephen E. *The Wild Blue*. Simon & Schuster, New York 2001.
Anson, Robert Sam. *McGovern: A Biography*. Holt, Rinehart & Winston, New York, San Francisco, 1971.
MacLaine, Shirley. *McGovern: The Man & His Beliefs*. W. W. Norton & Company, Inc., New York 1972.

BOOKS BY GEORGE McGOVERN

War Against Want. Walker and Company, New York 1964.
Agricultural Thought in the Twentieth Century. Bobbs-Merrill Company, Inc., Indianapolis, New York 1967.
A Time of War, A Time of Peace. Random House, New York 1968.
The Great Coalfield War (and Leonard F. Guttridge). Houghton Mifflin Company, Boston 1972.
An American Journey. Random House, New York 1974.
GRASSROOTS: The Autobiography of George McGovern. Random House, New York 1977.
Terry. Random House, New York 1996.
The Third Freedom. Simon & Schuster, New York 2001.

BOOKS ABOUT THE 1968 PRESIDENTIAL CAMPAIGN

Chester, Lewis, Hodgson, Godfrey, and Page, Bruce. *An American Melodrama.* Viking Press, New York 1969.
White, Theodore H. *The Making of the President 1968.* Atheneum Publishers, New York 1969.

BOOKS ABOUT THE 1972 PRESIDENTIAL CAMPAIGN

Crouse, Timothy. *The Boys on the Bus.* Random House, New York 1973.
Dougherty, Richard. *Goodbye, Mr. Christian.* Doubleday & Company, Inc., Garden City, New York 1973.
Hart, Gary Warren. *Right from the Start.* Quadrangle/New York Times Book Company, New York 1973.
Kimelman, Henry L. *Living the American Dream.* Vincent Lee Publishing, Inc., Hong Kong 1998.
McGovern, Eleanor with Hoyt, Mary Finch. *Uphill.* Houghton Mifflin Company, 1974.
O'Brien, Lawrence F. *No Final Victories.* Doubleday & Company, Inc., Boston 1974.
Thompson, Dr. Hunter S. *Fear and Loathing: On the Campaign Trail '72.* Straight Arrow, San *Francisco 1973.*
Weil, Gordon L. *The Long Shot.* W. W. Norton & Company, Inc., New York 1973.
White, Theodore H. *The Making of the President 1972.* Atheneum Publishers, New York 1973.

BOOKS ABOUT THE 1984 PRESIDENTIAL CAMPAIGN

Germond, Jack W., and Witcover, Jules. *Wake Us When It's Over.* Macmillan Publishing Company, New York 1985.
Goldman, Peter, and Fuller, Tony. *The Quest for the Presidency 1984.* Bantam Books, New York 1985.

BOOKS ABOUT PRESIDENTIAL POLITICS

Barone, Michael and Ujifusa, Grant. *The Almanac of American Politics 1986*. National Journal, Inc., Washington, D.C. 1985.

Burns, James MacGregor. *The Power to Lead: The Crisis of the American Presidency*. Simon & Schuster, New York 1984.

Germond, Jack W. *Fat Man in a Middle Seat*. Random House, New York 1999.

Haldeman, H.R. *The Haldeman Diaries*. G.P. Putnam's Sons, New York 1994.

Monagan, John S. *A Pleasant Institution*. University Press of America, Lanham, Md. 2002.

O'Neill, Thomas P. "Tip," with Novak, William. *Man of the House*. Random House, New York 1987.

Schlesinger, Arthur M. Jr. *The Imperial Presidency*. Houghton Mifflin Company, Boston 1973.

Witcover, Jules. *MARATHON: The Pursuit of the Presidency 1972–1976*. Viking Press, New York 1977.

INTERVIEWS WITH GEORGE McGOVERN

"APIC Interview: Senator George McGovern." Joseph Wasserman with John Vargo. *Keynoter* 82, no. 4 (winter 1982).

"'I Have Earned the Nomination.'" An Interview by Richard Meryman, *LIFE*, July 7, 1972.

"An Interview with George McGovern." *Playboy*, August 1971.

GEORGE McGOVERN ON THE ISSUES

Book

McGovern, George S., Westmoreland, William C., Luttwak, Edward M., and McCormick, Thomas J. *VIETNAM: Four American Perspectives*. Purdue University Press, West Lafayette, In. 1990.

Campaign Brochures

"George McGovern: The Kind of Man He Is," McGovern for Senate Committee, 1968.

"McGovern on the Issues," McGovern for President Committee, 1971.

Index

About the Author

RICHARD MICHAEL MARANO is a board certified criminal trial attorney who practices law in Waterbury, Connecticut. Among his earlier publications are *Connecticut Criminal Legal Forms* and *Growing Up Italian and American in Waterbury* with Sando Bologna.

"As an American bomber pilot in World War II, I saw clearly the devastation of war. During the time that I flew with the Army Airforce most of my close friends were blown out of the skies. When my own navigator was killed, I decided that if I survived the war, I would dedicate the rest of my life to the cause of peace."
—George McGovern, 1956

For further information on preserving the legacy of one of our country's finest statesmen, contact:

The George and Eleanor McGovern Library
and Center for Public Service
Dakota Wesleyan University
1200 W. University Avenue
Mitchell, South Dakota 57301
(605) 995-2603
www.mcgovernlibrary.com